The Southern Shores of the Mediterranean and its Netw

T0353047

The majority of scholarly conceptions of the Mediterranean focus on the sea's northern shores, with its historical epicentres of Spain, France or Italy. This book seeks to demonstrate the importance of economic, political and cultural networks emanating from the Mediterranean's lesser-studied southern shores. The various chapters emphasise the activities that made connections between the southern shores, sub-Saharan Africa, the lands along its northern shores, and beyond to the United States. In doing so, the book avoids a Eurocentric approach and details the importance of the players and regions of the southern hinterland, in the analysis of the Mediterranean space. The cultural aspects of the North African countries, be they music, literature, film, commerce or political activism, continue to transform the public spheres of the countries along the northern shores of the Mediterranean and beyond to the whole of the European continent. In its focus on the often overlooked North African shore, the work is an innovative contribution to the historiography of the Mediterranean region.

This book was originally published as a special issue of *The Journal of North African Studies*.

Patricia M.E. Lorcin is Professor of History at the University of Minnesota-Twin Cities, Minneapolis, MN, USA. She is the author of *Imperial Identities* and *Historicizing Colonial Nostalgia*, four edited or co-edited volumes, two special issues and numerous articles. Her present project is tentatively entitled *The Cold War, Art, Politics and Transnational Activism in the era of Decolonization.*

The Southern Shores of the Mediterranean and its Networks

Knowledge, trade, culture and people

Edited by
Patricia M.E. Lorcin

LONDON AND NEW YORK

First published 2016 by Routledge

2 Park Square, Milton Park, Abingdon, Oxon OX14 4RN
711 Third Avenue, New York, NY 10017, USA

Routledge is an imprint of the Taylor & Francis Group, an informa business

First issued in paperback 2017

British Library Cataloguing in Publication Data
A catalogue record for this book is available from the British Library

ISBN 13: 978-1-138-93196-1 (hbk)
ISBN 13: 978-1-138-09924-1 (pbk)

Typeset in Times New Roman
by RefineCatch Limited, Bungay, Suffolk

Publisher's Note
The publisher accepts responsibility for any inconsistencies that may have
arisen during the conversion of this book from journal articles to book chapters,
namely the possible inclusion of journal terminology.

Disclaimer
Every effort has been made to contact copyright holders for their permission to
reprint material in this book. The publishers would be grateful to hear from any
copyright holder who is not here acknowledged and will undertake to rectify
any errors or omissions in future editions of this book.

Contents

Citation Information

The chapters in this book were originally published in *The Journal of North African Studies*, volume 20, issue 1 (January 2015). When citing this material, please use the original page numbering for each article, as follows:

Chapter 6

The diaspora and the cemetery: emigration and social transformation in a Moroccan oasis community
Paul A. Silverstein
The Journal of North African Studies, volume 20, issue 1 (January 2015) pp. 92–108

Chapter 7

Beur/Maghribi musical interventions in France: rai and rap
Ted Swedenburg
The Journal of North African Studies, volume 20, issue 1 (January 2015) pp. 109–126

For any permission-related enquiries please visit:
http://www.tandfonline.com/page/help/permissions

Notes on Contributors

Michael Bonine was Professor of Near Eastern Studies and Geography, and founding Director of the School of Middle Eastern & North African Studies at the University of Arizona, Tucson, AZ, USA, until his death in 2011.

Aomar Boum is Assistant Professor in the Department of Anthropology at UCLA, Los Angeles, California, USA. His research is concerned with the social and cultural representation of, and political discourse about, religious and ethnic minorities in the Middle East and North Africa.

Timothy Cleaveland is Associate Professor in the Department of History at the University of Georgia, Athens, GA, USA. His book, *Becoming Walata: A History of Saharan Social Formation and Transformation*, was published in 2001.

Shamil Jeppie is Director and Associate Professor at the Institute for Humanities in Africa at the University of Cape Town, South Africa. He is the author of *Language, Identity, Modernity* (2007), the editor of the journal *History in Africa*, and the books *The Struggle for District Six* (1990), *Towards New Histories for South Africa* (2004) and *The Meanings of Timbuktu* (2008).

Patricia M.E. Lorcin is Professor of History at the University of Minnesota-Twin Cities, Minneapolis, MN, USA. She is the author of *Imperial Identities* and *Historicizing Colonial Nostalgia*, four edited or co-edited volumes, two special issues and numerous articles. Her present project is tentatively entitled *The Cold War, Art, Politics and Transnational Activism in the era of Decolonization*.

Beverly Mack is Professor of African and African American Studies at the University of Kansas, Lawrence, KS, USA. She has published extensively on African literature and Muslim women's lives in West Africa. Her books include: *Hausa Women in the Twentieth Century* (1990); *The Collected Works of Nana Asma'u, daughter of Shehu Usman dan Fodiyo, 1793–1864* (1997); *One Woman's Jihad: Nana Asma'u, Scholar and Scribe* (2001); and *Muslim Women Sing: Hausa Popular Song* (2004).

Ismael M. Montana is Assistant Professor in the Department of History at Northern Illinois University, DeKalb, Illinois, USA. His research interests include the social and economic history of slavery in Northwest Africa, and the Mediterranean Islamic world in the eighteenth and nineteenth centuries. His most recent book is *The Abolition of Slavery in Ottoman Tunisia* (2013).

Paul A. Silverstein is Professor of Anthropology at Reed College, Portland, Oregon, USA. His research interests include immigration, race and ethnicity, nationalism, cultural politics, and colonialism/post-colonialism. His most recent book is *Bourdieu in the Field: Colonial Politics, Ethnographic Practices, Theoretical Developments* (2009).

Ted Swedenburg is Professor in the Department of Anthropology at the University of Arkansas, Fayetteville, Arkansas, USA. His research is primarily focused on popular music. He is currently working on a book manuscript, tentatively titled *Sounds from the Interzone*, that deals with 'border' music of the Middle East as well as Middle Eastern-inflected music of the West.

Introduction

Patricia M.E. Lorcin

Department of History, University of Minnesota-Twin Cities, Minneapolis, USA

From the time the Romans dubbed the Mediterranean, *Mare Nostrum*, the history of the Mediterranean as an environment, a space of networks or a site of civilisational conflict has been overshadowed by its northern shores. The concept of 'our sea' introduced by the Romans was picked up in the nineteenth century by the French, who justified their conquest of the Maghrib, by maintaining that they were following in Rome's footsteps and re-claiming the southern shores for western civilisation (Lorcin 2002). In the twentieth century, the Italians, in the guise of 'new Rome', similarly justified their imperialism and the incursion into Libya and the horn of Africa (Ben-Ghiat and Fuller 2008). In the intervening period between the decline of Roman hegemonic influence in the region and the rise of France and Italian aspirations to emulate Roman imperialism, the Mediterranean has been as much a site of contestation as it has of peaceful networks of migration and trade. Correspondingly, the historiography of the sea from the northern perspective has been one of an enclosed space, a space whose specific characteristics, whether environmental or cultural, set it apart (Braudel 1949; Horden and Purcell 2000; Tillion 1983). In this image of the Mediterranean, the southern shores are envisioned as sites whose interaction is essentially across the sea to its bordering territories, rather than far beyond it.

A significant historiographical thread has been the discordant relationship between the northern Christian states and the southern Islamic ones. The Belgian historian, Henri Pirenne, in his posthumously published work, *Mohammed and Charlemagne*, argued, in what is now known as the 'Pirenne thesis', that it was not the Germanic tribes who invaded the southern shores, but the advance of Islam that eventually disrupted trade and led to the West's decline in the Middle Ages (1939). His thesis has been debated (Frank 1993; Havighurst 1976; Hodges 1983; Horden and Purcell 2000), but as Horden and Purcell point out, although his thesis is mistaken, it is invigorating in that it is 'immensely valued for its assertion of continuity' in the area (33). It is worth pointing out, however, that at the time it was written, it (consciously or inadvertently) reflected the historiographical conceit of French colonial scholarship on the area – and in particular colonial Algeria – which claimed that Islam had been a negative force in the region obliterating the culture of classical antiquity and shattering the unity of the area.

In the second half of the twentieth century, the historiography of the Mediterranean has developed under the shadow of Braudel's *magnum opus* on the Mediterranean world during the era of Philip II of Spain (1949). Braudel refuted Pirenne's claim arguing that the area's unity brought together its various shores through trade, diplomacy and travel, but his conceptualisation of the

Mediterranean world was also developed at a time when France was still a colonial power in North Africa, a fact, according to Strachan, that permeated his work (2011). Furthermore, inclusive though it is, the centre of gravity of the work was the northern shore of Spain. Braudel's work has had a profound influence on Mediterranean scholarship (Piterberg, Ruiz, and Symcox 2010). As a result, much of the ground-breaking scholarship on the area has remained centred on the medieval or early modern periods (Abulafia 2011; Horden and Purcell 2000). The focus on the Mediterranean as a single analytical field has not only created the concept of a unified space, whether environmental, economic or cultural, but also promoted the idea that its uniqueness came from this unity.

Recent scholarship has argued that the notion of unity is a western ideological construct that served the purposes of European hegemonic inclinations (Cooke, Erdag, and Parker 2008; Matar 2013). Indeed, Matar argues that Arab scholarship only saw the Mediterranean as 'the in-between sea' in the twentieth century, before which it had had multiple names, usually associated with a specific place along its shores, thus fracturing its unity and providing an image of multiplicity rather than unity[1] (Matar 2013). Be that as it may, the notion of a unified space has not gone away. With the advent of globalisation and the creation of subordinate trading or commercial organisations, Mediterranean unity has become a political and commercial actuality. The Mediterranean Union, first mooted in 1995, now comprises the member states of the European Union and most of the countries from the southern and eastern shores of the Mediterranean. The Secretariat, created in 2008, and headquartered in Spain, enjoys the 'privileges and immunities of an international organization'.[2] In 2013, the inaugural conference of the Society for Mediterranean Law and Culture chose the term, *Mare Nostrum*, for its title. The concept of unity seems to have come full circle.

The articles in this special issue take a somewhat different view of the Mediterranean. They are the result of a workshop held at the University of Minnesota in 2013 during which the importance of the southern shores of Mediterranean was discussed and debated. Although they do not contest the significance of the Mediterranean as a space of unique exchanges, networks and environmental influences, they do contest the notion of a space circumscribed solely by the territories along its shorelines. The activities emanating from or transiting through the southern shores are, according to these articles, multi-directional and wide reaching. Hence the concept of the influence of the Mediterranean is no longer limited to the sea and its shores but extends South beyond the Sahara and North beyond the bordering nations, as far afield as the USA.

The first two articles in the collection deal with trade networks, albeit of very different commodities. Aomar Boum's article examines the export from sub-Saharan and North Africa of ostrich feathers, a luxury product that reached a fashionable high point in late nineteenth-century Europe and the USA before being revitalised in the twentieth. The later-day renewed interest in ostrich feathers as a fashion accessory was, according to Boum, coupled with growing importance in ostrich meat consumption. Boum's arguments centre on the economic and environmental consequences of European and American demands for ostrich products on North and sub-Saharan African societies from both an environmental and economic perspective. The article thus demonstrates the multi-directional networks emanating from and encompassing the Mediterranean's southern shores and their long-term impact.

The second article, by Ismael Montana, examines the slave trade between sub-Saharan Africa and Ottoman Tunisia, countering the argument that the rise of maritime trade in the Mediterranean in the modern period diminished the commercial importance of trans-Saharan trade. Rather, he argues, capitalist penetration in the western Mediterranean from the late eighteenth century had a profound impact on the Saharan slave trade. By analysing the interactions of the this trade in conjunction with the economic and political changes that were taking place during this period, Montana provides a more complex picture, demonstrating the importance of the triangular relationship between North Africa, Africa and Europe.

Tim Cleaveland picks up the topic of slavery in the third article of this collection. His is the first of three articles that look at the intellectual or social impact of African or North African personalities beyond the borders of their individual residences. He considers the work of the Berber scholar, Ahmad Baba al-Timbukti, who sought to put an end to racial slavery by persuading North African scholars to accept the Islamic status of Muslims in West Africa, which, in accordance with standards laid down in Islamic law, should prohibit their enslavement. He focuses on Ahmad Baba's legal treatise, *Mi'raj al-Su'ud*, which catalogued the Muslim and non-Muslim populations of West Africa with the aim of clarifying their status with regard to enslavement. Cleaveland does not, however, attempt to present Ahmad Baba as a prototypical anti-slaver, but rather demonstrates the ambiguities of Ahmad Baba's thought as expressed in his treatise.

Shamil Jeppie's article moves us into the twentieth century by focusing on the role of the Timbuktu bibliophile, Ahmed Bul'araf, in the circulation of manuscripts and books throughout the Maghrib and the Middle East. Jeppie makes the all-important point that the dominance of Area Studies, which divided the African continent into distinct areas of scholarly research, has short-changed Africa in that it has obscured histories and historiographies in the interstices between the areas. Thus, networks, links and movements cross the Sahara from south to north or east to west are either overlooked or ignored. By examining the intellectual trajectory and activities of Bul'araf, Jeppie demonstrates the importance of the well-connected individual in establishing long-lasting networks radiating through and beyond the southern shores in many directions. Books and manuscripts become the object, and individuals the conduit, via which these networks are created and maintained. Books and manuscripts are a unique commodity in that their lifespan can not only be long-lasting but also uncommonly influential in diverse social and cultural spheres, thus time and space are reconfigured in compelling ways.

The third article in the trilogy about the centrality of personalities is Beverley Mack's examination of the ramifications of the scholarly reputation of the nineteenth-century teacher and activist, Nana Asma'u dan Fodio. Her intellectual reach extended beyond her homeland of what is today Nigeria through the Maghreb to America, where it had a formative influence on American Qadiriyya groups. Of particular note is the method by which these American groups adapted Asma'u's nineteenth-century educational model to suit twentieth- and twenty-first-century technological contexts. Connected to this adaptation is of course the way in which the West African and Maghribi practices of Islam are modified to accommodate the politics and needs of Muslim converts in the USA. Crucially, Mack reminds us that in the pre-colonial era there was no political divide between the Maghrib region and what is now Nigeria. In fact the region called the Maghrib extended far beyond the present northern shores into Mali and Mauretania. She thus reinforces the issue's central contention that the southern shores of the Mediterranean extend well beyond the countries making up its coastline.

The remaining two articles, whose directional networks are the two-way exchanges between the southern and northern shores, concern developments since the early 1990s. Paul Silverstein looks at the impact that Berber emigration has had on south-eastern oases in Morocco. He points out that whereas the oasis discourse on emigration is often of social abandonment and cultural death, emigration has also been instrumental in the survival of many of these oases, which have been challenged by overpopulation and the vagaries of weather or crop infestations. In such cases, emigration remittances have been a boon, providing the wherewithal for families to palliate, or even overcome, economic and financial difficulties. Silverstein provides a complex picture of the history and social structures of the oases, while examining the symbolic and material relationship of Berber mobility. His analysis makes an important contribution to diasporic politics.

Ted Swedenberg's contribution examines music as a form of protest and as a vehicle for potential political change. He traces the trajectory of Rai and Rap as interpreted by Maghrebi and African musicians from the ethnic margins to the mainstream of French popular music, thus shadowing the emerging political and cultural presence of Algerian-French and African-French in the metropole. The 1980s saw the rise throughout Europe of nationalist groups that used racism as a rallying point in their political platforms. Initially a response to these developments, the protest lyrics of Rai and Rap caught the imagination of a younger generation, an audience that extended beyond the milieu of its ethnic origins. Although Swedenberg stops short of claiming a casual relationship between the music and political change, it is incontestable that Rai and Rap have had a cultural and social impact. If the political goals remain elusive, the music has certainly contributed to raising the awareness of the problems facing both non-French immigrant and French nationals of immigrant origin and, in the process, firmly established their presence in French society.

Taken together these articles reconsider the concept of the Mediterranean as an enclosed sea where exchanges occur essentially between its immediate shores and highlight the importance of the southern shores in creating commercial, social and intellectual links far beyond the territories along its coastlines.

Notes

1. 'The Sea of Andalus, the Sea of Maghrib, the Sea of Alexandria, the Sea of Syria, the Sea of Constantinople, the Sea of the Franks, and the Sea of the Europeans/Byzantines … are one sea.' Yāqūt al-Ḥamawī (d. 1229), Mu'jam al-buldān. Quoted by Matar, unpublished manuscript.
2. http://ufmsecretariat.org/who-we-are/ (accessed July 7, 2014).

References

Abulafia, David. 2011. *The Great Sea: A Human History of the Mediterranean*. New York: Oxford University Press.
Ben-Ghiat, Ruth, and Mia Fuller. 2008. *Italian Colonialism*. Basingstoke: Palgrave Macmillan.
Braudel, Fernand. 1949. *La Méditerranée et le monde Méditerranéen à l'époque de Philippe II*. Paris: Colin.
Cooke, Miriam, Göknar Erdag, and Grant Parker, eds. 2008. *Mediterranean Passages: Readings from Dido to Derrida*. 1st ed. Chapel Hill: University of North Carolina Press.
Frank, Kenneth A. 1993. "Pirenne Again: A Muslim Viewpoint." *The History Teacher* 26 (3): 371–383.
Havighurst, Alfred F. 1976. *The Pirenne Thesis: Analysis, Criticism and Revision (College)*. Lexington, MA: Heath.
Hodges, Richard Whitehouse David. 1983. *Mohammed, Charlemagne & The Origins of Europe: Archaeology and the Pirenne Thesis*. Ithaca, NY: Cornell University Press.
Horden, Peregrine, and Nicholas Purcell. 2000. *The Corrupting Sea: A Study of Mediterranean History*. Oxford: Wiley-Blackwell.
Lorcin, Patricia M. E. 2002. "France and Rome in Africa: Recovering Algeria's Latin Past." *French Historical Studies* 25 (2): 295–329.
Matar, Nabil. 2013. "The 'Mediterranean' Through Arab Eyes: 1598–1798." The Mediterranean Re-imagined (CCAS Annual Symposium), Georgetown University, Washington.
Pirenne, Henri. 1939. *Mohammed and Charlemagne*. New York: Norton.
Piterberg, Gabriel, Teofilo Ruiz, and Geoffrey Symcox. 2010. *Braudel Revisited: The Mediterranean World 1600–1800 (UCLA Clark Memorial Library Series)*. Toronto: University of Toronto Press, Scholarly Publishing Division.
Strachan, John. 2011. "The Colonial Cosmology of Fernand Braudel." In *The French Colonial Mind: Mental Maps of Empire and Colonial Encounters*, edited by Martin Thomas, 72–95. Lincoln: University of Nebraska Press.
Tillion, Germaine. 1983. *The Republic of Cousins: Women's Oppression in Mediterranean Society/Uniform Title: Harem et les cousins. English*. London: Al Saqi Books, Distributed by Zed Press.

The elegant plume: ostrich feathers, African commercial networks, and European capitalism

Aomar Boum[a] and Michael Bonine[b†]

[a]Department of Anthropology, UCLA, CA, USA; [b]School of Middle Eastern and North African Studies,
University of Arizona, Tucson, AZ, USA

Ostrich feathers have long been an important export from Africa to different European markets.
The ostrich plume was a key part of the luxury trade across Mediterranean shores for centuries.
The main source of ostrich feathers was from wild ostriches especially from North and West
Africa. By the middle of the nineteenth century, the rising economic value of ostrich plumes
triggered colonial French and British competition over this luxury commodity, leading to the
establishment of domesticated ostrich farms by the French in North and West Africa and by the
British in South Africa. This article uses an economic historical framework to understand
colonial ostrich feather trade and its impact on French and British relations during the
nineteenth century in Africa. We examine the ostrich feather commercial networks that began
to emerge particularly by the middle of nineteenth century, and focus on the sources of ostrich
feathers and the local practices for hunting and raising ostriches. We argue that by looking at
the need for ostrich plumes in European markets and the rise in public consumption of fashion
goods based on the ostrich plume, nineteenth-century European capitalism destroyed not only
the wild African ostriches, but also local African livelihoods based on wild ostriches.

The ostrich plume has had an important symbolic significance in the Old World since antiquity, as
well as being important among numerous non-literate tribes in Africa and the Middle East for mil-
lennia. This elegant feather was often the symbol of authority, power, and prestige among the
royalty of the ancient Near East and was also adopted by the monarchs and their courts in
Europe. Warriors and rulers in ancient times might have had a single plume or perhaps an
elaborate headdress, or an ostrich fan or ostrich feathers on a staff. The ceremonial display of

---

†This paper is part of a large project that the late Michael Bonine and I have worked on since 2001. The ostrich feather was
one of Michael Bonine's passions. On his deathbed, he requested that I write this paper that summarizes our main ideas
about the topic. I dedicate this article to him and to his memory as my mentor and also include his name as co-author
because many of the ideas in this article were his.

headdresses and emblems that contained ostrich feathers were part of many cultures. First in Europe, and then in the United States, as of the seventeenth century, the ostrich plume became more common and fashionable, although it remained an expensive elite luxury item. By the last half of the nineteenth century, however, the display of ostrich feathers expanded considerably (in size and clientele), as plumes of ostriches and other birds became the fashion among the well-to-do women of Europe and America, both for elaborate hats with long plumes as well as ostrich fans, boas, stoles, muffs, and pompoms (Figure 1).

In the twenty-first century, many African farmers have benefited from the rising price of ostrich meat and feathers outside the continent. Europe and North America have renewed their historical interest in the African ostrich (Gillespie et al. 1998). South African ostrich meat is today the driving force rather than feathers, as it had been in the nineteenth century.

An online website describes this phenomenon:

> European confidence in red meat products plummets after successive health scares. Ostrich meat has the color and consistency of beef but provides a healthy red-meat alternative, being low in fat and cholesterol. The price of ostrich carcasses has risen by 25% in recent months.[1]

The fashion industry is also rediscovering the ostrich feather (Nixon 2001). Recently a Gucci advertisement read: 'Wear the ostrich feather with pride again'.[2] In Paris, New York, Los Angeles, London, and other global fashion capitals, ostrich feathers are used for fashion accessories such as evening wear, hats, and even wedding dresses. In 2002, ostrich accessories were presented at a fashion show in Paris attended by the famous fashion designer Pierre Cardin. The fashion for ostrich feathers is also evident in Rio de Janeiro's annual *Carnival* where

Figure 1. Postcard of Queen Mary wearing a hat with ostrich feathers (Courtesy Michael Bonine).

Figure 2. An advertisement of a Jean-Paul Gaultier ostrich dress in Klein Karoo Cooperative, Oudtshoorn, South Africa (Courtesy Michael Bonine, 2008).

dancers wear entire outfits of ostrich feathers, mostly imported from South African farms. Although the ostrich feather market has not yet regained its former historical success, from the rising export numbers and increasing ostrich farming, it appears that Europe and the Americas are again falling in love with Africa's ostriches (Williams 2012) (Figure 2).

Ostrich eggs (Green 2006) and feathers (Stein 2008) have also been an important export from North Africa to European markets (Schroeter 1988). As commodities, they were part of the valuable luxury trade crossing the southern shores of the Mediterranean as far back as the Roman, Assyrian,

Table 1.   Ostrich feathers brands, origin, qualities, and values in 1875[a]

Feather brand	Origin and characteristics	Exports (£)
Aleppo	Syrian desert; most perfect in feather quality, breadth, grace, and colour; very rare	?
Barbary	Tripoli	100,000
Senegal	Saint Louis	3000
Egypt	Good colour; do not bleach	350,000
Mogador	Morocco	20,000
Cape	Good colour; inferior quality	230,000
Yemen	Arabia; commonly but erroneously designated 'Senegal'; inferior in feather quality, thin, and poor	?

[a]Quoted in Mosenthal and Harting (1877, 224–225).

and Babylonian empires (Lefèvre 1914). Until the late nineteenth century, the source of feathers was principally from wild ostriches hunted in Syria (Mosenthal and Harting 1877, 236), the Arabian Peninsula, and North and West Africa (Table 1). Table 1 summarises the origins and characteristics of African ostriches during 1875. Of note is that by the 1870s, South African merchants were starting to redirect world exports of ostrich feathers from the traditional North African ports (Mogador, Tripoli, and Cairo) towards Cape Town. The historical value of ostrich plumes triggered a colonial French and British competition leading to attempts to establish domesticated ostrich farms (Daumas 1971, 61), by the French in North and West Africa and the British in South Africa; an industry that soon spread to a number of other countries, such as Australia in 1873, Argentina in 1880 (Douglass 1881, 4), and the USA in 1883 (Duncan 1888, 686).

In her work on ostrich feathers, Stein looks at the key role of Jews in the global trade of this commodity. She explores the way Jews

> fostered and nurtured the supply side of the global ostrich feather industry at all levels and stages – from feather handler to financier and from bird to bonnet – and over the varied geographical and political terrains in which the plumes were grown, plucked, sorted, exported, imported, auctioned, wholesaled, and manufactured for sale. (2008, 26)

We take a different perspective without overlooking the importance of the Jewish role in our historical narrative. Our focus is not only on the relationship between the bird's consumption and the feather fashion, but also on the larger economic and environmental consequences of European interest in this luxury item, and its impact, from an environmental economic perspective, on North Africa and sub-Saharan African tribal societies.

We examine in particular the feather trade that had developed by the late nineteenth century, focusing on the sources of feathers and the local practices for hunting and raising ostriches. We contend that by looking at the need for ostrich plumes in European and American markets and the rise in consumption of fashion goods based on the ostrich plume, Europe destroyed not only the wild North African ostriches, but also disrupted traditional trans-Saharan trading routes and shifted major Jewish networks to maritime routes on the southern African shores and further inland to places like Oudtshoorn. By expanding the local European luxury consumption of the African ostrich feather, France and Britain transformed the ordinary indigenous consumption of the ostrich egg, leather, and feather into a cash crop (Lefèvre 1914). Hence, they put traditional African economies and their environmental stability at risk, especially as the number of

Figure 3. Postcard of indigenous hunting of ostriches (Courtesy Michael Bonine).

ostriches used for food decreased. By the early 1900s, European fashion industries showed little interest in the ostrich feather following the anti-feather crusade, led by the Audubon society, which was against killing birds for elegance (Doughty 1972, 4) (Figure 3).

Ostrich plumes and eggs in local African contexts

Without any attempt to be comprehensive, either geographically or chronologically, examples of the wearing of ostrich plumes by African cultures illustrate their widespread use as a statement of status and importance. These are mainly from nineteenth- or twentieth-century descriptions, rock drawings (de Puigaudeau and Senones 1965) or photographs by travellers (Jackson 1968, 113–115; Monteil 1951, 98; Margueritte 1888, 51), ethnographers, anthropologists, and other scholars and professionals. To be sure, other types of feathers did adorn the head, similar to the significance of displaying cowry shells, but ostrich feathers were often the most prominent and important plume indicating either authority or a particular status and accomplishment.

Hats and headdresses were part of the representation of social and ceremonial practices and the visualisation of power and status relations in specific societies. As Arnoldi and Kreamer emphasise:

> Headgear and hair styles can no longer be viewed simply as passive reflections of culture. […] Hats and hairstyles, as well as other material objects, need to be understood as one of the technologies that people use to construct social identities and to produce, reproduce, and transform their relationships and situations through time. (1995, 9)

Within sub-Saharan African tribes, the head (and rest of the body) often was highly decorated, an expression of identity and social standing as well as a metaphor for the larger community. 'In the thought and moral imagination of many African and African diaspora societies, the head, itself, is a potent image that plays a central role in how the person is conceptualized' (Arnoldi and Kreamer 1995, 11). Hence headwear and headdresses (and hair styles) are attempts 'to transform their heads and by extension their whole bodies into cultural entities' (Arnoldi and Kreamer 1995, 13). The Pari in southeastern Sudan are part of a *monyomiji* system, which consists of four generations of age-sets. Similar age-set systems are common among many tribal/ethnic groups in this part of Sudan. When ceremonial dancing occurs, a Pari member of the *monyomiji* wears a hat with long white ostrich plumes (Kurimoto and Simonse 1998, 34).

Bedouin (and other) nomadic tribes in the Middle East and North (and Northeast) Africa often transported women, or at least the higher status females, on a litter or palanquin that was fitted upon a camel (Viré 1993). These were frequently quite large and elaborate. Some were used for special events, such as weddings, or they might be used during warfare. Black ostrich feathers were a prominent feature of many palanquins, particularly for ceremonial or special occasions. One of the most elaborate structures was the *markab* or sacred litter of the Rwala Bedouin, described by Jabbur (1995, 380–390). The *markab* was a 'vessel' or throne-like litter made of wood placed on the back of a female camel on which only women could ride. Called the *'utfa* by the Rwala, it was a 'throne' rectangle made of poles and several metres in height and width. Of relevance to this discussion is the fact the *'utfa*

> is decorated with black ostrich feathers, which, to the Rwala, represents a sacred symbol and a standard bearer used only in times of danger. It is always kept in the tent of the *amir*, and leaves it only when the *amir* is traveling with his tribe to the desert. (Jabbur 1995, 382)

The *'utfa* with its ostrich plumes was so sacred that if it were captured, 'the tribe will be defeated and forced to submit to its opponent and acknowledge their ascendancy and primacy'

(Jabbur 1995, 386). The *'utfa* also was possessed by the leader or strongest shaykh of the Rwala, and Jabbur (1995, 389–390) gives an account of how when the principal shaykh of the Rwala died in 1904, several sons or uncles vied for the tribe's leadership, each killing the supposed successor and removing every time the *'utfa* to their own tent.

Ostrich feathers evidently held a similar importance and played a role in many Arab (Bedouin) and Berber nomadic tribes in North Africa. For instance, Tristram (1860, 222) gives this account (in the late 1850s) of an Arab tribe encampment on the outskirts of the town of Waregla [Ouargla]: 'We ... entered the Arab encampment, where we saw several sheikhs' tents larger than the others, and adorned with tall plumes of black ostrich-feathers'. In a book published in 1934 by Lieutenant d'Armagnac, *Le Mzab et les pays Chaamba*, he includes several photographs of women of the Ouled Naïls, a Berber tribe in the Hauts Plateaux of northern Algeria. One of the photos (1934, 27) shows the *bassour* (French for palanquin) used to transport women with black ostrich feathers atop of the structure. In the early twentieth century, MacMichael photographed an elaborate *'utfa* among the Kababish Arabs, used 'to transport the daughter of the wife of the sheikh from one camping ground to another' (1912, 192). Black ostrich feathers are on the tall staff as well as on top of the camel's head.

Even though ostrich feathers were a sign of status and royalty, the ostrich egg was also of practical and symbolic importance. First, equal to approximately twenty-four chicken eggs, an ostrich egg was a desirable food item that was consumed by hunters, nomads, and villagers. Obviously, before modern refrigeration fresh ostrich eggs would be preserved – and traded. In fact, ostrich eggshells have been found in a number of archaeological sites, from the Bronze Age in Crete and Greece (where the ostrich would certainly have had to be an item of trade) to those in ancient Egypt and elsewhere (Phillips 2000). In the latter case, 'during the New Kingdom there is even a hint at ostrich domestication'; eggs for consumption may have collected from such 'farms' (Phillips 2000, 332). Ostrich eggshell jewellery is found in some Neolithic and Pre-dynastic and Archaic Egyptian graves and archaeological sites, and the speculation is that at least some these were used as amulets (Nordström 1972; Needler 1984; Phillips 2000; Green 2006, 30). The depiction of ostrich eggs also occurred in Egyptian funerary art. In the later Ptolemaic period, for instance, an ostrich egg was part of the mortuary ritual symbols in the catacombs of Alexandria (Green 2006, 30).

The ostrich egg makes an excellent container for water (or other liquids), and various nomadic, tribal groups used the eggshells in this manner. Ostrich eggs were used as cups in ancient Mesopotamia at least 5000 years ago (Laufer 1926). It is probable that they were one of the first liquid containers used in Africa and the Mediterranean world. The ostrich egg has also had a sacred role, both in the past and the present. Green has shown the widespread use – chronologically and geographically – of ostrich eggs (2006). Eggs shells have been found in temple excavations from the Greek and Roman periods to the Islamic era and were important not only in the Mediterranean world, but also across the Iranian plateau and into India. They were displayed in ancient temples, probably at the front of the religious building, either just the egg itself or as part of a lamp – such practices passed into Christianity and Islam. Although ostrich eggs can be found hanging inside mosques and churches in northern and Western Africa, they are most frequently found in mosques, churches, and monasteries of the Eastern Mediterranean region. Ostrich eggs are still found in churches and monasteries associated with Eastern Orthodox Christians in the Mediterranean, including Egypt (and Sinai), Syria, Palestine, Greece, and Cyprus. The reason for the hanging of ostrich eggs within Islamic and Christian buildings most probably goes back to their use in sacred space in antiquity. Green (2006) has effectively argued for the antiquity of the sacredness of the ostrich (eggs, feathers, and the bird itself), as well as the great spatial – and cultural – extent of various displays and sacrosanct utilisation of this bird. He discusses the common occurrence of hanging ostrich eggs in churches and monasteries among Eastern Orthodox groups in the Eastern Mediterranean and the way their display made its way into the western European churches, where 'the cultic usage of ostrich eggs had already become widespread by the thirteenth century' (35). Carswell states that 'the symbolic meaning of their [hanging ornaments] shape is not certain, but the egg is a universal symbol of fertility, and egg-shaped ornaments may have their origins in some sort of fertility cult' (1972, vol. 2, 63).

The maraboutic tombs in North Africa sometimes have ostrich eggs hanging within the tombs. For instance, the Teda of the Tibesti region, who were influenced by the Sanussi brotherhood, had such tombs. A possible reason that an ostrich egg might be hanging in a religious building is not only because the ostrich (and particularly the egg) represented fertility, but also because the ostrich egg has long been a symbol of the sacred and especially of purity. The ostrich egg in pre-Islamic Arabian (*Jahiliyya*) poetry, for instance, was often equated with a pearl:

> She is like the choicest of pearls, wherewith the Persians light up the
> Or like an ostrich's eggs on a sand-hillock, laid gently in the earth;
> Fair as a nest full of ostrich eggs betwixt rock and sand.

As Flood explains, in this pre-Islamic Jahiliyya poetry, 'the radiance and purity of hue possessed by both pearls and ostrich eggs enable these to function as interchangeable metaphors for the virginal maiden and female purity' (2001, 40). The quality of 'whiteness' is a desirable attribute of beauty. In fact, the common root in Arabic for egg (*bayda*) and white (*abyad*) also engenders the association of the colour white and virginity, and early Islamic traditions ascribed to Paradise and its inhabitants a brilliant whiteness (Flood 2001, 40–41; Wendell 1974) (Figure 4).

Figure 4. Ostrich egg on the minaret of a mosque in Mali (Courtesy Michael Bonine, 2006).

Ostrich eggs also were – and still are – found on the top of minarets and various spires or pinnacles of mosques and tombs. Occurring principally in West Africa, ostrich eggs on mosques can be found in Mauritania, Mali, Niger, Burkina Faso, Ivory Coast, and Ghana. These eggs are usually associated with the Sahelian-style mud or earthen (or sometimes stone) architecture and only one egg might be on a minaret – or as in the example of the renowned mud-brick Grand Mosque at Djenné, Mali, there may be eggs on all the small minarets and pinnacles. In Mauritania, for instance, the major mosque of Chinguetti has five ostrich eggs on its minaret. While ostrich eggs are frequently found on religious architecture in West Africa, their occurrence in North Africa appears to be less common. In the later 1850s, however, Tristram recorded the presence of ostrich eggs on a number of minarets and tombs in northern Algeria, a drawing of tombs in N'Goussa (near Ouargla) being particularly striking, each with six pinnacles and ostrich eggs – and black ostrich feathers as well (1860, 250). Typical of an ostrich egg on a minaret in northern Algeria is the drawing of 'Semaur Tower (Minaret), El At'f, Beni M'zab' (Tristram 1860, 170). In fact, ostrich eggs still did appear on many of the minarets of mosques and pinnacles of tombs in the Mzab (and in nearby rest of northern Algeria) in the twentieth century. This includes, for instance, ostrich eggs on the major minarets of mosques in Laghouat, and Ouargla, but particularly on top of maraboutic tombs. As one of the few examples in the rest of North Africa, Prussin (1986, 202) provides a photograph of a marabout's tomb at Kassenine (Al-Qasrayn) Tunisia, with an obvious ostrich egg (or representation thereof) above the dome of the tomb.

Ostrich eggs are put on the top of mosques (as well as within) due to 'the fact that [they] are associated with purity and the apotropaic ability to ward off evil around the Mediterranean [and elsewhere]' (Green 2006, 48). Green suggests that

> this custom [of placing ostrich eggs on minarets and pinnacles of mosques and tombs] was reflected in the formerly widespread practice of placing sets of ostrich eggs upon the points of the crosses that dominate the rooftops of Ethiopia churches. (2006, 53)

This does not explain why ostrich eggs placed on mosques are so much more common in parts of Saharan/Sahelian West Africa than in North Africa, with the exception of the M'zab of Algeria, and the Middle East. Nor is it known whether or not the use of ostrich eggs on minarets came into practice with the spread of Islam – and mosques – into West Africa. It is clear, however, that the use of ostrich eggs on minarets in this region is not just a recent phenomenon. The 1828 drawing of the Djenné Ber Mosque by René Caillié shows what are clearly ostrich eggs on both the main minaret and a secondary one and, arguably, on the many pinnacles across the entire top of the walls. However, by the beginning of the twentieth century, the Great Mosque was in complete ruins, without most of its minarets, or its ostrich eggs. The mosque was rebuilt in 1906–07, and a 1911 photograph of the Djenné Grand Mosque shows that ostrich eggs were (once again) atop the mosque.

Just how long ostrich eggs have been used on mosques in the Sahel has not been determined. Yet, one might speculate that perhaps the greater availability of ostrich eggs in the Sahel (and earlier in the North) might have led to their greater use. It might be that the symbolic importance of fertility (and purity) as expressed by a huge egg might have been more easily displayed in the context of the characteristic syncretic West African Islam, where the origins and creation of life are acknowledged and celebrated more publicly. Thus sexuality may be more explicitly expressed in architecture (and arts and crafts) than in the typical North Africa and Middle Eastern Islamic context.

During his journey in North Africa (mainly in Libya) between 1818 and 1820, Captain George Francis Lyon described ostriches in the region of Marzouk (capital of Fezzan):

Figure 5. Postcard of ostrich hunting during Captain Buchanan expedition into the Sahara (Courtesy Michael Bonine).

There are ... in these mountains great quantities of ostriches ... . It is during the breeding season that the greatest numbers are produced, the Arabs shooting the old ones while on their nests. At all the three towns, Sockna, Hoon, and Wadan, it is the custom to keep tame ostriches in a stable, and in two years, to take three cuttings of their feathers. (1966, 76–77)

This personal report and others like it provided accounts of the uses of the ostrich, its feathers, meat, and leather by North African local tribes during the eighteenth and nineteenth centuries.

The ostrich feather gained unprecedented value in the growing world economy when it became one of the most exported articles from Africa to Europe during the second half of the nineteenth century (Miège 1981–1982). Its rising economic value had a negative impact on the future of the wild North African ostrich and its local usage. The introduction of guns and the continuous unrestricted killing, hunting, capturing, and wounding of wild ostriches in North Africa led to its quick extinction in southwestern Morocco, Algeria, and other parts of the Barbary and *Bilad al-Sudan* regions during the twentieth century (Campus-Fabrer 1990) (Figure 5).

During the first half of the nineteenth century, ostrich feathers could only be obtained through hunting the wild North African bird. The rising demand in European markets and the limited supply of this valuable article, led the French and subsequently the British colonial authorities to think of ways to ensure that trading in ostrich plumages and its circulation in European market continued. Henceforth, the domestication and farming of the ostrich began timidly in French colonies in North Africa and later grew in South African British colonies. By the turn of the nineteenth century, the European fashion industry turned out to be the driving force for a western interest in North Africa's ostrich plumes. This colonial infatuation with ostrich feathers came to be seen in the feathers put on top of women's hats as adornment and to add more height to their natural posture (Johnson 1881, 136).

Economic morality, colonial industries of luxury, and Ostrich plumes

In *the History of Everyday Things: the Birth of Consumption in France, 1600–1800*, Daniel Roche discusses major social and economic shifts in France during the seventeenth century when the rich identified mostly with the 'landowners and to less extent the leaders of commerce ... In the market of spiritual goods superfluity is converted into spiritual riches for the giver and necessary goods for the poor who are helped' (2000, 72). The rich enjoyed their wealth by redistributing part of it through almsgiving. The public display of luxury was not only condemned by society, but also frowned upon based on economic and moral grounds. Christian beliefs about consumption were partly grounded on a moral economy that stressed the obligations of rich people towards the poor and needy; at the same time, people were asked to engage in moderate consumption of goods.

Economic morality became less important as religious principles ceased to define the economic and social practices of individuals and social groups. This transformation took place in England by the early eighteenth century and gradually found its way into France. European society began to take a positive attitude to luxury and opulence. According to Roche: 'The necessity of super-fluity asserts itself through a new relation to the world and to objects … Virtue is no longer the fruit of renunciation but of moderate and reasonable use of goods and of benefits they lavish' (2000, 75). By the eighteenth century, changes in consumption by the privileged aristocracy gradually influenced all society, and the spread of luxury articles changed the traditional European model of social conduct. Preachers' influence over the social renunciation of lavish behaviour, the squandering of goods, and rejection of luxury as anti-morality declined over time.

Luxury came to be part of mainstream Europe as European economies entered a phase of wide-scale consumption in the early nineteenth century. European villagers and city-dwellers were no longer confined to an economy of ordinary consumption of necessities. Despite the slow accep-tance of luxury goods by society as a whole and their concentration in elite circles, other social classes started to be able to afford the vanities of life (Smith 1976; Fitzgibbons 1995). In the nine-teenth century, British and French colonialism competed not only for new economic markets for their mercantile expansionism, but also for local and exotic material and products that could be imported and sold in Europe. In this context, the fashion for ostrich feathers turned into a booming industry, and was later closely tied to colonial environmental policies of ostrich farming and domestication.

Besides being an important and often sacred symbol in the African environments, the ostrich feather also became a significant part of the dress of the wealthy and prominent and especially part of the ceremonial costume of Europe in mediaeval and later periods, and in the more recent several centuries in the USA as well. An examination of the costumes of England, for instance, gives an indication of the growing use of ostrich plumes as imparting a particular status and importance to both men and women. The wearing of ostrich feathers as hat embellishment differs depending on the period but, in general, becomes more fashionable over time – and, hence, more common – especially in the nineteenth and early twentieth centuries. It is this rather constant and increasing demand for these elegant plumes in Europe (and later America) that fuelled the trans-Saharan trade in ostrich feathers (as well as from other routes and sources), which is also discussed in this article.

Peacock (1986) provides hundreds of drawings of costumes for both men and women in England from 1066 to 1966, arranged by the chronological reigns of the kings and queens of England. A cursory examination of the English dress patterns over time in this 'sketch-book' indicates the expanding use of feathers in general and ostrich plumes in particular, for 'feather-trimmed hats' in England. In the centuries immediately following 1066, no feathers were appar-ently used, and, in fact, hats are rather minimal, with 'caps' or no headpiece worn by men, and often veils or no headpiece for women. Feathers as part of hats among the English, for both men and women, appear to be first used in the late fourteenth and early fifteenth centuries – although the feathers depicted in the hats do not appear to be ostrich plumes and they do not seem to be very common (1986, 21, 23). Feather-trimmed hats seem to be worn mainly by English men from the mid-fifteenth century until the mid-sixteenth century, with clearly identified ostrich plumes only showing up by the end of the fifteenth century.

Starting at the beginning of the sixteenth century, Peacock (1986, 36–39) begins to use the term 'ostrich plume' to describe the feathers of the men's hats. It is not until the mid-sixteenth century that ostrich plumes are shown on a woman's hat (1986, 43). By the seventeenth century, ostrich plumes were used on hats of the English elite for both sexes, although it appears to have been more common for men's hats. By the eighteenth century, however, English men's hats generally lose their ostrich feathers, and it is also less common among women. In the nineteenth century, men are wearing mainly top hats with no plumes or any other decoration, whereas women now begin to wear more and more ostrich (and other) feathers throughout that century (1986, 79–107), and into the beginning of the twentieth century. Many of these women's hats could be quite large and elaborate.

Having given a very general overview of the sartorial use of ostrich feathers in England, more specific information is warranted to explain the extensive wearing of the elegant plume in Europe (and America), the demand for which created the lucrative feather trade from Africa and the Middle East. It should be stressed that the ostrich feather as part of ceremonial dress, particularly for military and other official and royal orders, remained an important and necessary accessory in England, even after its usage declined following the First World War. Mansfield (1980) examines how English court dress and ceremonial uniforms and dress remained elaborate throughout the last four centuries, with ostrich feathers often being part of that dress. For the Most Noble Order of the Garter, by the time of Charles II (r. 1660–1685), the cap or hat had become 'a narrow brimmed hat with a stiff pleated crown, all of black velvet, and a towering plume of white ostrich and black heron's feathers' (Mansfield 1980, 54). The painting of King Charles in his Garter robes shows this rather spectacular crown of ostrich feathers (Mansfield 1980, 51; Ashmole 1672). By the nineteenth century, however, the

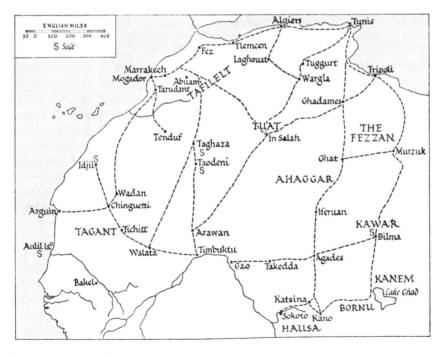

Figure 6. Trans-Saharan trade routes.
Source: Wright (2007).

crown was lower and the number of ostrich plumes was restricted to three (Mansfield 1980, 54). Mansfield points out that the feathers were one of the most expensive items in the earlier days.

Ostrich plumes were also important for most of the other British orders of chivalry. In a photograph from 1953 at least one large plume is shown on the cap of the Order of the Thistle (Mansfield 1980, 71), while a 1725 statute of the Order of the Bath shows that 'the hat was of white silk, high crowned, and decorated with a towering plume of white ostrich feathers', and 'as with the [order of the], Garter the ostrich feathers were a very heavy item: in the early 1800 s they could cost over £20' (Mansfield 1980, 77, 79). White ostrich feathers were also once part of the headpiece of the Order of St Michael and St George, but were abandoned by about the mid-twentieth century (Mansfield 1980, 86) (Figure 6).

Trade routes and their caravans

Before French colonial penetration in North Africa, Saharan caravans transported ostrich feathers as well as other goods to Mediterranean coastal ports. The caravan traffic between the Barbary and *Bilad al-Sudan* was carried out via three major routes. They included the Mogador–Taoudeni–Timbuktu route in the west, the Ghadamis–Air–Kano and the Tripoli–Fezzan–Bornu routes in the centre, and the Cyrenaica–Kufra–Wadai route in the east (Adu Boahen 1962, 350; Bovill 1958, 235). The western Taoudeni–Timbuktu route ended in Marrakesh and Fez. It also led to Mogador in the coast for European trade. This route had two small arteries, which ended up in Timbuktu: Goulimime–Taoudeni and Touat–Tafilalelt. Second, the central route had two arteries: Touat–Mzab and Gadames–Gabes. Finally, the Egyptian routes linked the Delta to *Bilad al-Sudan* by two networks: Darfour and Sennar (Lydon 2009) (Figure 7).

These three routes were always affected by the political and economic conditions in Bilad al-Sudan and the security provided by local tribes. Newbury summarised the causes of the decline of trans-Saharan trade as:

> [The] (1) political instability in the Timbuctu area following the fall of Songhai; (2) nineteenth-century wars in Bornu, the Fezzan and at Agades; (3) the French occupation of Algeria; (4) the abolition of the slave trade; (5) commercial competition from the Senegal and Niger posts. (1966, 234)

During the nineteenth century, local and international political events led to major transformations along these routes. The rivalry between numerous Arab and Tuareg groups as well as the Fulani

Figure 7. Postcard of a caravan carrying ostrich carcasses (Courtesy Michael Bonine).

and Bambara tribes in the Sahara put the caravans at risk along the western route. This contributed to a shift in commercial movement from the western route to the eastern route leading to two highly used routes: the Ghadames–Air–Kano and the Cyrenaica–Kufra–Wadai routes. Adu Boahen debunked the theory put forward by Bovill who contended that until the nineteenth century the western route was 'pre-eminent in the gold trade and still more important as a cultural high-way' (Bovill 1958, 235). Instead, Adu Boahen argued that this route was active during the sixteenth century. However after the Sa'dian conquest of the Sudan, anarchy and insecurity reigned in the region. Therefore, 'by overwhelming the peace and order of the Askias', Adu Boahen noted, 'the Moroccans killed the goose that more or less literally laid the golden eggs' (1962, 351). The Tripoli–Fezzan–Bornu route also lost its commercial importance because of the fall of the Songhai Empire. Adu Boahen explains this decline as a result of significant political developments:

> In the first place, the revolutions brought that traffic to a complete standstill between 1830 and 1842 and part of it was therefore diverted into the Wadai-Benghazi and the Soudan routes. Secondly, the substitution of the feeble Turkish administration, whose influence did not even reach the southern provinces of Fezzan, for the oppressive though relatively powerful Karamanli government, enabled the Tuareg and the Tibu, the two great peoples of the Sahara, to revive their traditional raids and plundering expeditions against each other. (1962, 351)

The political stability of the Sokoto Empire, on the other hand, led to the Ghadames–Air–Kano route becoming one of the most active commercial routes. In northern Algeria, however, the networks were deeply affected by the French conquest. Miège contended that Algerian commercial activities declined as caravans turned from the French-controlled markets towards Morocco and Libya (1989, 74). During the second half of the nineteenth century the Cyrenaica–Kufra–Wadai route was the most active. Established in 1843, the Sanusiyya brotherhood maintained political stability in southern Cyrenaica. For Slouschz,

> The Senussiya have stretched across the desert a chain of Zawya which recall the hospices of the Middle Ages, and through which the Senussiya exert a profound influence on the surrounding nomad tribes. The Zawya has become a sort of center of exchange and barter for the nomads, which carry on transactions both in money and in kind. They give shelter to all wayfarers excepting Christians, even extending their hospitality to Jewish merchants. (1927, 82)

All trade routes were affected by political, social, and climate factors; tribal alliances and control of regions; availability of wells, entrepôts (*nzala)*, and relief. The size of each caravan, measured in camel numbers, varied from a few persons and camels to several thousand people (Ollive 1880, 5; Schroeter 1988, 92–95). The trade was maintained and financed in general by minority groups. According to Miège, they were Algerian Mzabi Jews, Egyptian Greeks and Copts, Arabs of African coasts and the Red Sea as well as Zanzibar, Indians of the Red Sea and Central Africa, and the Jews of other North African urban and rural places from Mogador to Egypt (1981–1982, 96). Jews were stationed throughout the northern and southern termini and the refreshment centres of the trans-Saharan trade North African commercial entrepôts, such as Mogador, Goulmime, and Tripoli (Miège 1982; Schroeter 1988; Stein 2008; Boum 2013).

'Jews are Ostrich feathers:'[3] Jewish merchants and saharan trade

Although European trade started to shift to the coastal ports of West and South Africa, the percentage of commercial transactions through trans-Saharan routes towards the north did not decline (Newbury 1966; Dunn 1971; Miège 1981–1982; Fituri 1982). By the middle of the nineteenth century, northern Mediterranean and other European ports (Marseille, Livorno, Gibraltar, Liverpool, and London) maintained intensive commercial links with the Sahara through northern termini ports of the Saharan trade routes. These ports, especially Essaouira (Schroeter 1982, 1989) and Tripoli (Stein 2008), had large Jewish communities of merchants, traditionally called *Tujjar al-Sultan* (merchants of the sultan). In Essaouira (Mogador), the sultan protected the Jewish merchants and granted them the authorisation to engage in trade (Boum 2013). Jews also benefited from Othman protection in Tripoli. The patron–client relationship between Jews and Muslims in North Africa during the nineteenth century was central to the long distance trade. When Jews travelled outside the territory controlled by the central governments in Morocco and Libya, they were 'compelled to pay tribute to the tribesmen who ruled the regions that they crossed. A kind of passage toll called *zattata* ... was required by those guaranteeing safe passage (*zattat*)' (Schroeter 1989, 124).

Jewish merchants played a central role in the Saharan trading centres because of their multiple connections in the southern regions. This network of patron–client relations enabled Jewish peddlers and merchants along the Cyrenaica and southern Morocco to travel without being harmed. In Cyrenaica, the Sanusiyya also enabled the Jewish communities to establish themselves in many towns of the interior. Slouschz described the relationship between the Jewish merchants of Cyrenaica and the religious order. He wrote:

> I have given a good deal of attention to the question of the relations between the Senussiya and the Jews, carrying on an investigation at first hand. I must begin by stating that nowhere in my travels have I come across a single complaint against the Senussiya as such on the grounds of injustice and extortion .... All the Jews of whom I have made inquiry are of the opinion that the Senussiya, besides being well disposed towards them, are, on the whole, a peaceful people, living a simple and austere life. (1927, 80–81)

In southwestern Morocco, The Nasiriyya Zawiyya in Tamgrout also extended its protection to Jewish peddlers and merchants in Dar'a. Jews also attended annual fairs like the moussem of Sidi Ahmad ibn Mousa of Tazeroualt in Sous (Pascon 1980; Schroeter 1988). In Tripoli and Mogador, Jewish merchants traded among other articles in ostrich feathers with Bilad al-Sudan and the Sahara. Before the French occupation of Algeria, they shipped ostrich feathers through Algeria. At the same time, they were involved in the importation and distribution of European commodities, such as sugar and tea in the southern regions (Miège 1961, 246–251). The Jewish wholesalers operated through a network of Jewish communities in trading centres throughout southwestern Morocco and Fezzan (Libya).

By the middle of the nineteenth century, the ostrich trade was entirely in the hands of the Jewish traders of Essaouira and Tripoli and their co-religionists of the Saharan fringes. Local tribes captured ostriches in the southern fringes of the Sahara (Boum 2013). Then they were loaded to Tindouf and Oued Noun to be sold to agents of Jewish merchants in Essaouira (Schroeter 1988) and Tripoli (Stein 2008). These Jewish merchants relied on Muslim transporters to ship their commodities from the interior to the coastal port of Essaouira. The trading system involving ostrich feathers was based on long-term credit where the Ait Baha acquired commodities such as Manchester goods from the merchants of Essaouira before they 'proceeded to the frontier of the Sahara where they gave their goods to the Sahrawi traders until the season for the caravan of ostrich feathers, gold and slaves' (Schroeter 1982, 379).

In the 1880s, trading in ostrich feathers through the Saharan routes started to decline due to the political reasons already stated. In the meantime, the ostrich feather industry became firmly established in the Cape colony (Aschman 1955, 121). As ostrich farming started to grow in the Cape, hundreds of Jews migrated to the district of Oudtshoorn, where they became actively involved in the ostrich feather industry. According to Aschman,

> Most of them had never seen an ostrich, not even in a zoo, but realizing the potentialities of the industry, they begin to make a study both of the birds and their feathers. Some dabbled in feather buying and selling while running their stores. Others traveled round from farm to farm buying feathers and later even buying the feathers on the birds before they have been clipped. (1955, 129–130)

While the ostrich feathers were contributing to the economic boom of South Africa, the decline of the Saharan trade led to the decrease in trade through the western route as caravans continued to move through eastern routes. Walz maintained that by the end of the eighteenth century, Jewish intermediaries already controlled the feather industry in Egypt. He noted that, in Cairo, 'feathers were almost exclusively bought up by Jews, who specialised in sorting and packing them for shipment to Europe' (1978, 38). After the French conquest of Timbuktu in 1893, much of the trade was channelled through Benghazi, Tripoli, and Cairo.

In North Africa, and Algeria in particular, France justified its colonial presence as a legitimate successor of Rome arguing that the natives had ruined the North African environment. Davis notes that 'one of the ways the French thought they could fulfill their Roman and Imperial legacy was to "restore" the North African landscape to its former glory and fertility with large reforestation and other environmental and agricultural improvement projects' (2011, 65). The French colonial environmental policy blamed the indigenous population and mainly nomadic tribes for ruining the North African environment, and therefore gave the moral authority to French administrators in Algeria and later Tunisia and Morocco to confiscate private and tribal lands and develop them. Agricultural development and reforestation were at the centre of a policy 'driven by the legend of the granary of Rome, especially in the cereal sector' (Davis 2011, 73). Accordingly, in addition to its 'wheat policy', France also developed a domestication of ostriches for its feather fashion.

From wild Ostrich hunting to domestication

The domestication of the North African ostrich dates back to antiquity. Yet, it is very difficult to trace its origin. Campus-Faber (1990, 96) assumed that the demand and use of the plumes by

Figure 8. Postcard of indigenous domestication of ostriches in Tchad (Courtesy Michael Bonine).

the Eastern Libyans (Bates 1914, 99) and the difficulties in hunting ostriches might have pushed them towards domestication. However, there is no clear and strong scientific evidence of early attempts of the bird's domestication in North Africa. We had to wait until the beginning of the nineteenth century to hear the first North African explorers' testimonies of ostrich farming (Haïdara 1999, 140; Cristobal 1987, 140). Oudot wrote that Moroccans raised ostriches at the beginning of the nineteenth century in the royal palace (1880, 94). He also noted that many explorers observed cases of domestication of ostriches in Egypt and Kurdufan (Sudan). These native domestication attempts yielded good profits from plumes sales (Oudot 1880, 94; Camps-Fabrer 1990, 97). In South Africa, M. Jules Verrieux witnessed a farmer named M. Korsten in Algoa-Bay in 1818 who owned six domesticated ostriches: two males and four females. These birds were fed in the morning and afternoon, allowed to leave their enclosure during the middle of the day and roamed in the vast lands that surrounded the farm before they returned to their coop at sunset. They laid and brooded their eggs off the farm (Oudot 1880, 94) (Figure 8).

These European eyewitness accounts show that the domestication of ostriches started before Oudot, a French civil engineer, asked M.A. Chagot to set up the first ostrich domestication project in North Africa. If the Victorian fashion led to the growing demand of African plumes in the middle of the nineteenth century, the decreasing numbers of wild North African ostriches was behind the preliminary ostrich farming and domestication attempts. The first attempts of domestication were conducted in Laghouat (Algeria) and Saint Louis (Senegal). They turned out not to be profitable. In 1857, M.A. Chagot, member of the *Société Zoologique d'Acclimation de Paris*, offered a prize of 2000 francs for the domestication of the ostrich. This amount was given to M. Hardy, the director of the *Pépinière du Gouvernment à Alger*, in 1859. During the same period, other attempts at domestication were carried out in Europe, but they failed. Some of these were in San Donato near Florence by prince Demidoff; in Marseille by Noël Suguet; in Grenoble by M. Bouteille; and in Madrid by Graelles (Oudot 1880, 96). These projects demonstrated that if certain conditions (temperate latitude, dry barren waste land, soil, etc.) were met ostrich domestication could be achieved (Figure 9).

The British followed these experiments with unprecedented interest and managed to set up their own ostrich farms in the Cape Colony in 1866. Mosenthal and Harting noted that the first experiments of artificial incubation of the wild ostrich took place in 1866 in Beaufort,

Figure 9. Postcard of ostrich farming at the Jardin d'Essai d'Alger (Courtesy Michael Bonine).

Cape Colony (1877, 190–191). In 1870, ostrich chicks were successfully raised in the George District. In 1874, a farmer by the name of M. Murray wrote to the journal *The Field* that he was the first to successfully reproduce ostriches through domestication in his farm in Kuyl Fonteyn at Cape Bonne Esperance (Oudot 1880, 97–98). It appears from Oudot's *Le fermage des autruches en Algérie: Incubation artificielle* and Julius de Mosenthal and Harting's *Ostriches and Ostrich Farming* that there was strong competition between the British and the French over the domestication of the bird. It is clear that, though the French did not reach the same successful results the British did, Chagot succeeded in domesticating the ostrich seven years before it was introduced into the Cape territories.

Despite French colonial projects, the ostrich domestication ultimately failed in Algeria. The British who started late in their ostrich domestication in the Cape achieved a remarkable success. The high Jewish immigration to the Cape in the middle of the nineteenth century contributed to this achievement. The new Jewish community of Oudtshoorn drew heavily on its knowledge of the world markets for ostriches. Among the most successful businessman of ostrich feathers in South Africa was Max Rose, also known as the 'ostrich feather king of South Africa'. Aschman describes him as someone who not only had

> A greater knowledge of the ostrich feather market than any man alive, but also knew vastly more about the breeding of birds and the growth of the right sort of feathers than most other farmers in the Oudtshoorn and surrounding districts. He took a scientific interest in the life of the ostrich … . He knew the historical background of the ostrich as a creature of the desert, he knew the bird's idiosyncrasies from the day it was hatched until old age … . His knowledge of the world markets for the ostrich feathers was limitless, and the local farmers drew heavily upon this at all stages of the industry's mercurial career. (1955, 130)

In the early stage of the industry, South African merchants (such as Rose) were able to analyse and anticipate the market tendencies and fashion in the cities of New York, Paris, London, Vienna, and Berlin. Their profit from the feather trade steadily rose from '£87,074 in 1870 to £304,933 in 1875; £883,632 in 1880, and more than £1,000,000 in 1882' (Aschman 1955, 125). Thereby, South Africa controlled the world market by the 1880s. The French could not improve their ostrich farming and were not aware of the British colonists' success in the Cape until the latter managed to gain control of the industry.

The French decided to respond to the British success by following the steps outlined by Chagot to compete with British colonists in Cape. For this purpose, some French merchants met to examine how they could challenge the British monopoly of ostrich feather exports from North African ports. The solution was to establish a large farm of ostriches in a geographical area close to the European market. A disagreement rose between the members of this committee regarding the choice of farming land between Egypt and Algeria. In November 1878, French settlers formed a company for ostrich farming in Algeria. In a carefully chosen area of 200 hectares, they set up a huge park at Aïn Marmora, near Algiers. The owners faced some major problems in obtaining wild ostriches because most of the wild Algerian ostriches retreated to the interior. The ostriches were bought from the *Jardin d'essai d'Alger* (Oudot 1880, 102). Hence although, the park had all the resources for the domestication of a population of 500 ostriches, it actually started with 20 including some adult couples.

Apart from this experiment, Oudot, the only known source on ostrich farming in Algeria during the second half of the nineteenth century, gave other examples of parks set up by French *colons*. He cited the *Jardin d'essai du Hamma* directed by Charles Rivière, which housed eight adult couples, four young ostriches, and eighteen chicks. Equally important, Captain Crépu produced ostriches by natural incubation in the *Parc de Misserghim* (Oran) in 1873. However, other colonial priorities impeded his interests in improving ostrich farming in Algeria. Finally, in 1876, an unnamed English lady, the wife of a French advocate at Algiers, started ostrich farming in Kouba, near Algiers. This park was also supplied with ostriches in 1876, 1877, and 1879 by the *Jardin d'essai d'Alger*.

All these parks including the original *Jardin d'essai du Hamma* contained a total population of approximately 108 ostriches, the majority of which were adults. Ostrich farming in the Cape started in 1865 with 80 ostriches, and rose to 35,000 birds. Oudot hoped that Algeria would have a population of 40,000 ostriches by 1889. This objective, he thought, could be achieved by utilising both natural and artificial incubations. Since 1873, ostrich egg artificial incubation in South Africa changed the reproduction of ostriches. The system of farming in Cape Town differed from Algeria. For British farmers, ostrich farming depended on free space and good fencing for its success. It was estimated that the land of farming should be five hectares per ostrich; other farmers however thought that a hectare per bird was enough. South African farmers also maintained that ostriches must be let loose in these lands.

Oudot, however, had a different perspective. As long as the enclosed space is rich in terms of food, it was not necessary for farmers to have a large amount of land. The farmers penned up their ostriches by couples within a relatively small fenced terrain of about 500–1000 metres. This enabled the closure of 10–20 couples per hectare (1880, 106). Oudot went beyond this statement, maintaining that French ostrich farming methods were more efficient than the one practiced in Cape Town. He provided a number of reasons to favour small farms, namely (1) farmers did not need to occupy lands with fertile valuable soil; (2) small terrains meant good surveillance of the ostrich; (3) a very controlled breeding pattern between the couples was important; (4) eliminating fights between males when it was very hot was critical; (5) ensuring the tranquillity of the bird during brooding was beneficial, and finally (6) small plots enabled the farmer to handle the ostrich easily and thereby ensure quick domestication.

Ostrich feather trading fluctuations and the end of the boom

The trans-Saharan trade was part of a worldwide economic system. Economic, social, and cultural changes that took place in London and Paris reverberated in the different commercial centres of the *Bilad al-Soudan* as well as western and northern African commercial markets. Between 1860 and 1900, a number of political and economic changes took place in the centres and the periph-

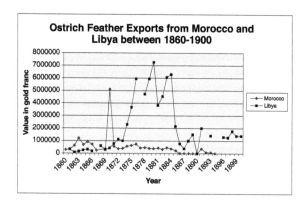

Figure 10. Ostrich feather exports from Morocco and Libya between 1860 and 1900.

eries of this world system economy bringing major changes at the level of feathers trade. Although the ostrich feather industry shifted largely to South Africa partly because of the Jewish community of Oudtshoorn, the value of ostrich feathers trade with Europe through Essaouira and Tripoli continued to increase in the second half of the nineteenth century.

Figure 10 shows that before 1872 trade in ostrich feathers through Essaouira was flourishing compared to Tripoli. While the western route was relatively safe between 1863 and 1867, the Sanusiyya order had not yet made a big impact in securing the safety of the routes that led to Tripoli and Benghazi. Unlike France's role in North Africa, the Turks were not 'a regional power, trying in any real sense to influence the trade or the regional struggles for hegemony' (Vikor 1985, 741). After 1870, the ostrich feathers trade through Essaouira started to plummet because of the political conditions along the western route. The central government could not control the tribal revolts in the south although Morocco tried to reaffirm its control in the region and its supervision of the trans-Saharan trade through intermittent military expeditions.

Although the French authorities in Algeria launched many ostrich farms in Algiers and other cities, exports through North Africa fell short of competing with British exports through South Africa. Ostrich feather exports through Morocco represented about 2% of the value of the European consumption in 1878 (Pascon 1980, 717). Trade routes through Libya, however, became very active when compared to Morocco, mainly because of security. The European market had more faith in the South African representatives because of their safe and reliable maritime route. The existence of a network of Jewish merchants in South Africa replaced the dwindling Jewish intermediaries along the western route. Rabbi Mardochée Aby-Serour described how caravans in the 1860s were continuously attacked and pillaged by Arab tribes (Boum 2013). He travelled to Timbuktu at the end of 1864 when looters from the Arab tribes of Rguibet, Ait-el-Hassen, and Ygout stopped his caravan on multiple occasions, kidnapping him, and almost killing him. When he finally reached Timbuktu he borrowed 12 sirat of gold, which he used to buy ostrich plumes for his associate in Essaouira (Beaumier 1870, 361).

By the end of the nineteenth century, Paris and London supplied the bulk of ostrich feathers to the USA. Yet, as the supply of ostrich and other birds' feathers increased in London and the USA, British and American organisations against the feather trade launched a massive popular movement (Adams and Donovan 1999) against not only the destruction of nests of wild birds and their killing but also wearing feathers as ornaments (Doughty 1972, 4, 1975). For instance, in the 1890s the American Audubon Society managed to gain wide support among women 'who agreed never to wear plumage of wild birds other than the ostrich … and set out to inform other people of the plight of plume bird species' (Doughty 1972, 4). The Audubon society built close contacts with other anti-plume organisations in Europe especially the London-based Society for the Protection of Birds. However, although restrictions on the ostrich plume were relative, women were asked to boycott any wild African ostrich feathers. The 'plume guilt' was not only based on a critique of Europe consumption behaviour and its lack of consciousness about the environment, but also on its lack of concern for traditional African societies which partly based their survival on ostrich meat and eggs.

Acknowledgements

We thank Patricia Lorcin, Daniel Schroeter, Thomas Park, Diana Davis, and Norma Menozda-Denton for their valuable comments and editing. We are responsible for the ideas and opinions made in the final version.

Disclosure statement

No potential conflict of interest was reported by the authors.

Notes

1. Available at: www.ostrichemporium.co.za/index.htm (last checked on 15 March 2014). There are other websites that provide a great deal of information about the growing ostrich meat industry and its markets across Europe and the Americas.
2. Many tutorials including fashion magazines and webpages offer new trends of how to wear the ostrich feather and use it in home decorations. An example is the Sydney Style A-Z Trend Guide for Fall/Winter 2013 posted on YouTube and last accessed on 29 March 2014. Available at: http://www.youtube.com/watch?v=B77HgAWYT-c.
3. Quoted in Aschman (1955, 121).

References

Adams, C., and J. Donovan, eds. 1999. *Animals and Women: Feminist Theoretical Explorations*. Durham, NC: Duke University Press.

Adu Boahen, A. 1962. "The Caravan Trade in the Nineteenth Century." *Journal of African History* 3 (2): 349–359.

Armagnac, D. L. 1934. *Le Mzab et les pays Chaamba*. Alger: Baconnier.

Arnoldi, M., and C. Kreamer. 1995. *Crowning Achievements: African Arts and Dressing the Head*. Los Angeles, CA: Fowler Museum of Cultural History.

Aschman, G. 1955. "Oudtshoorn in the Early Days in the Jews." In *South Africa: A History*, edited by Gustav Saron and Louis Holtz, 121–137. Cape Town: Oxford University Press.

Ashmole, E. 1672. *The Institution, Laws and Ceremonies of the Most Noble Order of the Garter*. Baltimore, MD: Genealogical Pub.

Bates, O. 1914. *The Eastern Libyans: An Essay*. London: MacMillan.

Beaumier, A. 1870. "Premier établissement des israélites à Timbouktou." *Bulletin de la société de geographie* May–April: 345–370.

Boum, A. 2013. *Memories of Absence: How Muslims Remember Jews in Morocco*. Stanford: Stanford University Press.

Bovill, E. W. 1958. *The Golden Trade of the Moors*. London: Oxford University Press.

Camps-Fabrer, H. 1990. "Autruche." *Encyclopédie Berbère* Volume VIII, 1176–1187. Aix-en-Provence: Edisud.

Carswell, J. 1972. *Kütahya Tiles and Pottery from the Armenian Cathedral of St. James, Jerusalem. 2 vols*. Oxford: Clarendon Press.

Cristobal, B. 1987. *Voyage a Tombuctù*. Madrid: Laertès.

Daumas, E. 1971. *The Ways of the Desert*. Austin: University of Texas Press.

Davis, D. 2011. "Restoring Roman Nature: French Identity and North African Environmental History." In *Environmental Imaginaries of the Middle East and North Africa*, edited by Diana Davis and Edmund Burke III, 60–86. Athens: Ohio State University.

Doughty, R. 1972. "Concern for Fashionable Feathers." *Forest History* 16 (2): 4–11.

Doughty, R. 1975. *Feather Fashions and Bird Preservation: A Study in Nature Protection*. Berkeley: University of California Press.

Douglass, A. 1881. *Ostrich Farming in South Africa*. London: Cassell, Petter, Galpin.

Duncan, T. C. 1888. "Ostrich Farming in America." Report of the Commissioner of Agriculture, 1888, 685–702. Washington, DC: U.S. Department of Agriculture.

Dunn, R. E. 1971. "The Trade of Tafillalt: Commercial Change in Southeast Morocco on the Eve of the Protectorate." *African Historical Studies* 4 (2): 271–304.

Fituri, A. S. 1982. "Tripolitania, Cyrenaica, and Bilad as-Sudan: Trade Relations during the Second Half of the Nineteenth Century." PhD thesis, University of Michigan.

Fitzgibbons, A. 1995. *Adam Smith's System of Liberty, Wealth and Virtue: The Moral and Political Foundations of the Wealth of Nations*. Oxford: Clarendon Press.

Flood, F. B. 2001. *The Great Mosque of Damascus*. Leiden: Brill.

Gillespie, J., G. Taylor, A. Schupp, and F. Wirth. 1998. "Opinions of Professional Buyers Toward a New, Alternative Red Meat: Ostrich." *Agribusiness* 14 (3): 247–256.

Green, N. 2006. "Ostrich Eggs and Peacock Feathers: Sacred Objects as Cultural Exchange Between Christianity and Islam." *Al-Masaq* 18: 27–78.

Haïdara, I. D. 1999. *Les Juifs à Tombouctou: Recueils des sources écrites realtives au commerce juif à Tombouctoo au XIXème siècle*. Bamako: Editions Donniya.

Jabbur, J. S. 1995. *The Bedouins and the Desert: Aspects of Nomadic Life in the Arab East*. New York: State University of New York Press.

Jackson, J. G. 1968. *An Account of the Empire of Morocco and the District of Suse and Tafilalelt*. London: Frank Cass.

Johnson, M. 1881. "Tijarat rish al-na'am fi al-nisf al-awwal min al-qarn al-tasi' 'ashar." *Majallat al-buhut al-tariykhiyya* January (1): 133–151.

Kurimoto, E., and S. Simonse. 1998. *Conflict, Age and Power in North East Africa: Age Systems in Transition*. Athens: Ohio University Press.

Laufer, B. 1926. *Ostrich Egg-Shell Cups of Mesopotamia and the Ostrich in Ancient and Modern Times*. Chicago: Field Museum of Natural History.

Lefèvre, E. 1914. *Le commerce et l'industrie de plume pour parure*. Paris: Edmond Lefèvre.

Lydon, G. 2009. *On Trans-Saharan Trails: Islamic Law, Trade Networks and Cross-Cultural Exchange in Nineteenth Century Western Africa*. Cambridge: Cambridge University Press.

Lyon, G. F. 1966. *A Narrative of Travels in Northern Africa in the Years 1818–1819 and 1820*. London: Franck Cass.

MacMichael, H. A. 1912. *The Tribes of Northern and Central Kordofán*. Cambridge: Cambridge University Press.

Mansfield, A. 1980. *Ceremonial Costume: Court, Civil and Civic Costume from 1660 to the Present Day*. Totowa, NJ: Barnes & Nobel Books.

Margueritte, A. 1888. *Chasses de l'Algérie et notes sur les Arabes du sud*. Paris: Jouvet et Cie Editeurs.

Miège, J.-L. 1981–1982. "Le commerce trans-saharien au XIXe siècle: Essai de quantification." *Revue de l'occident musulman et de la Méditerranée* 32 (1): 93–119.

Miège, J.-L. 1982. "Les juifs et le commerce transaharien au dix-neuvième siècle." In *Communautés juives des marges sahariennes du Maghreb*, edited by Michel Abitbol, 391–406. Jérusalem: Institut Ben-Zvi.

Miège, J.-L. 1961. *Le Maroc et l'Europe, 1830–1894*. Paris: Presses Universitaires de France.

Miège, J.-L. 1989. *Le Maroc et l'Europe (1830–1894). Tome III les Difficulté*. Paris: Editions La Porte.

Monteil, V. 1951. *Contribution à l'étude de la faune du sahara occidentale: du sanglier au phacochère-catalogue des animaux connus des Tekna, des Rguibat et des Maures*. Paris: Éditions Larose.

Mosenthal, J. D., and James Harting. 1877. *Ostriches and Ostrich Farming*. London: Trübner.

Needler, W. 1984. *Predynastic and Archaic Egypt in the Brooklyn Museum*. Brooklyn: Brooklyn Museum.

Newbury, C. W. 1966. "North African and Western Sudan Trade in the Nineteenth Century: A Re-Evaluation." *The Journal of African History* VII (2): 233–246.

Nixon, R. 2001. *Dreambirds: The Strange History of the Ostrich in Fashion, Food, and Fortune*. New York: Picador.

Nordström, H.-A. 1972. *Neolithic and A-Group Sites*. Uppsala: Scandinavian Joint Expeditions to Sudanese Nubia.

Ollive, C. 1880. "Commerce entre Timbouctou et Mogador." *Bulletin de la Société de Géographie de Marseille* 1: 5–8.

Oudot, J. 1880. *Le fermage des autruches en Algerie incubation artificielle*. Paris: Challamel.

Pascon, P. 1980. "Le commerce de la maison d'Iligh d'après le register comptable de Husayn b. Hachem (Tazerwalt, 18501875)." *Annales: économies, sociétés, civilisations* 35 (3–4): 700–729.

Peacock, J. 1986. *Costume, 1066–1966*. New York: Thames and Hudson.

Phillips, J. 2000. "The Ostrich Eggshells." In *Ancient Egyptian Materials and Technology*, edited by P. T. Nicholson and I. Shaw, 332–333. Oxford: Oxford University Press.

Prussin, L. 1986. *Hatumere: Islamic Design in West Africa*. Berkeley: University of California Press.

de Puigaudeau, O., and M. Senones. 1965. "Nouvelles gravures rupestres de l'Oued Tamanart (sud marocain)." *Bulletin de l'institut français d'afrique noire* xxvii (série B, 1–2): 282–285.

Roche, D. 2000. *History of Everyday Things: The Birth of Consumption in France, 1600–1800*. Berkeley: University of California Press.

Schroeter, D. 1982. "The Jews of Essaouira (Mogador) and the Trade of Southwestern Morocco." In *Communautés juives des marges sahariennes du Maghreb*, edited by Michel Abitbol, 365–390. Jerusalem: Institut-Ben-Zvi.

Schroeter, D. 1988. *Merchants of Essaouira: Urban Society and Imperialism in Southwestern Morocco, 1844–1886*. Cambridge: Cambridge University Press.

Schroeter, D. 1989. "Trade as a Mediator in Muslim–Jewish Relations: Southwestern Morocco in the Nineteenth Century." In *Jews Among Muslims: Contacts and Boundaries*, edited by Mark Cohen and Abraham Udovitch, 113–140. Princeton, NJ: Darwin Press.

Slouschz, N. 1927. *Travels in North Africa*. Philadelphia: The Jewish Publication Society of America.

Smith, A. 1976. *The Wealth of Nations*, edited by R. H. Campbell, A. S. Skinner, and W. B. Todd. Oxford: Oxford University Press.

Stein, S. 2008. *Plumes: Ostrich Feathers, Jews and a Lost World of Global Commerce*. New Haven: Yale University Press.

Tristram, H. B. 1860. *The Great Sahara: Wanderings South of the Atlas Mountains*. London: J. Murray.

Vikor, K. S. 1985. "An Episode of Saharan Rivalry: The French Occupation of Kawar, 1906." *The International Journal of African Historical Studies* 18 (4): 699–715.

Viré, F. 1993. "Na'am." *Encyclopedie de l'Islam* 7: 628–631.

Walz, T. 1978. *Trade Between Egypt and Bilad al-Sudan, 1700–1820*. Cairo: Institut Français d'Archéologie Orientale de Caire.

Wendell, C. 1974. "The Denizens of Paradise." *Humaniora Islamica* 2: 29–59.

Williams, E. 2012. *Ostrich*. London: Reaktion.

Wright, J. 2007. *The Trans-Saharan Slave Trade*. London: Routledge.

The trans-Saharan slave trade in the context of Tunisian foreign trade in the western Mediterranean

Ismael M. Montana

Department of History, Northern Illinois University, DeKalb, USA

The paper explores effects of local Tunisian reforms and broader economic and political developments occurring in the western Mediterranean shores during the late eighteenth and early nineteenth centuries on the trans-Saharan slave trade. While the scanty available literature stresses the insignificance of the trans-Saharan slave trade to Tunisia, this paper examines the complex interplay of Tunisian economic reforms and the burgeoning European commercial expansion that shaped the Tunisian economy and, in turn, the trans-Saharan slave trade. Impact of these developments was not limited to Tunisian trade with Europe and the Levant. A significant increase in trade activities between the Regency of Tunis and the African interior can be observed on a number of levels. In particular, aside from the favourable conditions arising from Hammuda Pasha's reform and economic policies, expanding European trade in Tunisia, mainly after 1788, was a major force behind a continuation and growth of the trans-Saharan slave trade which continued until outlaw in 1841. In addition to Hammuda Pasha's economic reform policies that led to the integration of the Ghadames caravan trade into burgeoning economy, trade growth between Tunisia and the African interior was further fuelled by European capital infusion in the western Mediterranean.

Introduction

Beginning in the late 1780s, the trans-Saharan slave trade from the African interior, while becoming a principal branch of the Regency of Tunis' network of overland trade, was typically not considered important for burgeoning European commercial expansion that stimulated agricultural production, commerce and Tunisian economy. Nearly a century prior to the late 1780s, the Muradites, who undertook the consolidation of various economic infrastructures following the Ottoman conquest of Tunisia in 1574 (along with corsair expeditions, they developed as a 'legitimate commerce' of the Ottoman province), integrated the trans-Saharan slave trade into the nascent Tunisian foreign trade. Successors of the Muradids, the Husaynids

(1705–1957), maintained the trade via Ghadames. Until the early 1780s, however, it remained a marginal branch of the Husaynids' foreign trade.

Between 1786 and 1808, the slave trade peaked at 1300 to 1000 slaves per annum. Yet, after reaching this peak, the trade declined slightly and then grew even more, particularly during the 1830s and early 1840s, reaching levels above the previous peak. Shortly after its second peak, in April 1841, the slave traffic from Tunis across the western Mediterranean was outlawed. Four months later, in August 1841, the slave trade from the African interior was prohibited, and within less than half a decade, slavery itself was abolished throughout Tunisia (see Montana 2013).

This paper provides a broad overview of interplay between the trans-Saharan slave trade and economic and political developments underway in late eighteenth to early nineteenth century Ottoman Tunisia. Contrary to the widely held assumption that economic developments after 1500 in North and West Africa, particularly the rise of sea-borne and maritime trade, had rendered the trans-Saharan trade ' … less commercially significant and more vulnerable to competition from the sea,' (Anene 1965; Anderson 1986; Chater 1987; Austen 1990) it is argued here that increased European capitalist penetration in the western Mediterranean from the late eighteenth century on had profound and dynamic implications on the Saharan slave trade.

Using a combination of secondary sources and available contemporary European travellers' accounts and memoirs in North Africa, consular official reports, and local Tunisian chronicles, the paper attempts to rehabilitate the trans-Saharan slave trade from the African interior into the directional trends and patterns of expanding Tunisian foreign trade and European capital infusion in the western Mediterranean. The paper maintains that exploring the interactions of the trans-Saharan slave trade and the economic and political changes underway reveals a much more complex and parallel relationship than existing scholarly literature assumes.

Several scholars and historians have examined the above economic and political developments and assessed their implications on Tunisian economy with Europe, the western Mediterranean and Levantine countries. A number of these scholars, however, have bracketed off the trans-Saharan slave trade from the broader implications of these economic processes and developments. This neglect has led to attributing the implications of the economic and political developments on the trans-Saharan slave trade solely to the 1846 mass emancipation of slavery under the reign of Ahmad Bey (r. 1825–1855). Within this scholarship, the close relationship between the abolition of slavery, the trans-Saharan slave trade, and the economic and political changes underway has been overlooked. By failing to take into account the Saharan slave trade, scholars have shown only a partial understanding of the dynamics of the economic and political processes shaping the Tunisian economy from the late eighteenth century onwards. In the following sections, the paper outlines the intellectual and historical contours for placing the trans-Saharan slave trade at the core of the economic and political developments shaping the Tunisian foreign trade in the period under examination.

The intellectual context

In the historiography of the modern history of the Maghreb, the effects of the major economic and political transformations underway during the mid-eighteenth and early nineteenth centuries on the Tunisian branch of the trans-Saharan slave trade received marginal attention. Within this historiography, the themes of 'decay', 'decadence', and 'regularity' but 'insignificance' run through the early phase of this literature, which mentions the trans-Saharan commerce as a component of North African foreign trade. In the mid-1970s, Lucette Valensi, a leading French historian on

Tunisian economic history in the eighteenth century, wrote that after the late eighteenth century, Tunisia became a centre for growing maritime trade, particularly with Europe, the Mediterranean and the Levant. Throughout this period, she opined, the trans-Saharan slave trade remained a regular feature of Tunisian overland commerce, but increased maritime trade across the Mediterranean superseded its importance (Valensi 1977, 43–46). Consequently, the Saharan trade was 'static' and 'unimpressive' (Valensi 1967, 1275–1276). What is more, the Saharan slave trade was privately operated by poor Ghadames merchants and did not follow the same pattern of Tunisian trade from the late eighteenth century onwards (Valensi 1977, 44). André Raymond and Lisa Anderson took a similar approach in different ways (Raymond 1953, 25–26; Anderson 1986, 59). Raymond discussed the consequences of European influence from 1816 onwards and shows how Tunisian exports of foodstuffs from the late eighteenth century onwards decreased as a result of epidemics and foreign debts. While epidemics caused crop failure (resulting in heavy taxation for overland trades), foreign debts led to unprecedented European influence, leading to the control of Tunis's economy and the eradication of corsairs and Christian slavery in the Regency (Raymond 1953, 31). For this reason, Raymond posited, the Tunisian Saharan trade was ruined by the action undertaken by European Powers for the abolition of [Christian] slavery in Tunis (Raymond 1953, 25). According to him, European pressure against Christian slavery diverted the Saharan slave trade to Tripoli (Raymond 1953, 25). This aggressive European influence led Lisa Anderson to subscribe to the thesis that the Saharan slave trade from the African interior declined. Similar to Raymond, she argued, it reduced the Saharan slave trade to 'a mere fraction of its earlier value' (Anderson 1986, 59). However, while Raymond believed that trade declined as a result of direct European action against Christian slavery between 1816 and 1830, Anderson assumes that the decline of the Saharan slave trade (which she believes already lost its vitality to the trans-Atlantic trade along the West African coast) was caused by the increased European trade's erosion of the rural economies of both Tunis and Tripoli.

Khalifa Chater, a well-established Tunisian historian of the period under study, cautioned the decadence thesis (Chater 1987, 137–141). Taking into account the response of the Saharan trade, including the inland and inter-Maghreb caravan networks, to the growth of Tunisian trade, he argues the Saharan trade adapted to the new economic milieu characterising the Mediterranean. According to Chater, owing to Tunisia's strategic location as a transit point, it remained vibrant as liaison and transit commerce. Consequently, instead of decline, the caravan trade sustained both Tunisian and European commerce (Chater 1987, 143). Other historians such as Rachad Limam demonstrated the proliferation of the Saharan slave trade during the height of Tunisian economic growth. Limam perceived this growth as a by-product of Hammuda's trans-Saharan trade policy (Limam 1974, 194–196, 1981, 349–357; Abun-Nasr 1982, 57–58). Limam argued that, along with the Regency's ever-increasing trade with Europe and the Levant, Hammuda also promoted commerce with the African interior because of self-interest in the commerce (1980, 302).

Political and economic developments

Any serious attempt to examine interdependence and interaction between the trans-Saharan slave trade and the burgeoning Tunisian foreign trade will be incomplete without a closer look at changes in Tunisian state's politics, economy, as well as vast array of unprecedented regional transformations occurring around the western Mediterranean during the late eighteenth and early nineteenth centuries. Domestically, the decades-long succession crisis that marked the early phase of the Husaynid dynasty – compounded by frequent encroachment by the Turkish Deys from the Regency of Algiers in Tunisian affairs – ended with the ascension to the throne of Husayn bin Ali's eldest son, Mohammad Bey (reigned, 1756–1759). During the last years of Ali Bey I's rule, the Algerian Deys profited from internal disputes between Ali and his son. After decades of solid control of the Regency, the Deys took advantage of infighting and managed to capture and assassinate Ali Bey I. This development paved the way for the relinquishing of the throne to Husayn b. Ali's faction, which had been locked in succession crises for nearly half a century (see, e.g. Hédi Chérif [1983] on discussion of the succession crisis).

Despite the assassination of Ali Bey I and the accession to the throne of Husayn's faction, which put an end to the lingering infighting among the Husaynid ruling class, the coup d'etat was aided by the Algerian Deys. Thus, ascension to the throne of Husayn's faction increased Algerian encroachments in the Regency's affairs. From Mohammad Bey's enthronement by the Algerian Deys in 1756 until his death in 1759, the Regency was nominally reduced to tribute status. In addition to an annual tribute that the Deys imposed on Tunis, Mohamed-Hédi, Chérif and other historians described this phase of the Husaynid dynasty as a period, which witnessed the Algerian Deys intrusion on Tunis's political and financial affairs. Bin Diyaf, the nineteenth-century Tunisian chronicler, concluded that by the end of Mohammad Bey's rule, the Tunisian treasury had been emptied by the Algerian Deys' frequent plunder (Limam 1980, 302–303).

Due to the circumstances of his accession to the throne, Mohammad had no choice but to succumb to the Deys' successive encroachments on Tunisian affairs. His successors, however, did not tolerate the Algerians' frequent meddling in the Regency's political and economic stability. Mohammad's rule lasted only three years. After his death in 1759, he was succeeded by his younger brother, Ali Bey II (reigned 1759–1782). Ali Bey II put an end to the Deys' intrusion in Tunis' affairs. To ensure Tunis's independence, the Bey not only embarked upon serious reforms aimed at strengthening Tunis's political independence but also at refurbishing Tunis's treasury, which had been emptied by Algerian troops and by the diversion of Tunisian trade to Algiers.

Ali Bey II's determination to strengthen Tunis' autonomy was a turning point (see Kraiem 1973 vol. 2, 49–60). Besides strengthening Tunis's political independence, the Bey introduced – by sanction of a *fatwa* issued by the Hanafite grand Mufti – a series of institutional and fiscal reforms (Julien 1970, 330–331; Abun-Nasr 1982, 39–40). For instance, the Bey commissioned the Hanafite grand Mufti, Mohamed Bayram I (d. 1800) to compose for him a treatise on governance (*siyasat al-Shar'iyat*) and fatwas to support his political and economic reforms. Among the Bey's measures designed to take advantage of European commerce in Tunis, which slowly began to increase, Ali Bey II accorded rights to coral fishing and a factory in Bizerte to a French company. Similar trade incentives were granted to Tunisian Jews, particularly the *grana,* who had been at the forefront of Tunisian foreign trade with Europe since the late seventeenth century. Furthermore, as foreign trade began to rejuvenate, Ali Bey II regulated the selling of crops before their harvest. This measure was taken to curb abusive trade practices in the Regency by European traders, mainly Genoan and Venetian merchants.

While historians have often stressed that Ali Bey II's role in strengthening Tunisia's political and economic prosperity in the late eighteenth century marked a turning point, these reforms did not end with his death. They laid the foundation for further political and economic progress in the Regency. Thus, in the same spirit as his father, Hammuda Pasha (r. 1782–1814), who succeeded Ali Bey II, embarked upon a series of ambitious political, military, social and economic reforms. Except for the tenth Husaynid successor, Ahmad Bey, no Husaynid statesman has been as praised as Hammuda. Historians have unanimously depicted his reign as the 'Golden Age' of Tunisia (Julien 1970, 331).

Soon after his accession to the throne, among the first steps Hammuda took was to discontinue Tunis' dependence on Algiers as a tribute state (Limam 1980, 261). Over and above the earlier reforms initiated under his father, Hammuda introduced a series of political reforms including the reduction of the number of Turkish Janissaries by replacing them with Mamluks. He introduced new ministries, led by a Prime Minister (Mustapha Khaznadar), a Minister of Finance, and a Keeper of the Seal (Sahib al-Taba). These positions were also filled by his Mamluks.

By the mid-1780s, the peace and stability brought about by Hammuda's solid social and political reforms led to the *fellahin* (peasants) producing foodstuffs that surpassed the Regency's consumption. Limam notes that during the early phase of Hammuda's rule, agricultural lands were greatly expanded (Limam 1980, 261). Thanks to his subjugation of the nomadic tribesmen, who inhabited the region inland from Sfax, and had been fervent enemies of the sedentary population of the town, Hammuda's security reforms paid off greatly (Limam 1974, 195). The Bey implemented an annual *mahalla* (military expedition), which not only defeated disloyal elements to the regime, but also imposed a hefty taxation system aimed at assuring their allegiance to the regime. His coercive measures paving the way for peace led to the abundant production of wheat, barley, and livestock. They also augmented the cultivation of olive oil, whose production expanded, providing the Regency with considerable trade benefits in the export of olive oil.

By the late 1780s, the results of Hammuda's reforms in the agricultural sector not only resulted in a bumper crop and harvest but also to an unprecedented level of economic growth. This period, which also marked the early phase of the Industrial Revolution in Europe, saw increased European commercial interests in Tunis. One of the most significant results of the unprecedented growth of Tunisian agriculture during this period was that it rejuvenated Tunisian foreign trade, particularly the export of grain and olive oil to Europe and the Levant. Yet, unlike Ali Bey II, who accorded trade concessions to European traders to promote Tunisian trade, Hammuda pursued a different economic course (Limam 1974, 195–196).

First, Hammuda revisited the existing commercial arrangements between various European states and the Regency of Tunis. Prior to his rule, many of the European merchants trading in Tunis had secured trade agreements and preferential treatment. Some of these agreements dated back to 1600 and had been granted under the Ottoman capitulation system, allowing Christian European states, mainly Genoa, Venice, France and later, Great Britain, to trade in the country. To curb the European merchants' monopoly on Tunis's burgeoning trade, Hammuda abolished existing trade agreements. At the same time, he restricted European merchants from purchasing goods directly from Tunisian *fellahin* (peasants) by introducing the system of *teskere* (Bill of Right of Export). According to this stringent trade control measure, European traders were forced to purchase *teskeres* directly from the Beylik's authorities, including the Bey himself. European merchants worked assiduously through their respective consuls to exert pressure on Hammuda to rescind the restrictive and prohibitive measures, but the Bey did not yield to pressure and upheld his strict control of the foreign trade.

Secondly, while imposing stringent trade restriction on European traders, Hammuda encouraged indigenous Tunisians to participate in Tunisia's burgeoning foreign trade by reducing their duties on goods exported to Europe to 5.5%, down from 11% *ad valorem*. Hammuda's encouragement of the traders included special preferential trade privileges accorded to local Tunisian Jews. To guarantee competitive advantage for indigenous Tunisians' participation in the foreign trade, the Bey imposed some restrictions on the Jewish merchants' monopoly of certain trade articles such as grain and olive oil (Limam 1974, 195–196). Ultimately, within a single decade, the Bey succeeded in stamping out foreign and local Jews merchants' monopoly of Tunisian foreign trade to the advantage of the *beldi*, (local traders).

By the late 1790s, the growth of Tunisian trade economy stemming from its burgeoning agricultural production had reached an unprecedented level. One could readily agree with John Jackson, who fervently advocated for the British government and British merchants to take advantage of the Tunisian booming agricultural trade and economy in the Mediterranean in 1798:

> The commerce carried on at present between the Christian states, on the northern shores of the Mediterranean and the kingdom of Tunis, is very extensive … Tunis is the most considerable state in Barbary for commerce, and even that was but trifling, until Sidi Mustapha, late prime minister, encouraged the cultivation of corn and olives, now the two chief articles of export from that kingdom. This has served much to civilize the inhabitants, who, from a state of perpetual warfare with Christians, and often among themselves, begin now to feel the advantage of commerce; and the duties on exports, at the present form the greatest part of the Bey's revenues. (Jackson 1804, 55)

Like Jackson, many contemporary Tunisian and European writers could not emphasise enough the new pattern of economic growth that characterised the Regency – particularly towards the start of the 1780s. According to the author of *Kitab al-bashi*, an eighteenth-century Tunisian chronicler (who served under Ali Bey II and Hammuda Pasha), the Regency's 'population was growing, building programs abounded, agriculture was thriving, and the economy was prosperous, at least for the elites.' (see Gallagher 2002, 34). Even those nineteenth-century writers such as Louis Frank, Hammuda's medical aide who lived in Tunis between 1802 and 1806, and who wrote his account of Tunis in 1811, viewed Tunis in terms of its economic prosperity and its relations with North Africa, the West and Central Sudan, as similar to London, Marseilles and Amsterdam's relations with the rest of Europe as financial capitals.

Not surprisingly, a number of historians have devoted systematic attention to the major economic changes discussed above. In examining the scholarly literature, one sees numerous examples of glorifying terms such as 'l'age d'or de la Tunisie precoloniale,' (Chérif 1970, 719; Kraiem 1973, Vol. I, 52). 'Shanghai of the Mediterranean,' (Gallagher 2002, 33) and 'Apogée de l'expansion' (Chater 1984, 175) to define the late eighteenth-century Tunisia. Others have interpreted these developments as heralding 'the high point of [Tunisian] independence and wealth before European pressures in the nineteenth century deprived the state of major revenue resources and led to its "detachment" from its hinterland' (Hunter 1986, 24).

Valensi has documented the pattern of Tunisian exports and imports during the late eighteenth century through an analysis of the ratio of regional and inter-state trade. Valensi, for instance, repeatedly emphasised that in the late eighteenth century, 'Tunisia was one of the countries that fed Europe'. She concluded that many of the exports of grain, dried vegetables, and other less important foodstuffs to France, Malta and Italy during this period came from Tunisia (Valensi 1981, 722). Valensi's claims are attested to by the French consular authorities in Tunis in the 1780s, who themselves were involved in Tunisian foreign trade. Writing during the height of France's importation of foodstuffs from Tunis, the French consular records at the time attributed this to a

> simultaneous poor harvest in Europe and the abundance of crops in the Kingdom of Tunis … [This] led a throng of ships to the port of Tunis which in less than four years, had become the richest and most commercially active of the Levant. (Gallagher 2002, 35)

By 1808, Thomas MacGill, an English merchant, found that 'trade of [Tunis] on the coast of Barbary has … declined considerably'. As well as Hammuda's stringent economic policies and the plague of 1804–1805, MacGill attributed the decay in Tunis's trade to political factors, particularly Hammuda's wars within 1807–1808. Despite this, MacGill noted that this trade which 'was at a former period much more extensive and lucrative', was still 'worthy of attention' (MacGill 1811, 120–123).

Tunisian trade continued to thrive – though only intermittently – due to the results of the 1804–1805 plague and certainly due to Hammuda's lingering wars with Algiers. Soon after his death, the state of economic affluence characterising his reign ended. By the second decade of the nineteenth century, Tunisia, like most non-European states, could not escape the political and economic consequences arising from the end of the Napoleonic and the Revolutionary Wars that shook continental Europe to its foundation.

After 1798, as was the case in the North African states of Algiers, Tripoli and Morocco, Britain and France's preoccupation with the Napoleonic Wars and the balance of power in the Mediterranean opened up avenues of profit for Tunisian corsairs. Between 1798 and 1814, the number of corsair campaigns organised by the Tunisian state, while never reaching the scale they had during their apex in the seventeenth century, nonetheless reached alarming rates targeting series of Mediterranean islands such as Sicily and Sardinia.

In 1814, the Napoleonic Wars came to an end. Like the Regencies of Algiers and Tripoli, the end of the Napoleonic wars in 1814 marked a major shift in the power politics of Tunis's relations with Europe. A few months after the Napoleonic Wars ended, European countries had gathered at the Congress of Vienna to look at the political and economic consequences of the wars in continental Europe. Among the many goals of the Congress was to find solutions not only for the growing European nationalism that resulted from the Napoleonic Wars, but also to address concerns surrounding Europe's Industrial Revolution, which occurred after the 1760s and led to the profound transformation of methods of commodity production. It reached its peak during the first quarter of the nineteenth century. Advancement in industrial and production methods helped Europe's population to boom. So did improvements in various industrial sectors, which forced Europeans to look beyond Europe for colonies. By 1815, many European states were searching if not for colonies, then at least for outlets for trade.

The abolition of the slave trade and slavery was also an issue at the Congress of Vienna. Here, it must be stressed that by 1814, a number of the European powers that gathered at the Congress, such as Denmark and Great Britain, had already outlawed the slave trade in their colonies – Denmark in 1792 and Britain in 1807. In fact, it was in the same year as the Congress that the Dutch abolished the slave trade. Clearly, promotion of 'legitimate commerce' – a direct result of the Industrial Revolution – was a major factor in the decision to abolish the slave trade. Several reasons have also been cited, including humanitarianism ideals and the European Enlightenment. Not surprisingly, since Europe perceived corsair activity and piracy as hindrances to its trade interests in the Mediterranean, their termination was considered a prerequisite for legitimate commerce. During the Napoleonic Wars, the USA had already complained that the corsair campaigns in North Africa were injurious to their commerce.

A year after the congress, Europe dispatched Admiral Lord Exmouth with a naval fleet to suppress the corsair activity and piracy in North Africa. By April 1816, only a month after he had forced the rulers of Algiers and Tripoli to free Christian captives, Exmouth headed to Tunis. Mahmud Bey (reigned 1814–1824) could not but follow the examples of the Deys of Algiers. With British and European naval fleets anchored at Tunis Bay and ready to bombard the city, Mahmud complied with all of Exmouth's conditions, notably terminating the corsair campaigns and freeing every Christian captive in the Regency.

By 1830, this show of European political and military prowess had not only successfully freed the Mediterranean from corsair activity and piracy, but had also paved the way for a new economic and political environment dominated by Europe in the Mediterranean. These developments also triggered a downturn in the Regency of Tunis's thriving economy. Thus compared to the period from the mid-1780s to 1814 – the 'Golden Age' of Tunisian trade economy – during which Hammuda Pasha solidly regulated European commercial practices in the Regency, after 1816 his successors were deprived of the ability to control European traders. The years between 1816 and 1830 ushered in a period of growing European political influence over the successive Beys. During this period, the Husaynid Beys witnessed aggressive exploitative behaviour on the part of European merchants who exacted economic concessions from them whenever possible. As Woodford puts it:

> Th[is] moment marks the establishment of the consuls as a political force in Tunis, stemming not just from their direct influence on the Bey, but also from their peculiar civil status and judicial rights over their countrymen and protégés, to the exclusion of the local courts. The consuls were nominally the representatives of European government, but these were without exception too distant to have any influence on the day-to-day decisions consuls had to make. As their power increased, so also did their tendency to make independent political decisions, backed by the financial clout of their compatriots. (Woodford 1990, 123)

To illustrate the implications of this European dominance, Raymond has shown that after 1816, Tunisian foreign trade, which was estimated at 5,000,000 francs (imports) and 5,300,00 francs (exports) in 1788 had declined significantly to only 2,200,00 (exports). Interestingly, this decline in Tunisian foreign trade was matched by flourishing European imports to Tunisia worth 8,100,000 francs (see Raymond 1953).

What is startling about this imbalance in the Tunisian trade during this period is not only the great increase of imported European goods into the Regency, which surpassed Tunisian exports by over three times, but also, as Raymond and others have demonstrated, the fact that a significant proportion of the flourishing European imports into the Regency were contraband. According to Raymond, of the 8,100,000 francs in imports, there were up to 2,000,000 francs in imports worth being classified as 'illegal Tunisian trade economy after 1816, this phenomenon of increased illegal trade is unsurprising'. As Ganiage's masterly documentation of European migration to Tunis has demonstrated, unforeseen political and economic developments after 1816 had major European demographic implications in Tunis (1960).

Quite apart from the clear effects of the end of the Napoleonic Wars on the Tunisian political economy, many historians have stressed the role of internal Tunisian factors as contributing in the downturn of the economy. Soon after Hammuda's death in 1814 (after a rule of 33 years), political disequilibrium between Hammuda's successors was cited as a hindrance to stability. By the 1820s, the situation had worsened because of the 1818–1820 plague, which caused famine and disrupted agricultural production.

Fiscal reforms also compounded the situation. Soon after 1816, the Regency was deprived of its regular revenues previously obtained through taxes levied on corsair campaigns, overland trans-Saharan slave trade and thriving commerce with Europe and the Levant. By 1827, Hussein Bey (r. 1824–1835), who had tried to steer Tunis out of its continuing economic crisis, resorted to the finance minister, Shakir Sahib el-Tabà, a Georgian Mamluk, in an attempt to remedy the situation by an earnest programme encouraging agricultural production. In particular, as the value of the Regency's exports in primary products had declined, and hence instead of grain, barley and wheat, Hussein promoted the cultivation of olive oil, even though its price had fallen from a high 30 francs in 1820 to only 8.75 francs in 1827–1828.

As a result, the production of olive oil, which had reached 10,000 hectolitres during the eighteenth century, was increased to over 50,000 in 1817. Then, by 1827, it had risen to 76,000 hectolitres. To strengthen his efforts at fiscal reforms, Hussein reversed Ali Bey II's policy of banning the sale of crops before their harvest. Even though this measure was calculated to ensure his *de facto* monopoly on the trade, by selling oil to European merchants himself, particularly the French, in 'advance payments and cash loans,' (Valensi 1981, 722–723) only a year after its peak oil production failed to series of plagues. The lifting of the ban on pre-harvest sales proved catastrophic because it instituted the beginning of the Tunisian Beys' indebtedness to European foreign capitalists.

Whither implications on the trans-Saharan slave trade

Effects of the political and economic developments discussed above from the late eighteenth century onwards had major implications on the pace, the scale and broadening scope of the trans-Saharan slave trade. Beginning of the late eighteenth century, the slave trade had not only become the principal branch of the Regency of Tunis' network of inland trade, but an important medium for the increased and the expanding European commercial capitalism in the western shore of Mediterranean basin. Prior to the eighteenth century and even earlier, the trans-Saharan slave trade had been severed and disrupted as a result of the Hilali invasion of Ifriqiyya (Medieval Tunisia) at the turn of the eleventh century. As a result of political instability caused by the Hilali invasion, the slave trade between Tunisian and western and central Sudan was diverted westwards towards Morocco. In addition to political instability arising from the invasion, caravans were subject to sectarian banditry. Kharijites attacks on trade caravans between Gabés and Tripoli proved detrimental and with the exception of irregular diplomatic envoys between the Hafsid state and the rulers of Borno, regular trade operations were severed and came to a halt. Until Ottomans' occupation of the Regency in 1575 and its tight control, even the Hafsids who aspired to control the trans-Saharan slave trade as an extension of their diplomatic relations with the rulers of Borno in the central Sudan could not provide the security requisite needed for caravans' safe operations. In the aftermath of the Ottomans occupation and pacification, especially in the south-western parts of the interior where the Kharijites and other local tribes disrupting the trade were based, the trans-Saharan trade was revived and integrated into the Regency's nascent coastal economy.

During the first decades of the Ottoman rule and control of the interior, inland trading networks connecting the new Deylik (now Ottoman Muradite post) with the western and central Sudan by way of Ghadames slowly gained traction. The scanty and sporadic available evidence points to a gradual resumption of trade activities in the hinterland. These trade activities continued unabated till the fourth decade of the Husaynid Dynasty founded in 1705. Thanks to the economic policies of the Muradites ruler, Hammuda Pasha el-Muradite, who accorded the monopoly of the slave trade to Ghadames diasporan merchants in Tunis, by the early part of the sixteenth century, the trans-Saharan trade had become a regular branch of the regency's foreign trade. The Pasha's successor, Yusuf Dey (r. 1610–1637) consolidated the revival and integration of the slave trade and built *suq el-Berka,* (Tunis Slave Market) for the sole sale of black slaves. However, as Valensi rightly notes, until the eighteenth century, compared to overall volume of Tunisian foreign trade with Levant and across the Mediterranean, the slave trade remained a marginal branch of the foreign trade.

During the aftermath of the civil war that ravaged the Husaynid Dynasty, sources related to this period document political relationship between the Husaynid and the rulers of the central Sudan. The outcome of this relationship as Ibn Abi Diyaf and contemporary accounts reported culminated in enlistment of slave soldiers called *bawaba* or palace guards from the very cultural zone where the Hafsids had conducted diplomatic relationship with the rulers of Borno in the central Sudan. Writing during the middle of the civil war, Thomas Shaw, a well-known British clergyman who visited Tunis from Algiers in 1727, reported that the infighting between the Husayniyya and the Bashiyya factions of the Husaynid Dynasty had negative impact of the trans-Saharan slave trade and economic activities in the Regency as a whole. This prolonged civil war, which was exacerbated by Algerian janissaries intervention in favour of the Husayniyya faction, did not end until the late 1750s.

After the end of the civil war, Hammuda Pasha ushered in reforms that established the Regency as a major trade destination, as attested by Jackson in the previous section. Thus, with the return of political and economic stability, commercial relations between Tunisia and west and central Sudan resumed at a much greater pace than before. The most noticeable example of the trade resumption came four years, in 1786, following the start of Hammuda Pasha's rule. During this period, the slave trade increased abruptly and within less than a decade of Hammuda's rule, reached its apogee. Not surprisingly, this increase coincided with the climax of Tunisia's economic affluence discussed in the previous section. Throughout the late eighteenth to the first quarter of the nineteenth century, although with occasional interruptions, the extant evidence suggest that this increased momentum of the slave trade did indeed continue well into the first half of the nineteenth century. This increased pattern of the slave trade contests the statist view that the trans-Saharan slave remained marginal throughout eighteenth and early part of the nineteenth centuries. Furthermore, this increased trend highlights the slave trade's interaction and interdependence with the pattern of growth and declines occurring in Tunisia's foreign trade.

Early evidence of the increased trends of the slave trade and its interaction with the ebbs and flows of Tunisia foreign trade came a few years after Miss Tully's report of the active trade between the rulers of Tunisia and the central Sudan. In 1789, Robert Traill, the British Consul General in Tunis, writing to the British Commerce Secretary also came to a similar and even more promising conclusion about the level of trade interaction between Tunisia and the western and central Sudan. In the first of his several reports, which he wrote upon request from the British Government to obtain intelligence information about the level of Tunisian foreign trade, and especially its share of the trans-Saharan slave trade with the African interior, Traill revealed that the scope of the trade was expansive as the Ghadames merchants who conducted the trade penetrated deep across the Sahara into Yorubaland near the Atlantic coast of West Africa. The report showing the importance of the slave trade as a sector of Tunisian foreign trade also documents its interaction with the above economic and political developments underway, especially during the reign of Hammuda Pasha.

According to Traill's reports, the interaction and interdependence with the above economic developments is evident through the scope, the pace, and shifting pattern of the slave trade. For instance, Traill's reports showed that in 1789, Arab merchants conducting the Saharan slave trade between Ghadames and the African interior 'generally' procured 1000–1300 slaves per annum. Traill noted that 'the greatest part of this [quantity ... to the amount of one thousand [were re-exported] yearly into the Dominion of Tunis.' (FO 77/3; Hallett 1964, 79; Limam 1980, 303; Limam 1981, 350). Despite this voluminous scale, he noted that in some years, when caravans were not 'considerable', slaves imported to Tunis did not arrive at half that number. Consequently, about only 'one hundred or one hundred and fifty' slaves reached Tunis (Hallett 1964, 81–84). Over a decade later, Louis Frank provided another impressive statistical account of the Tunisian Saharan slave trade. Frank estimated that, at the time he resided, between 1802 and 1806, in the Regency, Ghadamissiyah caravans 'frequently' imported between 1000 and 1200 slaves per annum to Tunis. Like Traill, Frank noted the irregularity of the trade, observing that, in some years, only around 200 slaves entered Tunis (1851, 116–117). Contrary to Traill's report and Frank's account of the voluminous scale of the slave trade, Thomas MacGill, one of the most notable European writers in the early nineteenth-century Tunis, reported that three 'caravans of Gdamsi' linking Tunisia with the African interior frequented Tunis annually. His account – one of the best reports on Tunisian foreign trade – indicates that some of the Ghadames caravans he observed in Tunis brought around 200 slaves (1811, 148).

Despite the available evidence indicating a continuation and growth of the slave trade, the paucity of data on the slave trade when compared to other branches of Tunisian foreign trade has encouraged some scholars to assert that it does not suffice as a basis for sustained academic inquiry. As a result, with few exceptions, Tunisian and North African economic historians have not included the Saharan commerce in mainstream economic history. For example, Mark Dyer, who set out in the late 1970s to 'explore the role of Tunis as a market for trans-Saharan trade and a home for trans-Saharan merchants', assumed – after the preliminary phase of his research – that Saharan trade to Tunisia from the late eighteenth century on was insignificant. Dyer's main reasons for shifting the focus of his study are noteworthy:

> As I have become more familiar with Tunisian economic history, it became apparent that trans-Saharan trade was of little overall importance in that country, and that Tunis was merely a host to visiting traders from Ghadames rather than home of active trans-Saharan merchants.' As a result, I shifted the emphasis of the dissertation to western Libya, a region that was more directly involved in Saharan trade and more strongly influenced by it. (1978, vii–viii)

For the same reasons that discouraged Dyer from examining the Tunisian Saharan slave trade, Chedli Sehili, a Tunisian researcher whose proposal for his *doctorat d'etat* thesis (under Prof. Abdeljelil Temimi) sought to investigate Tunisian economic relations with Tripoli and West and Central Sudan, also abandoned his project (1986).

The above-stated reasons, which discouraged scholarly attempts to examine the Tunisian branch of Saharan commerce, have other noteworthy implications amongst scholars interested in 'counting the uncountable' (see Austen, 1979). For example, based on the sporadic statistical data from Traill's (1788), Frank's (1851) and MacGill's (1811) accounts of the size of the slave trade to Tunisia, Ralph Austen estimated that the total quota of the Tunisian share of the slave trade between 1700 and 1900 averaged 125,000. Using mainly sporadic data on the size of the slave trade indicated by Traill, Frank and MacGill, Austen suggests that between late 1780s and 1814, the annual average number of slaves imported to Tunis was about 700–800. In developing his estimates of the Tunisian share of the slave trade, Austen relied on a meticulous method of calculations and quantitative assessments of sources known to him on the trans-Saharan slave trade. While a few scholars dispute his estimates, unlike the Atlantic slave trade, relying on rough estimates in order to comprehend the directional trend of the slave trade is unavoidable (Wright 2002, 57).

During the late eighteenth century, the economic reforms undertaken by Tunisian state officials to take advantage of the expanding European trade led to a greater reorganisation of the Ghadames caravan trade. Therefore, this overall trade policy – pursued by the Tunisian state – integrated both the overland and inland branches of the burgeoning Tunisian trade. This integration, indeed, promoted a liaison between the caravan trade and expanding European commerce, especially after 1787. As Chater and others have shown, during this period, Tunisian imports and exports between Europe and the Levant grew. Similarly, these major economic developments influenced the Ghadames caravan slave trade. This development had a bearing on the increased frequency of Ghadames caravans entering Tunis from the interior.

When compared to previous periods before late 1788 and early 1789, the Traill report presupposes that 1788 and 1789, in particular, marked the height of the Ghadames caravan trade since its reintegration into the expanding Tunisian foreign trade. This height of the trade, indeed, is illustrated by the frequency of Ghadames caravans, especially their sudden leap between 1788 and 1789. Until 1788, the annual average number of Ghadames caravans entering Tunis was between one to three caravans. By the early 1789, Traill noted that 'there [we]re five or six yearly caravans'. Despite Valensi's belief that from the early eighteenth century on, the Ghadames caravan trade was static and unimpressive, increases in the number of caravans would suggest that, indeed, the Ghadames caravan trade adapted to the economic transformation that occurred from 1786 on, and, like the Regency's foreign trade in general, it enjoyed marked progress.

Apparently, the continuing trend of the Ghadames caravan trade's growth was further illustrated in Frank's estimate that at his time, the annual average number of slaves imported by the caravans amounted to between 1000 and 1200 slaves. Yet again, his estimate suggests that the annual average of slaves imported to Tunis stayed, consistently, at the same level or even increased after the late 1780s, especially if one considers that not the whole of the 1000–1300 slaves Traill reported did reach Tunis.

Besides the frequency of the Ghadames caravan and the scale of its slave trade, a noted diversification in secondary trade articles became evident. While slaves, gold dust, leather products and ivory had a long history as chief staples of the caravan trade, a number of secondary trade articles burst upon the scene from the late 1780s and began to assume more significance. However, they did not become as important as slaves. Especially noteworthy in this period were senna and ostrich feathers, which were re-exported in large quantities across the Mediterranean to European destinations, particularly to the Italian cities of Leghorn, Venice, and Genoa. Prior to the reign of Hammuda Pasha, these articles were not a major component of the Ghadames trade.

In 1789, after listing senna, gold dust, ostrich feathers and a few elephant teeth as the principal articles of commerce, Traill noted that 'the most considerable article of all these was senna'. Until the late 1780s, senna, a bush plant whose leaves were widely used in Europe for papermaking and other industrial purposes had not been a significant part of the Ghadames caravan trade to the Regency. However, from the late 1780s until the early 1840s, it did become a principal import of the Ghadames caravan trade. According to Traill, when entering the Regency from the African interior, Ghadames merchants brought up to 3100 weight of cantaar of senna to Jerba, which being the first place the Ghadames caravan stopped after returning from the interior in the Regency. There, they were forced by the Ben Ayeds Caidat family controlling the southwestern route of the caravan trade to dispose of at least two-thirds of the quantity to the governor of Jerba. Again, like Tunis, Jerba was an important commercial entrepôt for Jews and European merchants trading with Malta and other Italian cities such as Leghorn, Venice and Genoa. Jewish merchants monopolized the island's trade and shipped the bulk of the senna that was retained in Jerba to Italy. Traill stated that, indeed senna was of little use in Tunis and was generally sold for about £3.10–£4 Sterling per 100 weight and shipped to Europe. It is unclear if the gold dust, which he said seldom amounts to the value of £500 sterling was also re-exported to Europe. In addition to senna, trade in other trans-Saharan products such as ostrich feathers flourished. Ostrich feathers, used in the textile industry, did not become a well-known article until the late 1780s, with their increased re-exportation to European destinations across the Mediterranean. Traill noted that in early 1789, ostrich feathers were of little value and were sold at £5–£6 pounds sterling per skin. Between 1789 and 1808, however, they saw enormous growth as a result of continuous expansion of European trade in the Regency. While Frank described ostrich feathers as the main trade article of Ghadamisyyah caravan trade 'après la vent des esclaves noires', because of their value to the European commerce, Jackson divided them into three main classes according to their weight and quality.

Conversely, a survey of the shifting nature of European goods exported from the Regency of Tunis into the African interior also points to the diversification of Ghademes caravan trade goods. This trend can be seen clearly in the European products destined for retail in the African interior, particularly following the increased trade's interaction between the European and the Ghademes caravan trade after 1788. In 1799, Jackson, for instance, noted that in return for ostrich feathers, ivory, senna and gold dust, European goods that the Ghadames merchants took back to the African interior mainly consisted of 'coarse woollen, firearms, gunpowder, watches, and hard-ware'. Compared to the period before the late 1780s, Jackson was among the earlier writers explicitly to list firearms and gunpowder as among the European hardware re-exported from Tunis to the African interior. Throughout the previous period leading to the 1790s, firearms are hardly discernible in the extant Europeans account of European goods exported from Tunis to the African interior. Overall, the above-noted diversification of secondary trade goods was a by-product of the increasing interaction between the Ghadames caravan trade and the expanding European trade in the Regency.

Conclusion

While the economic and political developments occurring from the late eighteenth and early nineteenth century have stirred a burgeoning academic interest and have led scholars to conjure up a plethora of paradigms to explain the implications of these developments on the Regency's economic, political, and social history, this scholarship has done little to integrate the trans-Saharan slave trade into these studies. Except for selectively noting the 1846 much-celebrated abolition of slavery as an outcome of Ahmad Bey's modernisation and reform scheme, most scholars have bracketed off the Saharan slave trade from the implications of the above-discussed broader historical developments. One readily sees this discounting of the Saharan trade from implications of these developments in Anderson's fine comparative study of Tunisia and Libya. In pointing to the effects of these developments on transformation processes in Tunisia and Libya, she reinforces the thesis that stressed – as has already been indicated – that in the period after 1500, the trans-Saharan trade was 'more vulnerable to competition from the sea' and therefore 'insignificant'. Anderson concludes that:

> By the first quarter of the nineteenth century, the garrison-states of Tunisia and Libya had seen their resources from international trade erode. During the course of the eighteenth century, the value of the caravan trade declined as European traders along the western coast of Africa diverted the trade in gold and slaves – the major commodities of trans-Saharan commerce – to Atlantic Ocean ports. Although commerce remained important, and trans-Saharan trade would revive briefly in Libya late in the century, by then the caravan was a mere fraction of its earlier value. (Anderson 1986, 59)

This paper has argued, instead, that in order to understand the varying trends characterising the Tunisian trans-Saharan slave trade, the slave trade has to be studied within the broader context of Tunisian political and economic development underway. Over the past decades, many historians and political scientists have examined the implications of the above transformations as signalling a watershed moment. The periods following 1786, defined as the 'Golden Age' of Tunisia, and the aftermath of 1816, which saw European capitalist domination of the Mediterranean, have shaped modern Tunisian history.

As of 1786, the fluctuations and changes in the Ghadames caravan trade were consistent with the broader patterns of Tunisian trade with Europe, the Mediterranean and the Levant. The sources examined between 1786 and 1808 demonstrate a steady flow of Ghadames caravans as well as slaves into the Regency. During the course of the early 1780s, as they did with Europe, the Mediterranean and the Levant, the Tunisian Beys recognised the importance of trade with the west and central Sudan. In addition to the systematic importation of Sudanese gold to replenish the Tunisian treasury, the Beys regulated the Ghadames slave trade, leading to its integration into the network of inland and foreign trade that blossomed after 1786. In the few decades following the end of the civil war that disrupted economic activities in the Regency, Robert Traill wrote a detailed official report showing how the number of Ghadames regular caravans entering Tunis fluctuated from three to between five and six yearly caravans. The available contemporary accounts, both Tunisian and European, suggest that up until 1786, in an average year, the number of regular caravans was only two. Clearly, this increased in the number of the caravans makes 1788 and 1789, the same period in which Tunisian exports and imports flourished, an exceptional time for the slave trade.

Thus, the paper has emphasised the implications of the political and economic developments in the late eighteenth and early nineteenth century-Tunisia and the western Mediterranean on the trans-Saharan slave trade. From the early eighteenth century, the Ghadames caravan trade, which conducted the slave trade between Tunisia and the African interior, had been a marginal branch of Tunisian foreign trade. Despite the slave trade common depiction as insignificant, the political and economic developments processes that occurred after 1782 affected the dynamics of the trans-Saharan slave trade. It needs to be stressed that, in spite of the compounded economic effects of the civil war on the Ghadames caravans entering Tunis, after the end of the war and following the resumption of political and economic stability, the trans-Saharan slave trade enjoyed significant growth in scope, pace and scale.

The growth in scope and the scale of the trans-Saharan slave trade was particularly pronounced between 1786 and 1788. As shown above, this growth paralleled the growth of the Tunisian foreign trade with the Levant and western Mediterranean. After the end of the civil war, the solid economic and commercial reforms that Hammuda Pasha implemented led to the flourishing of the Ghadames caravan slave trade, especially in the last few years that followed the trade's reorganisation and its integration into the Regency's foreign trade. Then, from 1789 until 1808, increased European trade in Tunis further boosted the growth of the Ghadames caravan trade. The far-reaching implications of the increased European trade on the Ghadames caravan trade can be discerned, first, in the increased number of its caravans entering Tunis, mainly between 1788 and 1789. Similar to the effects of Hammuda Pasha's economic reforms, these developments signalled a turning point for the trans-Saharan slave trade, just as it did for Tunisian external trade. This is especially evident when trans-Saharan slave trade in this period is compared to that of the early part of the eighteenth century, a time that Valensi describes as static and unspectacular.

References

Abun-Nasr, Jamil M. 1982. "The Tunisian State in the Eighteenth Century." *Revue de l'Occident Musulman et de la Méditerranée*, no. 33: 33–66.

Anderson, Lisa. 1986. *The State and Social Transformation in Tunisia and Libya, 1830–1980*. Princeton, NJ: Princeton University Press.

Anene, J. C. 1965. "Liaison and Competition between Sea and Land Routes in International Trade from the 15th Century: The Central Sudan and North Africa." In *XIIe Congrés international des sciences historiques par la commission international d'Histoire maritime á l'ocassion de son VIle colloque*, 191–207. Paris: Ecole Practique des Haute Études.

Austen, Ralph A. 1979. "Trans-Saharan Slave Trade: A Tentative Census." In *The Uncommon Market*, edited by H. A. Gemery and J. S. Hogendon, 23–69. New York: Academic Press.

Austen, Ralph A. 1990. "Marginalization, Stagnation, and Growth: The Trans-Saharan Caravan Trade in the Era of European Expansion, 1500–1900." In *The Rise of Merchant Empires: Long-Distance Trade in the Early Modern World, 1350–1750*, edited by James D. Tracy, 311–350. Cambridge: Cambridge University Press.

Chater, Khalifa. 1984. *Dépendance et mutations précoloniales: la régence de Tunis de 1815 à 1857*. Tunis: Université de Tunis.

Chater, Khalifa. 1987. "Le Commerce Caravanier au Maghreb et ses mutations au cours de l'ère précoloniale." *The Maghreb Review* 12 (3–4): 99–104.

Chérif, Mohamed-Hédi. 1970. "Expansion européenne et difficultés tunisiennes de 1815 à 1830." *Annales Economies Sociétés Civilizations* 8 (mai-juin): 714–745.

Chérif, Mohamed-Hédi. 1983. "Pouvoir beylical et contrôle de l'espace dans la Tunisie du XVIII siècle et les débuts du XIX siècle." *Annuaire de l'Afrique du Nord* 22: 49–61.

Dyer, Mark Frederick. 1978. "The Foreign Trade of Western Libya, 1750–1830." Ph.D. Thesis, Boston University.

Frank, Loius. 1851. *Précédée d'un description de cette régence. Published with Jean-Joseph Marcel, Histoire de Tunis*. Paris: Firmin Didot Fréres.

Gallagher, Nancy E. 2002. *Medicine and Power in Tunisia, 1780-1900*. Cambridge: Cambridge University Press.

Ganiage, Jean. 1960. '*La population européenne de Tunis au milieu du XIXe siècle; étude démographique.*' *Université de Tunis. Publications de la Faculté des lettres. 4. sér.: Histoire, no. 2*. Paris: Presses universitaires de France.

Hallett, Robin. ed. 1964. *Records of the African Association, 1788–1831*. Toronto: Thomas Nelson and Sons Ltd for the Association for Promoting the Discovery of the Interior Parts of Africa.

Hunter, F. R. 1986. "Recent Tunisian Historical Writing on State and Society in Modern Tunisia." *Middle East Studies Association Bulletin* 20 (1): 23–28.

Jackson, John. 1804. *Reflections on the Commerce of the Mediterranean ... Containing a Particular Account of the Traffic of the Kingdoms of Algiers, Tunis, Sardinia, Naples & Sicily; the Morea ... the Manners and Customs of the Inhabitants, in their Commercial Dealings. And a Particular Description of the British Manufactures Properly Adapted for Each Country*. London: W. Clarke.

Julien, Charles-André. 1970. *History of North Africa: From the Arab Conquest to 1830*. Translated by John Petrie, Edited. C. C. Stewart and revised by R. Le Tourneau. London: Routledge and K. Paul.

Kraiem, Mustapha. 1973. *La Tunisie Précoloniale: Économie, Société*. 2 vols. Tunis: Societe Tunisienne de diffusion.

Limam, Rachad. 1974. "The Commercial Policy of Hammuda Pasha Al-Husayni." *Revue d'Histoire Maghrébine* 2: 194–196.

Limam, Rachad. 1980. *Siyasat Hammuda Basha fi Tunis, 1782–1814* [La Politique de Hammouda Pacha]. Tunis: Manshurat Jami'ah al-Tunisiyyah.

Limam, Rachad. 1981. "Some Documents Concerning Slavery in Tunisia at the End of the 18th Century." *Revue d'Histoire Maghrebine* 8 (11): 349–357.

Lord Sydney to Consul Robert Traill, Whitehall, 6 October, 1788, FO 77/3, National Archives, Kew.

MacGill, Thomas. 1811. *An Account of Tunis: Of Its Government, Manners, Customs, and Antiquities; Especially of Its Productions, Manufactures, and Commerce*. Glasgow: Longman Hurst Rees Orme and Brown.

Montana, Ismael M. 2013. *The Abolition of Slavery in Ottoman Tunisia*. Gainesville: University Press of Florida.

Raymond, André. 1953. "British Policy Towards Tunis, 1830–1881." Ph.D. Thesis, Oxford University.

Seheli, Chedli. 1986. "La Tunisie et l'Afrique sub-saharienne." *Revue d'Histoire Maghrebine* 49 (52): 41–42.

Valensi, Lucette. 1967. "Esclaves chrétiens et esclaves noirs à Tunis au XVIII siècle." *Annales Economies Sociétés Civilizations* 22 (6): 1275–1285.

Valensi, Lucette. 1977. *On the Eve of Colonialism: North Africa Before the French Conquest*. Translated by Kenneth J. Perkins. New York: Africana Publishing Company.

Valensi, Lucette. 1981. "The Tunisian Fallaheen in the Eighteenth and Nineteenth Centuries." In *The Islamic Middle East, 700–1900: Studies in Economic and Social History*, edited by A. L. Udovitch, 709–724. Princeton: The Darwin Press.

Woodford, J. S. 1990. *The City of Tunis: Evolution of an Urban System*. Cambridgeshire: Middle East & North African Studies Press Ltd.

Wright, John. 2002. "Morocco: The Last Great Slave Trade Market?" *The Journal of North African Studies* 7 (3): 53–66.

Ahmad Baba al-Timbukti and his Islamic critique of racial slavery in the Maghrib

Timothy Cleaveland

History Department, University of Georgia, Athens, GA, USA

This essay examines the life of Ahmad Baba al-Timbukti (1556–1627) and his efforts to end racial slavery and to persuade Maghribi scholars to accept the Islamic status of self-professed Muslims in West Africa. Towards this end, Ahmad Baba wrote a legal treatise that criticised the association of 'Black' Africans with slaves, especially through the racialised version of the curse of Ham. This treatise, entitled *Mi'raj al-Su'ud*, drew upon a century of jurisprudence produced in Timbuktu and set Islamic standards for enslavement that defined as illicit a substantial portion of the trans-Saharan slave trade as it then existed. However, the treatise also defined much of West Africa as non-Muslim or lightly Islamised, and thereby sanctioned the targeting of these peoples for enslavement. In a similar effort, Ahmad Baba also publicised the scholarly achievements of West African Muslims by compiling a huge biographical dictionary of scholars from West and Northwest Africa. This book, entitled *Nayl al-Ibtihaj*, could have substantiated the fact that many self-identified Black West Africans had been producing serious Muslim scholarship for at least a century, but it did not. On the contrary, Ahmad Baba included only one Black scholar in his biographical dictionary and instead featured nine scholars from his own 'Berber' patriline, including himself. The ironic characteristics of the *Mi'raj al-Su'ud* and *Nayl al-Ibtihaj* may best be explained by Ahmad Baba's own ambiguous status in Timbuktu and the broader society of Islamic West Africa – as a 'White' Berber living in the 'land of the Blacks'. The fact that his scholarship was ground-breaking, but not radical, facilitated its reception in the Maghrib while perhaps mitigating its practical effect on the slave trade and enslavement in that region as well as in West African trading towns such as Timbuktu.

Introduction

In the cool of a southern Saharan morning on the 9th of February 1615, Ahmad Baba sat in a quiet room of his Timbuktu home, leaned forward and pressed the moistened tip of his reed pen to paper.[1] He was completing a treatise or *fatwa* on the Islamic law of slavery, emphasising the illegality of enslaving West Africans on the basis of race rather than religion. It was a very conscious attempt to change the nature of the trans-Saharan slave trade and Northwest African slavery. As such, Ahmad Baba and his treatise were products of a vibrant commercial and cultural relationship between the Maghrib and West Africa that stretched back more than a millennium, predating the spread of Islam across North Africa in the seventh century. Shortly after the arrival of Islam in Northwest Africa, Muslim geographers began recording information about the kingdoms of West Africa and their roles in long-distance trade, which included slaves. By the eleventh century, the West African commercial and political elite had begun to adopt Islam and acquire literacy in Arabic, resulting in stronger bonds between the regions. West Africans often passed through the Maghrib on their pilgrimages to the holy sites of Arabia, sometimes stopping for extended periods of study and scholarly exchange. At this time, Berber speakers from the Sahara and as far away as Mediterranean North Africa also began to migrate to the southern Saharan trading towns of West Africa.[2] By the fourteenth century, Arabic-speaking nomads as well as some urbanites were following this pattern of migration, further diversifying these already cosmopolitan towns. Ahmad Baba was himself an embodiment of this diversity; his patriline claimed a noble Berber ancestry, but had spent generations in West Africa and maintained close relations with scholarly families belonging to the Mandé and Fulani language groups. Ahmad Baba's Timbuktu and the towns his patrilineal ancestors had lived in were home to families of many ethnic groups, but the Mandé and Fulani had a particularly strong history of scholarship in the region in the late sixteenth century.

Despite the diversity of urban West Africa, slavery and slave trading in the region were often justified by reference to ethnic and racial identities. The earliest North African texts that referred to West Africa described it as the *Bilad al-Sudan* ('the land of the Blacks'), often associating Black racial identity with slavery. Although West African Islamic scholarship was already centuries old when Ahmad Baba was born, many North Africans still perceived the region as a land of unbelief. Slave traders used these negative stereotypes to justify both the trans-Saharan slave trade and a form of racial slavery practised in North Africa. These stereotypes may have also facilitated the aggressive foreign policy of Mulay Ahmad al-Mansur, the sultan of Morocco, who invaded Timbuktu in 1591 as part of his conquest of the Songhay Kingdom.[3] Two years into the occupation, Mansur's forces arrested Ahmad Baba and many other Timbuktu scholars on suspicion of resistance and imprisoned them in Marrakesh. Ahmad Baba remained there until 1608, when he was allowed to return home to Timbuktu, where he resumed his career as a scholar until his death in 1627. The trauma of the violent invasion and occupation of Timbuktu, as well as Ahmad Baba's exile, shaped his prolific scholarly career.

This essay examines Ahmad Baba's efforts to persuade Maghribi scholars to accept the Islamic status of self-professed Muslims in West Africa and to reject racial slavery. Towards this end, Ahmad Baba wrote a legal treatise that suggested that Northwest Africans were illegally enslaving West Africans on the basis of race. This treatise, entitled *Mi'raj al-Su'ud*, drew upon a century of jurisprudence produced in Timbuktu and set Islamic standards for enslavement that defined as illicit a substantial portion of the slave trade as it then existed. However, the treatise also defined much of West Africa as non-Muslim or lightly Islamised, and thereby sanctioned the targeting of these peoples for enslavement. In a similar effort, Ahmad Baba also publicised the scholarly achievements of West African Muslims by compiling a huge biographical dictionary of scholars from West and Northwest Africa. This book, entitled *Nayl al-Ibtihaj*, could have substantiated the fact that many self-identified 'Black' West Africans had been producing serious Muslim scholarship for at least a century, but it did not.[4] On the contrary, Ahmad Baba included only one Black scholar in his biographical dictionary; instead, most of the scholars included from West Africa were his own Berber ancestors. While these two texts advocated on behalf of West Africans, Ahmad Baba could have defined legitimate enslavement more narrowly than he did, and he could have made a much stronger case for the scholarly achievements of Black West Africans. The ironic characteristics of these texts may best be explained by Ahmad Baba's own ambiguous status in Timbuktu and the broader society of Islamic West Africa. The fact that his scholarship was ground-breaking, but not radical, facilitated its reception in the Maghrib while perhaps mitigating its practical effect on the slave trade and enslavement in that region, as well as in West African trading towns such as Timbuktu, which maintained substantial slave populations through the nineteenth century.[5] The trans-Saharan slave trade and racial slavery in the Maghrib also persisted from Ahmad Baba's time through the end of the nineteenth century, and yet there are several reasons to believe that his efforts eventually had a significant effect on the region's perception of Islamic West Africa. And his scholarship has been extremely useful for historians of Africa who, over the past few decades, have begun to examine racial slavery and racism in North Africa and the Sahara (Figure 1).

The racial and ethnic diversity of Ahmad Baba's society

In order to understand Ahmad Baba and his scholarly critique of racial slavery, one must first consider the history of Timbuktu and the broader region, as well as Ahmad Baba's personal and family history. In particular, I will emphasise the ethnic and racial diversity of the West

Figure 1. Saharan Trade Networks c. 1600.

African towns where Ahmad Baba's ancestors made their careers, and the close relations between scholarly families of various backgrounds.

Ahmad Baba was born in Timbuktu on 26 October 1556 into a scholarly family (Zouber 1977, 15–22). His hometown was one of the provincial capitals of the Songhay Kingdom, and it lay on the southern edge of the Sahara Desert, but close to the great Niger River. Indeed, in Ahmad Baba's time, the region enjoyed greater rainfall than it did in the twentieth century, so that in the rainy season, the Niger would often flood to the edge of the city. At Timbuktu and similar trading towns along the northern bend of the Niger River, camel caravans bearing commodities southward across the Sahara would encounter boats laden with goods from the savannah and forest regions of West Africa. The caravans, sometimes numbering several thousand camels, brought blocks of salt from the central Sahara, as well as cloth, books and writing paper, and sometimes horses from North Africa. The boats from the south mainly brought grain, such as millet and sorghum, but also carried ivory, kola nuts, honey, gold and newly captured slaves.

Timbuktu was not the oldest centre of trade and Islamic scholarship in West Africa. Indeed, it seems not to have been a significant settlement before the thirteenth century, by which time, other West African towns such as Awdaghust, Kumbi Saleh, Dia, Jenné and Walata (originally Biru) had served as centres of trade for centuries. Earlier generations of Ahmad Baba's patriline, the Aqits, had lived in towns such as Dia and Walata before ultimately moving to Timbuktu, which grew rapidly in the thirteenth and fourteenth centuries and eventually replaced Walata as the premier trading town in the southern Sahara. This commercial growth attracted many scholars as well as traders, two professions that were very closely related in this region. Trading towns such as Timbuktu had long been multi-ethnic and multi-racial communities. In many ways, these towns were quite sophisticated, as families like Ahmad Baba's were highly mobile, well-educated and politically astute. Ahmad Baba's family was but one branch of the Aqit patriline, which had already produced at least five generations of 'ulama in the region, and a few chief judges of Timbuktu (Zouber 1977, 13–21; Hunwick 1964, 568–593).

Lineage groups such as the Aqits operated as small corporations, creating their own trading networks, strategic alliances and credit. Each new branch of the patriline would disperse several of its sons and daughters across the region to settle in the towns that made up their trading network. The settlement of these newcomers would be cemented by strategic marriages with elites in the network towns, who often did not belong to the same ethnic group or race. This meant that inter-ethnic and inter-racial marriages were much more common for the merchant families in the trading towns than was the case for peasant families living in agricultural villages. But even though these inter-ethnic and inter-racial relations were sophisticated and enlightened by modern Western standards, they were not completely without stereotyping and prejudice (Cleaveland 2002, 37–60, 191–197; Cleaveland 1998, 365–388).

In Ahmad Baba's day, the population of Timbuktu was multi-lingual and multi-ethnic. There were families of local origin, such as Zarma speakers, but also many families from ethnic groups whose centres were outside the immediate area. Prominent among these were the Mandé language groups such as the Soninké and Malinké as well as the unrelated Fulani (or Fulbé). Sixteenth-century Timbuktu also included families of northern origin, most from the Sahara, but some from North Africa or Arabia. These included Berber and Arabic speakers, each category being composed of multiple languages or dialects. Finally, during Ahmad Baba's life, Timbuktu and other major Niger River towns in the region were developing a new language that came to be called Songhay, drawing its name from the sixteenth-century kingdom that dominated the region (Heath 1998). Songhay is partly based on local Zarma languages, but includes prominent influences from all the major languages of the people who moved to cosmopolitan riverine towns such as Timbuktu.

Ahmad Baba identified his origins by describing himself in his texts as 'Sanhaja', an Arabised form of the Berber name 'Zenaga'. A Berber-speaking people, the Zenaga had lived in the southern Sahara of West Africa since at least the tenth century, and their name is the origin of the modern name 'Sénégal'. Ahmad Baba traced his patriline into the distant past, but the patronym 'Aqit' seems to have originated with Ahmad Baba's great-great grandfather Muhammad Aqit, who was a prominent scholar living in the Masina region of the Niger River valley, about 150 miles south of Timbuktu (Zouber 1977, 13–21).

Muhammad Aqit or his ancestors had moved south to Masina from the southern Saharan town of Tishit. Indeed, the Timbuktu historian 'Abd al-Rahman al-Sa'di asserted in the seventeenth century that many of the people of Masina were from Tishit, although it is highly unlikely that people from Tishit actually founded Masina, which had a majority Fulani population.[6] The family of Muhammad Aqit did not remain in Masina, but emigrated to Biru, a southern Saharan town also known as Walata. Al-Sa'di quoted Ahmad Baba when he described the reason for the Aqit family's emigration from Masina to Biru in the following passage:

> I heard the legal scholar Ahmad Baba say … [that Muhammad Aqit] only left Masina to go to Biru because of his hatred for the Fulani, who lived in his neighborhood. He was certain that he would never marry among the Fulani, but he feared that his children would, and that their lineage would be mixed with the Fulani. (Cleaveland 2002, 64)[7]

Al-Sa'di's statement about Muhammad Aqit, regardless of its accuracy, demonstrates the consciousness of race or ethnicity in seventeenth-century Timbuktu. Muhammad Aqit's alleged fear of intermarriage with the Fulani was not uncommon among Saharans who settled in non-Arab and non-Berber communities to the south. This story suggests that Muhammad Aqit and much of al-Sa'di's audience associated intermarriage with the potential loss of social or ethnic identity. In theory, Muhammad Aqit's intermarriage with the Fulani would not have altered the patrilineal identity of his male descendants, whose children would theoretically assume their fathers' identity no matter whom they married. However, his fear suggests that he recognised the power of affinal and matrifilial kin to shape one's identity (Cleaveland 2002, 64–65).

Despite the attitudes that al-Sa'di and Ahmad Baba attributed to Muhammad Aqit, the Zenaga of Tishit maintained close relations with Masina from Muhammad Aqit's time through the early nineteenth century when a conflict among the dominant families of Tishit resulted in the emigration of a group of Tishiti families to the Masina kingdom of Ahmadu Lobbo. According to the nineteenth-century historian, Muhammad Salih al-Nasiri, the Tishiti families took refuge there because the Fulani king honoured and protected them.[8] This evidence of close relations between Tishiti emigrants and their Fulani hosts in Masina suggests that Muhammad Aqit's fear of intermarriage was based on his experience of a common and largely accepted social practice (Cleaveland 2002, 173–184, 191–197; Saad 1983, 7–9, 69–70).

When Muhammad Aqit moved to Biru (or Walata), his sons found themselves in a mixed Mandé and Berber community, with few, if any, Fulani. Biru was the original name of the Mandé settlement, which had welcomed many Berber families before the arrival of the Aqits. Indeed, by the mid-fourteenth century, Biru was also known by the Berber name 'Iwalatan'. Furthermore, in the time of Muhammad Aqit's great-great grandson Ahmad Baba, scholars were starting to Arabise this Berber name to 'Walata', which became the dominant name for the town by the beginning of the nineteenth century. This history of name changes closely approximates historic changes in the predominant ethnicity of the town, which started out as a Mandé town, eventually became predominantly Berber, and, by the twentieth century, had become Arab (Cleaveland 2002, 46–60).

In Muhammad Aqit's day, Biru was on the northern edge of the Mandé Kingdom of Mali. It had long been one of the wealthiest towns in the region, but its importance as a regional centre of trade was already being eclipsed by the growth of Timbuktu. The historian 'Abd al-Rahman al-Sa'di, writing in 1655, described the decline of Biru and the rise of Timbuktu:

> The commercial center [of the region] used to be Biru. There flowed caravans from every land, and great scholars, and pious persons. Wealthy people from every race and every country settled there, including people from Egypt; Aujela; Fezzan; Ghadames; Tuwat; Dra'a; Tafilalt; Fez; the Sus; Bitu; and others. All of that was transferred to Timbuktu little by little until they were concentrated at Timbuktu. Additionally, all the tribes of the Sanhaja rejoined their elements [which had moved to Timbuktu]. The prosperity of Timbuktu was the ruin of Biru. Its (Timbuktu's) civilization came to it exclusively from the Maghrib, in matters of religion as well as trade. (Cleaveland 2002, 62)[9]

Although al-Sa'di asserted that the most prominent citizens of Biru were originally from North Africa, and that Timbuktu derived its civilisation from the Maghrib, other sources, including al-Sa'di's own work, suggest that this was an exaggeration. While it is true that Islam spread from North Africa to Biru (Walata) and Timbuktu, bringing with it many cultural influences, the culture of these towns in the sixteenth and seventeenth centuries was still predominantly West African (Cleaveland 2002, 37–66). Moreover, the Islamic scholarship produced in these towns in this period was almost exclusively the work of non-Arabs whose families had spent generations in the region. Some of these scholars were Berbers, as was the Aqit family, but al-Sa'di as well as other regional historians, who described the early development of Islamic scholarship in West Africa, included many important scholars of sub-Saharan origin. One of the earliest scholars in Timbuktu was Muhammad al-Kabari, who came from a town in the Masina region named Dia.[10] Timbuktu and the neighbouring towns supported several large families that enjoyed a scholarly reputation, among them the Gidadu, Gurdu, Baghayogho and Sila (Saad 1983, 38–72, 115–156). These Mandé and Fulani scholarly families generally enjoyed good relations with the various generations of the Aqit patriline. Indeed, Ahmad Baba's principal teacher and mentor (his *shaykh*) was Muhammad Baghayogho al-Wangari, whose lineage name and *nisba* indicate his Mandé origins (Hunwick 1990, 149–163).

Although Timbuktu's growth came partly at the expense of Biru, the town survived and even served as a haven for several scholarly Timbuktu families that fled to Biru when Timbuktu was forcefully brought into the expanding kingdom of Songhay in 1468. This Songhay expansion was led by Sunni 'Ali, who was based in Gao, located downstream on the Niger River some 250 miles east of Timbuktu. Sunni 'Ali's warriors from Gao took advantage of a weakening Mali Kingdom and seized its northern territories along the Niger River, which lay far from Mali's heartland in the south. Biru had also been a part of the Mali Kingdom, but successfully defended its newfound autonomy from the growing Songhay Kingdom in the late fifteenth century. This made Biru attractive to many of the scholarly families in Timbuktu, including many of the Aqits, who had difficulty adapting to a new and suspicious king.

A generation after the Aqits had fled to Biru, many members of this and other scholarly families moved back to Timbuktu, in part because of a change of dynasty in the Songhay Kingdom after the death of Sunni 'Ali. For much of the sixteenth century, life was good for the traders and scholars living in Timbuktu, as the economy remained prosperous. But all this changed in 1591 when Morocco's sultan sent an expeditionary force across the Sahara to invade the Songhay Kingdom. The invasion was successful, in part because the expeditionary force was armed with muskets, as well as a few canons. The initial Moroccan invasion focused on Gao, the capital of Songhay, and quickly routed the larger Songhay army, equipped only with arrows and spears. The surviving Songhay elite evacuated the city and sued for peace. The Moroccans then headed for Timbuktu, entering the city without opposition, as the Songhay military and administrators had already evacuated. The Moroccan soldiers immediately commandeered several homes, and set about turning some of the contiguous ones into a fortress, as the sultan had directed them to establish a permanent occupation. They also looted other Timbuktu homes of their valuables, especially their gold. The military leaders kept much of this loot, but did send 100,000 mithqals of gold to the Moroccan sultan (Hunwick 2003, 191–192).[11] This sum was insufficient to satisfy the sultan, but the confiscations were more than enough to engender small acts of resistance in Timbuktu. The Moroccan soldiers responded disproportionally, taking out their frustrations on the civil population. Several scholars were killed, and many others fled to Biru and other towns beyond the Moroccan reach. The worst of these disproportional responses occurred in 1593 when the Moroccans killed dozens of civilians, several scholars and one prominent member of Ahmad Baba's extended family. Many scholars, including Ahmad Baba and several of his family members, were arrested and exiled to a prison in Marrakesh (Hunwick 2003, 218–227).

The conditions of this exile seem to have been relatively harsh for the first two years, but once Ahmad Baba had a chance to demonstrate his knowledge and skills to Moroccan scholars, they apparently intervened in order to extricate him from the prison and to improve his living conditions. By 1596, although still not free, he was regularly interacting with several Marrakesh scholars, studying together as colleagues, and even teaching some of the local students in the main mosque.[12] Therefore, during much of his 15-year exile, he was able to continue his work as a scholar, and he compiled his long biographical dictionary of scholars while in Marrakesh (Zouber 1977, 24–31, 146–155). Still, his exile must have been a traumatising experience, and not just because he was separated from many of his family and friends. In addition to the material hardships imposed by the Moroccan invasion, there seems to have been an important ideological or cultural dimension for Ahmad Baba. His subsequent scholarship suggests that he believed that the attack and ensuing abuse were partly the result of the Moroccan sultan's contempt for the 'Sudan', the Black peoples of West Africa. Although Ahmad Baba belonged to a Sanhaja Berber patrilineage, it is quite possible that some of the people he met in Marrakesh identified him as 'Sudani'. Ahmad Baba addressed issues of race and identity in his treatise on enslavement entitled *Mi'raj al-Su'ud*, so I will examine the question of his identity in the next section devoted to his scholarship.

In 1603, Sultan Mulay Ahmad died and his successor, Mulay Zaydan, promised to free Ahmad Baba, which he eventually did in 1608. Ahmad Baba returned home to Timbuktu as a free man, but without some of the other prisoners, such as his paternal uncle 'Umar who had died in Marrakesh in 1597. Later historians in Timbuktu viewed 'Umar's death as such a gross injustice that they classified him as a martyr (Hunwick 2003, 44).[13] After Ahmad Baba's return to Timbuktu, he enjoyed a peaceful life and a productive career. Despite the hardships, his time and studies in Morocco enhanced his skills and his reputation, and he published many of his most noteworthy texts during this last phase of his life. He lived out the rest of his life in Timbuktu, ultimately dying on 22 April 1627, at the age of 71 (Zouber 1977, 31–34).

Ahmad Baba, race and his critique of racial slavery

Ahmad Baba's exile in Marrakesh may have facilitated his compilation of the *Nayl al-Ibtihaj bi tatriz al-Dibaj*, his long biographical dictionary of Muslim scholars in Northwest and West Africa. This book, and a slightly abridged version entitled *Kifaya al-Muhtaj*, profoundly interested the *'ulama* of Morocco, in part because they were featured in it.[14] The *Nayl* included more than a dozen scholars from West Africa, which served to educate the Moroccan scholars about the academic accomplishments of the West African Muslims. In 1615, now back in Timbuktu, Ahmad Baba wrote *Mi'raj al-Su'ud ila nayl hukm mujallab al-sud*, which translates as *The Ladder of Ascent Towards Grasping the Law Concerning Imported Blacks*.[15] The term 'imported Blacks' referred to 'Black' West Africans who had been enslaved and traded across the Sahara into North Africa. This trans-Saharan trade in slaves began at least two thousand years ago, but was not well documented until the spread of Islam across North Africa in the late seventh century. By the time Ahmad Baba was born, it was a flourishing trade that still dwarfed the incipient Atlantic trade in slaves (Austen 1979). Ahmad Baba's *Mi'raj* provides us with evidence about the ideological underpinnings of this trade in the early seventeenth century, especially with regard to notions of ethnicity and race, as well as Islamic law. But his text went far beyond a mere interpretation of law and practice, and made a specific attempt to change the behaviour of North Africans, whom he accused of sometimes purchasing West African slaves on the basis of race, rather than according to the regulations of Islam. In particular, he feared that free Muslims were being captured and traded across the Sahara, where they were enslaved by fellow Muslims, contravening the dictates of their religion.[16]

Besides the *Mi'raj* and the *Nayl,* there are more than 50 texts attributed to Ahmad Baba by other sources, though relatively few have been studied by modern scholars and some have yet to be found (Zouber 1977, 72–81). The *Mi'raj* has survived because it was copied and recopied generation after generation by scholars interested in the Islamic laws relevant to slave raiding and trading. Similarly, the *Nayl*, and its abridged version *Kifaya al-Muhtaj*, are still popular texts among scholars in West and Northwest Africa. The analysis of this essay is based mainly on these two texts; therefore, it cannot offer a definitive account of Ahmad Baba's views on the relevant issues, even if these texts do seem to be the most historically significant of his corpus.

The *Mi'raj*, written near the end of his career, is a detailed legal response to questions sent to Ahmad Baba in Timbuktu by Sa'id ibn Ibrahim al-Jirari, who lived in a northern Saharan oasis named Tuwat. We do not know much about al-Jirari, but apparently, he was a merchant who had some experience with West African captives who arrived in North Africa claiming that they had been free Muslims when they were enslaved. Al-Jirari may have heard that Ahmad Baba had questioned the legitimacy of some of the slave trade while he was exiled in Marrakesh, so he wrote to him to ask whether the claims of these captives might be true. Ahmad Baba's erudition seems to have surprised many in Marrakesh who believed that there were few, if any, learned Muslims south of the Sahara. And because of the Moroccan ignorance about the spread of Islam in West Africa, Ahmad Baba had been asked similar questions regarding Islam, race and slavery while in exile in Marrakesh (Hunwick 2000, 131–139).

The questions al-Jirari posed to Ahmad Baba suggest that the questioner associated the 'Black' racial category with slavery. Al-Jirari asked about several West African Muslim societies, claiming that an un-named *Sudani* judge had argued that these Muslim societies had been conquered by a Muslim *imam* before they converted to Islam, thereby implying that un-enslaved Muslims from these societies were not legally free and therefore were legitimate targets of Muslim enslavement. Citing Ibn Khaldun (1332–1406) and earlier scholars, Ahmad Baba responded that these Muslim societies had never been conquered but had voluntarily adopted Islam in the distant past. Whereas Ahmad Baba's answers to other questions were sometimes subtle, his answer to this question was direct and even disdainful. He responded by saying:

This we have not heard of at all, and it did not reach us. Ask this *Sudani qadi*, who was that *imam*, and in what time he conquered their land and which land he conquered? Let him, if he can, specify all this to you. Surely, his words do not bear any trace of the truth, and if you search now, you will not find any one who can ascertain the truth of what he said. (Barbour and Jacobs 1985, 128)

Al-Jirari then asked whether a slave-buyer would be required to investigate and confirm the religious status of a captive before a purchase if that captive was from a society that was known to contain Muslims. Ahmad Baba started by citing a variety of opinions, but ended by referring to three earlier scholars who argued that the burden of proof should fall on the slave-buyer, the first being the eleventh-century Andalusian scholar Abu al-Asbagh ibn Sahl. Ahmad Baba then described two sixteenth-century scholars based in Timbuktu who had referred to the opinion of Abu al-Asbagh in elaborating their own opinions on the issue. One was 'Ali ibn Salih ibn Makhluf al-Balbali (fl. 1533) and the other was Mahmud ibn 'Umar ibn Muhammad Aqit (d. 1548), Ahmad Baba's great-uncle, who had served as the *qadi* of Timbuktu for 50 years.[17] Ahmad Baba described the position of Qadi Mahmud and al-Balbali as recommending that slave-buyers defer to the claims of slaves and free them immediately, in order to protect their own souls against the sin of enslaving a free Muslim. This last point was important because al-Jirari had asked whether freeing captives on this basis was an act of piety or a religious obligation, so the historical position of the Timbuktu scholars was that it was an obligation (Barbour and Jacobs 1985, 131). According to Ahmad Baba, both Qadi Mahmud and al-Balbali claimed that the sale of free Muslims was a big problem in the region, in part because nomadic raiders, mainly Berbers and Arabs, regularly raided towns and sold their captives, regardless of their religious status. Both scholars also explicitly stated that regarding enslavement, Black non-believers were just like the other non-believers, and that Black believers were just like their co-religionists (Barbour and Jacobs 1985, 129–131). Besides confirming the legal equality of Black Muslims, this statement also implied that some slave traders were improperly associating race with slavery.

Al-Jirari's next question was about a tenth-century hadith that associated West Africans with slavery by describing the supposedly cursed descendants of Ham as 'blackened'.[18] The story of Ham's curse originally appeared in the Torah or Old Testament, written several centuries before the Common Era. The original version of the story had nothing to do with race, but sought to justify the enslavement of Canaanites by the Jews who left Egypt in the Exodus led by Moses. However, in the early centuries of the Common Era, a few Christian and Jewish texts began to add a racial dimension to the story, describing Ham or his cursed progeny as being darkened or blackened.[19] This racialised version of the story gradually became more popular and after the rise of Islam, it eventually spread to Muslim scholars as well, though there is no hint of it in the Quran. By the ninth century, Muslim geographers regularly described sub-Saharan Africans as 'Black' (*Sudan*) as opposed to 'White' (*Bidan*) North African and Mediterranean peoples. These geographers also regularly identified 'Black' Africans as descendants of the cursed and enslaved son of Ham.[20]

Ahmad Baba rejected this hadith's racialised version of the Hamitic curse by referring to three different environmental explanations for skin colour. First, he quoted Ibn Jawzi (1114–1201) who explained how the descendants of Noah's son's developed different skin colours by reference to the prevailing winds in the various lands they settled. Then, Ahmad Baba cited another hadith that described a people's skin colour as arising from the different soils from which they were derived. Then, finally, he quoted Ibn Khaldun's description of his climate theory of race, which was based on the effects of heat and cold on the skin. Thus, Ahmad Baba left it unclear which environmental explanation he favoured, though he clearly rejected the racialised story of Ham by quoting Ibn

Khaldun's statement pointing out that the Torah verses describing the curse of Ham made no mention of colour. This fact clearly undermined the basis of the hadith to which al-Jirari originally referred (Barbour and Jacobs 1985, 132–134).

Al-Jirari's next question was really a statement, and it seemed to reject the association of race and slavery that he had raised previously. He did this by first acknowledging that unbelief was not peculiar to the supposed descendants of Ham, and then by stating 'non-belief is that which makes enslavement permissible, whether the enslaved were Black or White'. Ahmad Baba immediately concurred with this statement and elaborated by stating that 'non-belief is not confined to the descendants of Ham. Any *kafir*, whether from the children of Ham or others, can be owned if he kept his original non-belief. In this respect, there is no difference between races' (Barbour and Jacobs 1985, 134). In an article published in the *Journal of North African Studies* in 2013, Chris Gratien referenced the previous quotation, out of context, to argue that Ahmad Baba rejected racism generally (2013, 465). However, the evidence clearly indicates that Ahmad Baba's statement only applied to unbelief and enslavement. At multiple points in the *Mi'raj*, Ahmad Baba made the point that there was no difference among the races regarding the rules of enslavement; that is, the rules of enslavement applied to all races in the same way.[21] Similarly, Ahmad Baba almost certainly believed that the rules of salvation applied to all races equally, because that was a well-established doctrine of Islam. However, there is evidence in the *Mi'raj* that suggests that Ahmad Baba believed that the races were not generally equal, even if they were equal before the law. For example, in response to another of al-Jirari's questions regarding a hadith that encouraged the early Muslim community to 'look after' or 'employ' Blacks, Ahmad Baba explained that the hadith statement aimed to prevent Blacks from being abandoned because of their 'bad characteristics' and 'lack of refinement'. In this same passage, Ahmad Baba also attributed to Blacks the qualities of 'docility, obedience, and readiness to convert to Islam'.[22] This passage, when considered alongside other scholarly representations of Blacks from the period and Ahmad Baba's representation of Black scholarship in the *Nayl*, strongly suggests that he did not view people of different races as being generally equal. As John Hunwick argued, Ahmad Baba's view of Blacks 'was affected by notions of the inferiority and enslavability of black Africans, though his legal mind rejected the simple equivalence of blackness with slavery' (Hunwick 1999, 51).

Although Ahmad Baba rejected the racialised curse of Ham, this was not the only assertion of black inferiority that was popular among Muslim scholars in his time.[23] Ibn Khaldun's climatic theory of race was the primary alternative to the story of Ham, but it employed very similar negative stereotypes. Drawing on the ideas of many earlier scholars going back to Hippocrates, Ibn Khaldun represented the Earth as divided into climate zones that stretched from south to north. The people on either extreme of these zones (sub-Saharan Africans and northern Europeans) were supposedly uncivilised because their brains were either too hot or too cold, whereas the people living in the temperate middle (the Mediterranean) were morally and intellectually superior. Below is a sample of Ibn Khaldun's views of the people living in the climate extremes:

> Their qualities of character, moreover, are close to those of dumb animals. It has even been reported that most of the Negroes of the first zone dwell in caves and thickets, eat herbs, live in savage isolation and do not congregate, and eat each other. The same applies to the Slavs. The reason for this is that their remoteness from being temperate produces in them a disposition and character similar to those of dumb animals, and they become correspondingly remote from humanity. (Khaldun 1988, 58–59)

One interesting nuance in Ibn Khaldun's version of the theory is that when individuals from one zone migrated to another, their behaviour and appearance were supposed to change accordingly. So if a Black man from the southernmost zone moved to the Mediterranean, he would become progressively lighter and more civilised, and his descendants would eventually become White. But this dynamic aspect of the theory does not render it less racist; according to the theory, a Black man could become civilised, but not without losing his blackness. The theory and its dynamism no doubt posed a serious intellectual and moral problem for Ahmad Baba because it suggested that his lineage, the Aqits, having lived for generations in the *Bilad al-Sudan*, must have been in the process of becoming Black. This brings to mind the fear expressed by Muhammad Aqit, cited above, that his family would be assimilated by the Fulani if it remained in Masina. The Aqits had moved northwards to Timbuktu in part because it had a substantial Berber and Arab community, despite still being part of the *Bilad al-Sudan*. But even if Ahmad Baba and his family could avoid the stigma of a Black identity, he knew that much of his community, his friends and colleagues had to live with it.

While Ibn Khaldun's theory is nuanced, it primarily provided a pseudoscientific explanation for the prevailing negative stereotypes of peoples who served as sources of slaves in North Africa, such as Blacks and Slavs. His version of the climate theory of race grew out of a long history of ethnic and racial stereotyping created for the purpose of justifying the oppression or enslavement of particular peoples. This includes the Torah's non-racial but ethnocentric disparagement of the Canaanites, the Greek and Roman portrayals of the 'Barbarians' and the racialisation of the story of Ham's curse in order to target Blacks. One might reasonably argue that Ibn Khaldun's climate theory of race was an important step towards the development of a pseudoscientific racism. While it is true that environmental theories of race and ethnicity varied over the centuries in the degree to which they emphasised negative stereotypes, in general, these theories were designed to explain and rationalise the dominant interpretation of difference. Some versions of environmental determinism may have been relatively benign, such as the one proposed by al-Jahiz al-Basri (Gratien 2013, 460–461). But al-Jahiz (776–869) was an outlier, and his views had much less influence than Ibn Khaldun's and other scholars of his ilk – and Ahmad Baba did not cite al-Jahiz.

Although Ahmad Baba seems to have accepted the racial dichotomy expressed by the terms '*Sudan*' and '*Bidan*' and at least some of the racial stereotyping associated with the dichotomy, in the *Mi'raj,* he clearly rejected the association of race and slavery. He also advocated standards of conduct designed to empower any *Sudani* Muslim who was illegally enslaved by another Muslim to sue successfully for his or her liberation, if that enslaved Muslim was from a predominantly Muslim society. However, his advocacy did not extend much beyond this narrowly defined group of Muslims. For that reason, some historians have been critical of Ahmad Baba for not being a better advocate for other victims of enslavement whose loss of freedom may not have conformed to a strict interpretation of Islamic law. The historian Chouki El Hamel has argued that the *Mi'raj* completely ignored the basic requirements outlined by Maliki jurisprudence for the enslavement of non-Muslims through *jihad* (El Hamel 2013, 82–83). For example, historically, there was a strong consensus among Muslim scholars that religious law should not allow the enslavement of non-Muslims except under fairly precise circumstances. Islamic law created 'protected' categories of non-Muslims, especially Jews and Christians, the *ahl al-dhimma*, who enjoyed special safeguards against enslavement. But the *'ulama* also generally agreed that even non-Muslims outside these categories should not be subjected to kidnapping and slave raiding or any other type of violence that did not conform to the laws of *jihad*. Ahmad Baba provided very little advocacy for these people in the *Mi'raj*. What is more surprising is that he did not advocate for one particularly important group of Muslims – those West African Muslims who lived as minority members of predominantly non-Muslim societies. Every West African community and society that adopted Islam must have gone through a period when

Muslims were a small minority of the population. These Muslim minorities no doubt acted as agents of conversion, and yet they received little consideration from the *Mi'raj*.

Thus, while Ahmad Baba's treatise sought to provide some protection for Muslims, it essentially did not question the broader patterns of enslavement and slave trading in West Africa and the Maghrib. And slavery and slave trading were very important aspects of Timbuktu's history, especially after the city was brought into the kingdom of Songhay by Sunni 'Ali in 1468. According to the seventeenth-century historians of Timbuktu, Sunni 'Ali was a particularly violent warrior who enslaved Muslims and non-Muslims alike throughout the region. Ahmad Baba was very familiar with this history. Although some of these captives were no doubt traded across the Sahara, most served out their enslavement in West Africa. One of the many victims of Sunni 'Ali was the great-great-grandmother of the Timbuktu historian 'Abd al-Rahman al-Sa'di, who was enslaved as a child and given as a gift to al-Sa'di's great-great-grandfather. Al-Sa'di implied that because the girl was Fulani, and therefore probably a free Muslim at the time of her enslavement, his ancestor freed and married her (Hunwick 2003, 95–96). But this girl should have been freed even if she were not a Muslim because al-Sa'di reported that the *'ulama* did not consider Sunni Ali to be a Muslim, hence none of his slaves was acquired through *jihad*.

While Sunni Ali enslaved many Muslims, it is likely that he enslaved just as many non-Muslims. Indeed, after Sunni Ali's reign, the large number of his non-Muslim slaves became an issue for which the new king, Askiya Muhammad, sought legal advice. In a famous exchange of questions and answers, the southern Saharan cleric Muhammad ibn 'Abd al-Karim al-Maghili advised the new king to free Sunni Ali's non-Muslim slaves, if they would agree to convert, because they had not been enslaved according to Islamic law (Hunwick 1985, 76–79). Ahmad Baba was well aware of this legal opinion, and he included a short biography of al-Maghili in both the *Nayl* and the *Kifaya al-Muhtaj*. But the problem of illegal enslavement was not limited to the reign of Sunni Ali. The much more orthodox Askiya Muhammad, whom the Timbuktu historians greatly admired, also engaged in widespread raiding, much of which targeted self-professed Muslim societies. Indeed, 'Abd al-Rahman al-Sa'di, who generally heaped praise on Askiya Muhammad, nevertheless, claimed that of his many military engagements that reaped captives, only one could be considered a legitimate *jihad*, and even that one did not lead the targeted society to accept Islam (Hunwick 2003, 106–107). Ahmad Baba was aware of this, but did not advise al-Jirari of it in the *Mi'raj*. He could have informed al-Jirari that purchasing any slaves from West Africa risked violating Islamic law because even the non-Muslim slaves were usually acquired in unlawful ways – but to do so would have amounted to advocating the abolition of the slave trade, a truly radical step.

Why was Ahmad Baba not more critical of slave raiding and trading in West Africa and the Maghrib? The historian Marta Garcia Novo has argued that the *Mi'raj*

> may have intended to remove the impediments to the trans-Saharan trade in slaves that a more rigorous interpretation of Maliki jurisprudence could have set up, thus benefiting the economic interests of his social group, the Berber (Masufa) elite that controlled it at the time. (2011, 3–4)[24]

Novo's critique reminds us that scholars (*fuqaha*) shared many attitudes with slave traders because they were not socially disconnected; indeed, they often belonged to the same family. Scholarly families in the commercial towns of Islamic West Africa in Ahmad Baba's time were almost always heavily involved in trade, and that trade had included a substantial volume of slaves for many centuries.[25] So, Ahmad Baba's proposed limitations on slave trading, limited as they were, nevertheless, risked undermining a portion of the livelihood of his own extended family, as well as that of Timbuktu and Songhay more generally.

While Ahmad Baba might have been influenced by economic interests that would have been harmed by a more critical assessment of the slave-trading business, an issue of history and legal reasoning may have also influenced his failure to defend the interests of Muslims living in predominantly non-Muslim societies. In a section of the *Mi'raj* regarding doubt about the status of slaves extracted from various kinds of societies, al-Jirari first raised the issue of the practice of the Prophet Muhammad, implying that he did not investigate the origins of slaves he purchased. Ahmad Baba answered that in the Prophet's time, one did not have to question the origin of slaves because the religious status of people was well known, presumably because Islam was still largely confined to Arabia. However, in this answer, Ahmad Baba also voluntarily conceded that there were exceptions to this generalisation, one being the conversion of a part of Abyssinia or Ethiopia (Barbour and Jacobs 1985, 131–132). From this point, the text moved on to the issue of the curse of Ham, but then returned to another question from al-Jirari asking whether the Prophet had hesitated in owning Abyssinians despite the fact that he knew that some Abyssinians had adopted Islam. Ahmad Baba answered by arguing that despite the mixed religious status of the Abyssinians, the status of slaves was well known back then. This answer was followed by a reiteration of the same question by al-Jirari: '[i]s the judgment concerning slaves brought from Abyssinia similar to the judgment that concerns those brought from the Sudan' (Barbour and Jacobs 1985, 135–136)? Ahmad Baba answered that all non-believers were the same except those who had a treaty with the Muslims or protected status (*ahl al-dhimma*), but he did not address directly the fact that Abyssinia was already predominantly Christian at the time of the Prophet. Instead, he launched into a brief description of the *jizya* tax that was generally demanded of the *ahl al-dhimma* who lived in the lands of Islam, and then indirectly suggested that the payment of this tax protected them from enslavement. Of course, this discussion was moot because the Muslims were never in a position to make such demands of Abyssinia during the Prophet's lifetime. Ahmad Baba did not return to the issue of Abyssinian slaves, but one can see the influence of the precedent the Prophet seems to have established in the last substantive statements of the *Mi'raj*. Ahmad Baba ended his treatise by naming several ethnic groups that were either non-Muslim or predominantly non-Muslim, stating that 'you may own people from these groups without questioning' (Barbour and Jacobs 1985, 137). This was certainly an unfortunate interpretation of law for the recent converts to Islam in predominantly non-Muslim societies, as it placed the interest of slave traders above their freedom.

Perhaps Ahmad Baba did not explore the issue of the Abyssinian slaves because the Prophet's purchase of them seemed to contradict the general consensus about the procurement of slaves under Islamic law. These Abyssinian slaves, if they were not Muslim, clearly were not taken in a *jihad* nor were they given an opportunity to convert or pay *jizya*, and that was precisely the point that al-Jirari was making. If we accept al-Jirari's characterisation of the Prophet's behaviour, which Ahmad Baba did not contradict, then we must conclude that Muhammad had no interest in the status of the Abyssinian slaves at the time of their enslavement. Therefore, if Ahmad Baba had demanded that the slave traders of the Maghrib prove the status of their slaves originating from lightly Islamised societies (like Abyssinia in 630 CE), then he would have been asking them to take a precaution that the Prophet appears not to have taken. If Ahmad Baba had advocated that the Maghribis abstain from purchasing non-Muslim slaves who may not have been enslaved through *jihad*, then he would have been asking them to go far beyond what Muhammad had done.

This examination of the *Mi'raj* suggests that Ahmad Baba rejected racial slavery in part because he sympathised with the Black Muslims of West Africa. His beloved hometown, Timbuktu, was a predominantly Black town in the predominantly Black kingdom of Songhay, and his *shaykh* was Muhammad Baghayogho al-Wangari, who identified as Mandé and therefore almost certainly as Black. But Timbuktu was a town that had internalised the concept of race long before Ahmad Baba was born. Most of the town's Berbers and Arabs, including Ahmad Baba, lived in the Sankoré quarter, which means the quarter of the 'White masters' or 'White nobles' in the Songhay language.[26] So, to what extent did Ahmad Baba identify with Black Africans and how might this have affected the opinions he expressed in his treatise on slavery? At the beginning of his exile, he might well have felt that he was being treated like a slave, and it is also quite possible that some Moroccans perceived him as Black, since they sometimes described him with the *nisba* al-Sudani. Still, the 'Sudani' label may have only referred to Ahmad Baba's residence, as does the *nisba* al-Timbukti, rather than his racial identity – at least that is what one of his Moroccan students argued (Zouber 1977, 15).[27] The fact that one of Ahmad Baba's students felt the need to clarify his teacher's racial identity strongly suggests its ambiguity. Indeed, some West African scholars described him as al-Takruri precisely in order to use a name for the region that was not race-specific. Ahmad Baba sometimes described himself as al-Takruri, but never to my knowledge as al-Sudani.[28]

Whatever the Moroccans thought of Ahmad Baba's race, it seems clear that he did not consider himself to be Black.[29] While Muslim scholars in West Africa as well as the Maghrib referred to sub-Saharan Africa as the *Bilad al-Sudan*, they almost always defined people who claimed Berber or Arab origins as '*Bidan*' or 'Whites', regardless of their actual skin colour. The Aqits, Ahmad Baba's patriline, claimed both Berber and Arab origins, and Ahmad Baba primarily identified himself with the *nisbas* al-Sanhaji, al-Masini and al-Timbukti.[30] As described above, the Sanhaji *nisba* refers to a Berber-speaking people who lived in the southern Sahara in close interaction with the West African kingdoms at least as early as the tenth century. An illustration of Ahmad Baba's view of the division between the Sanhaja and the Sudan can be found in his description of the southern Saharan town of Tegidda (or Takedda), which he stated was 'a town settled by the Sanhaja near the Sudan'.[31] According to Ahmad Baba, Tegidda was not part of the Sudan because it was a Sanhaja town.

Another important gauge of Ahmad Baba's view of the Sudan comes in his large biographical dictionary entitled the *Nayl*, which contains more than 800 biographies of Muslim scholars in the Maghrib and West Africa.[32] This was Ahmad Baba's chance to highlight the historic achievements of the West African *'ulama*, and demonstrate the maturity and sophistication of Islamic practice in the region. The fact that the text mainly focused on Maghribi scholars heightened its appeal in North Africa and therefore enhanced its potential for affecting the opinions of the northern *'ulama* concerning their southern colleagues. But as Novo has pointed out, while Ahmad Baba's biographical dictionary may have enhanced the Maghribi view of West African scholars, all but one of the West Africans he highlighted were Berbers, most from his own Aqit lineage. The one identifiably Black scholar he featured was his own mentor, Muhammad Baghayogho al-Wangari. Novo explained Ahmad Baba's omission of Black scholars, which so many previous historians had failed to note, by arguing that his motivation for compiling the *Nayl* was to promote his own personal, familial and ethnic interests (Novo 2011, 3–4).

Of course, there were many prominent Mandé, Fulani and other Black scholars from Ahmad Baba's time and the century before, about whom we know because seventeenth-century Timbuktu historians did not neglect them. Even the late eighteenth-century Walata scholar Talib Muhammad al-Bartayli included a dozen Black scholars in his biographical dictionary entitled *Fath al-Shakur*, which he conceived as a complement to Ahmad Baba's text.[33] Al-Bartayli did not primarily set out to correct Ahmad Baba's neglect of Black scholars; instead, he felt insulted that the *Nayl* had not included a single Walati scholar. In the process of correcting that omission, he featured several Black scholars (mainly Mandé) from Walata, as well as some from Timbuktu and Jenné. Among other omissions, Ahmad Baba referenced 28 *madrassas* or Muslim colleges across North Africa and the Middle East, but did not mention a single one in Timbuktu or anywhere else in the Bilad al-Sudan. How ironic this is, given the current proliferation of websites that expound on the 'University of Timbuktu' or the 'Sankoré University', which they sometimes claim to have been the first or oldest university in the world.[34]

Evidence for the effects of Ahmad Baba's scholarship in Morocco

It is very difficult to measure the effect of a discourse on actual events, even in our age of sophisticated polling. Individual actions are almost always the product of a complex interplay of factors, and individual explanations often conceal more than they reveal about the real motivations. Large events involving a multitude of actors are infinitely harder to unravel. Yet, in the case of Ahmad Baba's discourse with Maghribi scholars, there are very few known events that we might imagine to reflect the influence of his arguments. The evidence of events in Morocco suggests that the powerful people who shaped big events continued to define West Africans in racial terms and continued to associate the 'Black' racial category with moral inferiority and slavery. As for the historical popular opinion in Morocco, given the near silence of our sources, it is hard to argue that there was a significant change from the apparent earlier association of race and slavery, until after the institution was belatedly outlawed by French colonial authorities in 1923 (El Hamel 2013, 258–264).[35] There is, however, strong evidence that Ahmad Baba's arguments had an effect among the scholars that he primarily targeted, and that effect has echoed through the scholarly discourse for the subsequent three centuries.

There is no evidence for positive effects of Ahmad Baba's arguments on events in Morocco during the first three centuries after his death in 1627. Indeed, the social conditions for people defined as 'Sudan' or 'Haratin' dramatically declined in the seventeenth and eighteenth centuries, primarily because of the actions of two sultans – Mulay Ahmad al-Mansur and Mulay Ismail. The Moroccan term Haratin was of Berber origin and referred to people of supposed West African origin who had lived in Morocco for generations, usually as free Muslims.[36] Mulay Ahmad first created 'Black' units within the military, and Mulay Ismail greatly expanded this project and reinforced the historic association of race and slavery in order to force free Moroccans of supposed West African descent into military service. While these military units were sometimes well paid and politically powerful, they were also marked by a servile status that approximated slavery (El Hamel 2013, 155–240).

Mulay Ahmad al-Mansur (1549–1603), the sultan responsible for the invasion of Songhay and the imprisonment of Ahmad Baba, assembled 'Black' military units in Morocco, partly with slaves obtained from the initial invasion. The sultan's army was also composed of captives taken in battles against the Portuguese and Spanish: 'renegades', Moriscos and even some Turks, as well as free nomadic 'tribes'. Indeed, the expeditionary force that Mulay Ahmad sent across the desert to conquer Songhay was mainly composed of Iberian slaves and renegades.[37] So, while Mulay Ahmad did not single out the 'Sudan' in the creation of his servile military units, his unprovoked invasion of the clearly Muslim kingdom of Songhay suggests his negative attitude towards the peoples of West Africa. Ahmad Baba's appeals to the '*ulama* of Marrakesh succeeded in improving his condition from imprisonment to a loose house arrest, and this may reflect some change in Mulay Ahmad's attitudes towards these Songhay prisoners. But it must be remembered that Ahmad Baba was not freed to return to Timbuktu until after Mulay Ahmad's death.

The next powerful sultan to emerge in Morocco, Mulay Ismail (1646–1727), built on Mulay Ahmad's use of Black slave units in the Moroccan army to create an entire 'Black' army, which he named the 'Abid al-Bukhari.[38] Mulay Ismail built the army primarily through conscription of the so-called Haratin, and he justified the conscription through explicitly racial arguments.[39] The registers his administrators compiled of conscripted Haratin referred to the complexion of every conscript, which varied in shades from 'yellowish' to 'red' to 'liver black' (El Hamel 2013, 174–179). Similarly, when Mulay Ismail wrote to the *'ulama* of Cairo to ask for their scholarly legitimisation of the conscription, he claimed that the Haratin should legally be considered slaves, regardless of their current status as free Muslims, because of their distant origins in West Africa. In reference to the Haratin, he wrote ' ... these slaves were originally pagans from the Sudan' (El Hamel 2013, 312–315). Additionally, he stereotyped these 'Sudan' as outlaws, bandits, embezzlers, pillagers and usurpers. Ultimately, Mulay Ismail acquired at least 221,000 'Black' Moroccans for his army, most through conscription or purchase (El Hamel 2013, 188–190). These events were the very opposite of what Ahmad Baba advocated, especially with regard to where the burden of proof should lie regarding the enslavement of a professed Muslim.

Although the Sultan Mulay Ismail justified his conscription of the Haratin as necessary to defend Morocco from European infidels, who posed a very real threat, he in fact used his slave army as a police force to impose his will on the general Moroccan population. For this reason, and because the 'Abid al-Bukhari became involved in the political chaos and intrigue that followed the death of Mulay Ismail in 1727, the general population seems to have developed a negative view of the army, which may have reinforced their negative stereotypes about the Sudan or Haratin more generally (El Hamel 2013, 297–300). There is some anecdotal evidence for the persistence of these negative stereotypes. In 1898, a scholar from Timbuktu named Muhammad al-Sanusi wrote a treatise regarding the free status of West Africans, in which he stated:

> When I traveled to the land of the Farther Maghrib [Morocco] ... I found some of the uncouth Maghribis claiming that all Blacks without exception were slaves who did not deserve to be free, for how should they deserve that, being black of skin? (Hunwick 1999, 62)[40]

Similarly, in 1950, a French colonial official named Lapanne Joinville reported that in Morocco 'the Arabic word designating slave (*'abd*, pl. *'abid*) has taken on, in daily language, the meaning of "Black"' (El Hamel 2013, 258).

While Ahmad Baba's scholarship may not have had much effect on either the Moroccan political leaders or the general population, it did resonate with many scholars. During Mulay Ismail's conscription of the Haratin, there were several prominent scholars, especially in Fez, who publicly opposed it. Among the most important of those was a scholar named Jasus, who was executed by the Sultan Mulay Ismail in 1709 for refusing to sign the register of conscripted Haratin, which would have indicated his public acceptance of the legality of that forced recruitment. Jasus was a well-respected scholar from a wealthy family of long-time residents of Fez, so his execution was a great shock to the community. His *fatwa* denouncing the conscription was widely reproduced in chronicles written by Moroccan scholars in the eighteenth and nineteenth centuries (Batran 1985, 1–15).[41] Jasus did not cite Ahmad Baba, in part because his *fatwa* did not deal with the exportation of slaves from West Africa, but rather the enslavement of apparently free people in Morocco. Still, his argument resembled Ahmad Baba's in an important respect; they both argued that the burden of proof regarding the slave status of a Muslim should be on the person trying to enslave that Muslim. Several important Moroccan scholars did explicitly cite Ahmad Baba, especially his denunciation of the likely enslavement of free Muslims and the use of race to justify the enslavement of West Africans. Among these scholars were al-Fishtali (1549–1621), al-Ifrani (c.1669–1744) and al-Nasiri (1834/1835–97). In the *Kitab al-Istiqsa*, for example, al-Nasiri complained that 'many common folk believe that the reason for being enslaved according to the Shari'a is merely that a man should be Black and come from those [Sudanic] regions' (Hunwick 2000, 138–139).[42]

Perhaps Ahmad Baba's scholarly arguments gained their widest influence in the second half of the twentieth century, when West African Muslims were no longer at risk of falling prey to the trans-Saharan slave trade. In 1973, his name was attached to a new public archive and research centre in Timbuktu, which is now known as the *Institut des Hautes Etudes et de Recherces Islamiques – Ahmed Baba*.[43] This institution, in part because of the prestige of Ahmad Baba's name, received donations of many thousands of historic manuscripts and attracted scholars from far and wide. Three hundred and fifty years after his death, Ahmad Baba's legacy of scholarship was still helping to elevate the Islamic reputation of Timbuktu and the broader region. Both editions of his biographical dictionary of scholars were edited and printed in North Africa – the *Nayl* in Tripoli and the *Kifaya* in Rabat. His treatise on the law of enslavement, the *Mi'raj*, was edited and translated into English twice in the late twentieth century, and once into French. These edited and translated editions have made Ahmad Baba's work more accessible to a broader community of scholars.

In the twenty-first century, Ahmad Baba's scholarship has retained its importance. While slavery and the trans-Saharan slave trade are a matter of history, the historical legacy of slavery still weighs heavily on the descendants of its victims, especially in the form of racism. This lingering scourge still haunts parts of Africa as it does the Americas, and Ahmad Baba's scholarship reminds us that we still have work to do. In the last 15 years, Moroccan historians have seriously taken up the historical study of slavery in their country, a topic that previously was too sensitive to examine publicly. Scholars such as Mohammed Ennaji and Chouki El Hamel have joined scholars across the world in the study of the history of slavery and its legacy of racism.[44]

Conclusion

Ahmad Baba had a significant effect on the intellectual history of the Maghrib, but the Maghrib had a far greater effect on his life and the lives of generations to come in his home region of West Africa. After the Moroccans defeated the Songhay kingdom, the whole region fell into a long period of political chaos and violence, and the trans-Saharan slave trade continued as before. Even as the growing Atlantic markets diverted African trading patterns away from the trans-Saharan routes in the eighteenth and nineteenth centuries, the Saharan slave trade continued. The trade and slavery itself would persist into the twentieth century, belatedly ended by French colonialists. But the legacy of the association of race and servility has survived into the present, as it has in all former slave societies.

Ahmad Baba was able to influence Maghribi scholars in part because he identified with them and promoted their reputations in West Africa as well as across North Africa. But he did not influence scholars such as al-Fishtali, al-Ifrani and al-Nasiri by persuading them that racial slavery contradicted Islam, because that was already widely accepted among the *'ulama*. Instead, he persuaded them that negative racial stereotypes were leading to the enslavement of free Black Muslims, and that this was a significant problem. Even if Ahmad Baba and his North African interlocutors were themselves not completely free of these stereotypes, some scholars did recognise that stereotypes should not be used to justify the oppression of free Muslims. This recognition was a step in the right direction, but we do not know how widely it spread among the *'ulama* or whether it counter-balanced the old association of race with slavery, which was articulated through the racialised curse of Ham and some environmental theories of race.

Although Ahmad Baba was sharply critical of racial slavery, he did not advocate a strict interpretation of the law that would, if implemented, dramatically curtail slave raiding in West Africa or reduce the trans-Saharan trade in slaves. In this respect, he conformed to the jurisprudence on slavery produced in Timbuktu over the previous century. While he called for some reform of the practice of slave trading in West Africa and the Maghrib, his proposal gave at least as much consideration to the economic interests and property rights of slave traders as it did to individuals who may have been enslaved in ways that contravened the regulations of Islam.

Ahmad Baba became a respected scholar in Marrakesh during his exile there and maintained that reputation in the centuries after he passed away. He became a particularly popular subject of historians in the second half of the twentieth century as the breadth of his scholarship became better understood. The growing international interest in the history of slavery during this period also brought increasing attention to his treatise on racial slavery and to him more generally. Because of the volume of his scholarship and the historical importance of the key texts examined in this essay, he became a historical figure around whom the Malian state could build an international reputation for Timbuktu as a centre of Islamic learning – a reputation it richly deserves. As the namesake for Timbuktu's public archives, Ahmad Baba has served as a bridge between West Africa and the Maghrib, spanning an imaginary border that falls somewhere in the Sahara. Juxtaposed against the 2012 Tuareg rebellion in northern Mali, he represents a time when relations between the Saharan Berber speakers and the Black peoples of the Niger River valley were slightly less fraught. Yet, among the angry cries of the current conflict, surely, we are hearing some echoes of the violent past.

Despite his love of Timbuktu and his strong criticism of the worst manifestations of racism, Ahmad Baba nevertheless was somewhat constrained by the racial and ethnic prejudices of his time, mainly transmitted from North Africa and the Mediterranean. These prejudices helped to shape him into an enigmatic character of a type that historians of race find particularly revealing. He was from the Sudan, and through the common practice of inter-ethnic marriages among the urban elite, probably had many Black ancestors, and yet he chose to represent himself as separate in some essential way from the Black members of his society. In part because of his ambiguous status, he chose not to take full advantage of the opportunity provided by his education and experiences to advocate against slave raiding and for the intellectual achievements of Black Muslims. With regard to the latter, his enormous collection of scholars' biographies only reinforced the false impression among Maghribis that Blacks were intellectually inferior – how else could one explain why there was only one accomplished Black scholar in the broader Songhay region, while there were nine from Ahmad Baba's own Sanhaja Berber patriline? And how are we to understand Ahmad Baba's perplexing choice? It seems it was more important for him to clarify and enhance his own identity and status at home and across the great desert than it was to defend the intellectual abilities of his Black colleagues.

Notes

1. I dedicate this essay to Mahmoud Zouber and John Hunwick, who pioneered the modern scholarship on Ahmad Baba, and made this essay possible. John Hunwick supervised my dissertation at Northwestern University, and

Mahmoud Zouber was the Director of the Ahmed Baba archive in Timbuktu when I first conducted research there in 1991. Both men are kind and generous mentors, as well as academics of the first rank. I would also like to thank Patricia Lorcin, Chouki El Hamel, Daniel Schroeter and Njeri Marekia-Cleaveland for their editorial assistance in the revision of earlier drafts of this essay. And special thanks go to Eric Ross of Al Akhawayn University in Ifrane, for creating the map of Saharan trade networks.

2. The ethnic component of Ahmad Baba's identity is examined in greater detail later in this essay. Of course, the name 'Berber' was a foreign invention applied to people who often referred to themselves as Amazigh or some variation thereof. However, the identities of Berber-speaking peoples varied widely by region and status, and many elites claimed a patrilineal Arab origin even as they strongly embraced their Amazigh cultural heritage. See, for example, Keenan (1977), 1–25, 93–127.

3. The Arabic name Mulay is also sometimes transliterated as Moulay or Mawlay, which are equally legitimate.

4. This essay is concerned with race as a social construct and therefore examines how Muslim scholars categorised people by race and associated particular social, moral and intellectual qualities with different races. It does not assume that there is an objective criterion for defining race.

5. Timbuktu, like many commercial towns in the West African Sahel, maintained a substantial population of unfree residents – slaves, or freed slaves who became clients of their former masters. French Colonial administrators estimated the late nineteenth-century populations of towns such as Timbuktu, Gao, Gumbu, Nioro and Kayes to be at or just under 50% unfree, and a high proportion of these servile communities were female. See Meillassoux (1982), 94–5; and Klein (1983), 68–70.

6. Evidence for the Fulani in Masina comes from the chronicle of al-Sa'di (1898, reprint 1964). The evidence appears on folio 22, which refers to the edited Arabic edition of al-Sa'di's text compiled by Houdas. Subsequent references to this chronicle will also include a reference to John Hunwick's English translation of the same text, which appeared in *Timbuktu and the Songhay Empire* in the 2003 paperback edition. In this case, folio 22 corresponds to page 31 in Hunwick's translation. Al-Sa'di's statement should probably be interpreted as referring to the scholarly families that became associated with Masina through trade. It may be coincidence that a primarily nomadic group called the 'Masna' lived in the Tishit region in the nineteenth century, but there is much earlier documentary evidence linking the most prominent families of Tishit and Biru/Walata with various market towns in Masina.

7. Al-Sa'di (1964). For an English translation, see Hunwick (2003), 37–8, 58. For evidence on the Aqit family's origins, see Norris (1967), 637.

8. Muhammad Salih al-Nasiri (d.1854), *Al-Haswa al-baysaniyya fi 'ilm al-ansab al-hassaniyya*. MS 1275, in the Haroun Ould Cheikh Sidia Collection, University of Illinois (Urbana), ff. 22–3.

9. Al-Sa'di (1964). See Hunwick's (2003), 36–7.

10. Elias Saad spelled this name as 'al-Kaburi,' but John Hunwick and Chouki El Hamel spelled it 'al-Kabari'. For more on Muhammad al-Kabari, see Saad (1983), 60–64.

11. A mithqal equals 4.25 grams. Al-Sa'di (1964). See Hunwick's (2003), 192.

12. See al-Ifrani's description of Ahmad Baba's experience in Marrakesh, as translated by Hunwick (2003), 314–317.

13. Al-Sa'di (1964). See Hunwick's (2003), 44.

14. Ahmad Baba's biographical dictionary came in two forms: a long edition entitled *Nayl al-Ibtihaj bi Tatriz al-Dibaj* (Tarablus: Kulliyyat al-Da'wa al-Islamiyya, 1989) and an abridged edition entitled *Kifayat al-Muhtaj li-ma 'rifat man laysa fi al-Dibaj*, edited by Muhammad Muti' (Rabat: 2000).

15. Ahmad Baba also provided an alternative title for this same text, *al-Kashf wa al-Bayan li Asnaf Majlub al-Sudan*, (*The Exposition and Explanation Concerning the Varieties of Imported Blacks*). The *Mi'raj* drew and elaborated upon an earlier exchange of legal questions and answers that the author had recorded during his exile in Marrakesh. This exchange occurred between him and a student named Yusuf ibn Ibrahim ibn Umar al-Isi and is described in Hunwick's (2000), 131–39. The *Mi'raj* was translated and briefly analysed by Bernard Barbour and Michelle Jacobs, "The Mi'raj al-Su'ud: a Legal Treatise on Slavery by Ahmad Baba," in Willis, ed., *Slaves and Slavery in Muslim Africa* vol. I, 125–159. John Hunwick and Fatima Harrak also produced an edited and annotated Arabic edition of this text along with an English translation entitled *Mi'raj al-Su'ud: Ahmad Baba's Replies on Slavery*, (Rabat: University of Mohammed V, 2000). Mohamed Zaouit provided a French translation in his dissertation entitled, *L'esclavage au Bilad as-Sudan au XVIème siècle à travers deux consultations juridiques d'Ahmad Baba*, Thèse de Doctorat (Paris : Université Paris I Sorbonne, 1997). I only have access to a digital copy of this dissertation, so I cannot provide page numbers for citations. Because the Barbour and Jacobs translation is the most accessible, this essay's citations for the *Mi'raj* will refer to this translation, except in cases of discrepancies among the translators.

16. Many scholars have described and analysed Ahmad Baba's *Mi'raj*. Two recent analyses are those of Bruce Hall in *A History of Race in Muslim West Africa, 1600–1960* (Cambridge, 2011) and Hunwick's (1999).
17. See Saad, *Social History of Timbuktu*, 100–101 and John Hunwick, "Ahmad Baba on Slavery," 133.
18. In the text, al-Jirari referred to a quotation of this hadith made by Jalal al-Suyuti (1440–1505).
19. There is a growing and somewhat controversial literature on the story of the curse of Ham and the early development of racism. Edith R. Sanders initiated the debate in 1969 with her essay "The Hamitic Hypothesis: Its Origins and Function in Time Perspective" in the *Journal of African History*. See also Goldenberg (2003) and Isaac (2004).
20. See for example, Ibn Qutayba (d. 889) and al-Ya'qubi (d. 897) as translated in Hopkins and Levtzion, *Corpus of Early Arabic Sources for West African History* (2000), 15, 20–1; and al-Tabari (839–923) in al-Tabari (1986), Volume II, 21. For a general discussion of this literature, see El Hamel (2013), 60–77.
21. Additional examples of similar statements include: 'The answer to this is that you should know that the reason for slavery is non-belief and the Sudanese non-believers are like other *kafir* whether they are Christians, Jews, Persians, Berbers, or any others who stick to non-belief and do not embrace Islam. ... This means that there is no difference between all the *kafir* in this respect.' "Mi'raj al-Su'ud," 129–130; and 'The origin of slavery is non-belief and the black *kafir* are like the Christians, except that they are *majus*, pagans." "Mi'raj al-Su'ud," 130.
22. Some key words in this passage are difficult to translate and the three published translations all vary significantly, and in this case, the Barbour/Jacobs translation seems to be the least accurate (134). Instead, the Zaouit and the Hunwick/Harrak translations are preferable. Zaouit translated the text as ' ... il incite à l'adoption des noirs afin qu'ils ne soient pas abandonnés à cause de leur vice originel et de leur manque d'intelligence ... '. The Hunwick and Harrak translation reads ' ... there is a command in it to look after them so that people would not dislike them on account of some of their objectionable characteristics, and their general lack of refinement' (35).
23. Gratien argued that the racial egalitarianism he ascribed to Ahmad Baba also extended to Muslim scholars (*fuqaha*) more generally, 'While the *fuqaha* had long rejected the inferiority of particular races with Qur'anic, historical and scientific justification, the practice of Muslim rulers and slave traders was not as clearly informed by such a worldview' (Gratien, 461). He seemed to base this view on a misreading of Ibn Khaldun's climate theory of race, which, as we described above, helped Ahmad Baba to discredit the racialised version of the story of Ham's curse. Gratien misinterpreted this climate theory as debunking ideas about race difference, in particular negative stereotypes about Blacks.
24. The Sanhaja were divided into three groups, one of which was the Masufa, sometimes also spelled Massufa, and with a long 'u'. See Cleaveland (2002), 38, 49–51.
25. For the connections between scholars and traders, see Levtzion (1986, 21–37); and Lydon (2009, 11–12, 65, 384). For estimates of the trans-Saharan slave trade, see Austen (1979, 23–76); and Lydon (2009, 122–130).
26. For variant translations of the Songhay term *san-korey,* see Hunwick (2003), lviii; and Hall (2011), 244.
27. Ahmad Baba's student, Ahmad ibn Ali al-Susi, declared that his teacher was not Black. See Muhammad al-Qadiri's *Nashr al-Mathani*, vol. I, 152, as cited by Zouber (1977), 15.
28. Al-Bartayli (1981).
29. Lliteras (2008) mistakenly interpreted Ahmad Baba's Sudani *nisba* to mean that he identified as Black. This appeared in an essay she adapted and translated from Mahmoud Zouber's *Ahmad Baba de Tombouctou (1556–1627): Sa Vie et Son Oeuvre*. Zouber never attributed a race to Ahmad Baba but rather described him as self-identifying as Berber. See Susana Molins Lliteras, "Ahmad Baba of Timbuktu (1556–1627): Introduction to his life and works" in *Timbuktu Scripts and Scholarship: a catalogue of selected manuscripts from the exhibition*, 25.
30. See Ahmad Baba's short autobiography in the *Kifaya al-Muhtaj* written in 1603, in which he described himself using the *nisbas* al-Sanhaji, al-Masini and al-Timbukti. This is biography #704 in the edited and annotated edition of Ahmad Baba's text, published by the Moroccan scholar Muhammad Muti' under the title *Kifayat al-Muhtaj li-ma'rifat man laysa fi al-Dibaj* (2000), vol. 2, 281.
31. Ahmad Baba, *Kifaya al-Muhtaj*. See the edited edition by Muhammad Muti', vol. 1, 377.
32. The *Nayl al-Ibtihaj* has 802 biographies, and the *Kifaya al-Muhtaj* has 704.
33. Al-Bartayli (1981). See El Hamel's (2002).
34. See, for example, http://en.wikipedia.org/wiki/University_of_Timbuktu and http://www.africanecho.co.uk/africanechonews4-mar24.html.
35. Slavery was also officially outlawed in Algeria under French colonial rule, but about 75 years earlier, though the French allowed the institution to persist into the early twentieth century. In Mauritania, slavery persisted into the late twentieth century, if not to the present.

36. The term 'Haratin' or 'Haratine' (s. Hartani) seems to be an Arabised Berber term for 'mixed' or 'dark, originally *ahardan* (pl. *ahardanen*), and was commonly used in the Maghrib and the northern Sahara, though in the southern Sahara it is *hardanen* or *ashardan*. Colin (1971), 230–1; Taine-Cheikh (1989a), 395–396; and Taine-Cheikh (1989b), 90–105. The earliest known written etymology for the term Haratin (which seems to be wrong) is found in Ahmad ibn Khalid al-Nasiri (1835–1893), *Kitab al-Istiqsa li-Akhbar duwal al-Maghrib al-Aqsa*, E. Fumey, trans. (Paris, 1906), 75. For a history of the Mauritanian Haratin in the colonial and post-colonial period, see Ruf (1999); Brhane (1997); and McDougall (1988).
37. See 'Abd al-Rahman al-Sa'di, *Tarikh al-Sudan*, Garcia-Arenal (2009) and Yahya (1981).
38. The following account is based on multiple sources, including Aziz Abdalla Batran, "The Ulama of Fas, M. Isma'il and the Haratin of Fas," in Willis, ed., *Slaves and Slavery in Muslim Africa*, vol. II, 1–15. See also Meyers (1974), and "Class, Ethnicity, and Slavery: The Origins of the Moroccan 'Abid,'" *The International Journal of African Historical Studies* 10, 3 (1977): 427–442. Arabic documents relating to Mulay Isma'il's 'slave' army are archived at the al-Khizana al-'Amma, in Rabat, Morocco. See also El Hamel (2013).
39. Conscription was not legal according to the dominant interpretation of Islam at this time, and Mulay Ismail was imposing a permanent military service on the conscripts. For these reasons, the Muslim scholars interpreted conscription to be a form of enslavement. Evidence for the stereotypes used by Mulay Ismail and the ultimate scale of the conscription is from Chouki El Hamel (2013, 155–184).
40. This is John Hunwick's translation of Muhammad al-Sanusi ibn Ibrahim al-Jarimi, *Tanbih ahl al-tughayan 'ala hurriyyat al-Sudan* (c. 1898), f. 2, ms #1575, Centre de Documentation et de Recerces Historiques Ahmed Baba, Timbuktu.
41. The *fatwa* by Jasus was translated by Batran (1985), vol. II. Ch. 1 (1–15). The scholar's full name was Abu Muhammad Sidi al-Hajj 'Abdal Salam ibn Ahmad Jasus, sometimes also spelled Jassus.
42. This is John Hunwick's translation of Abu al-Abbas al-Nasiri (1955), 131. See also E. Fumey's translation (Paris, 1906), and al-Ifrani (1888), and Abu Faris 'Abd al-Aziz al-Sinhaji al-Fishtali, *Manahil al-safa fi ma'athir mawalina al-shurafa*. Editor: 'Abd al-Karim Kurayyim (Rabat, 1973).
43. Formerly known as the Centre de Documentation et de Recherches Historiques Ahmed Baba.
44. See Ennaji (1999), originally published *as Soldats, domestiques et concubines, le esclavage au Maroc au XIXeme siècle* (Maroc, 1994), and El Hamel (2013).

References

Ahmad Baba. 1615. *Mi'raj al-Su'ud ila nayl hukm mujallab al-sud*. Bibliothèque Général de Rabat, mss. nos. J100, D194, D478, D1724.
Ahmad Baba. 1989. *Nayl al-Ibtihaj bi Tatriz al-Dibaj*. Edited by A. al-Harama. Tarablus: Kulliyyat al-Da'wa al-Islamiyya.
Ahmad Baba. 2000. *Kifayat al-Muhtaj li-ma'rifat man laysa fi al-Dibaj*. Edited by M. Muti', 2 vols. Rabat: Wizarat al-Awqaf.
Austen, R. 1979. "The Trans-Saharan Slave Trade: A Tentative Census." In *The Uncommon Market: Essays in the Economic History of the Atlantic Slave Trade*, edited by H. Gemery and J. Hogendorn, 23–76. New York: Academic Press.
Barbour, B., and M. Jacobs. 1985. "The Mi'raj al-Su'ud: a Legal Treatise on Slavery by Ahmad Baba." In *Slaves and Slavery in Muslim Africa*, edited by R. Willis, vol. I, 125–159. London: Frank Cass & Co.
al-Bartayli, T. 1981. *Fath al-Shakur fi mar'ifa a'yan 'ulama al-Takrur*. Edited by Muhammad Ibrahim al-Kattani and Muhammad Hajji. Beirut: Dar al-Gharb.
Batran, A. 1985. "The Ulama of Fas, M. Isma'il and the Haratin of Fas." In *Slaves and Slavery in Muslim Africa*, Vol. II, edited by R. Willis, 1–15. London: Frank Cass & Co.
Brhane, M. 1997. "Narratives of the Past, Politics of the Present: Identity, Subordination, and the Haratines of Mauritania." PhD diss., University of Chicago.
Cleaveland, T. 1998. "Islam and the Construction of Social Identity in the Nineteenth-Century Sahara." *The Journal of African History* 39, No. 3: 365–388.
Cleaveland, T. 2002. *Becoming Walata: A History of Saharan Social Formation and Transformation*. Portsmouth: Heinemann Press.
Colin, G. 1971. "Hartani." In *The Encyclopaedia of Islam*, edited by B. Lewis, V. L. Ménage, C. Pellat, and J. Schacht, 230–231. Leiden: E.J. Brill.
El Hamel, C. 2002. *La vie intellectuelle islamique dans le Sahel Ouest Africain*. Paris: l'Harmattan.
El Hamel, C. 2013. *Black Morocco: A History of Slavery, Race, and Islam*. Cambridge: Cambridge University Press.
Ennaji, M. 1994. *Soldats, domestiques et concubines, le esclavage au Maroc au XIXeme siècle*. Tunis: Cérès Editions.

Ennaji, M. 1999. *Serving the Master: Slavery and Society in Nineteenth-Century Morocco*. Translated by S. Graebner. New York: Saint Martin's Press.

al-Fishtali, A. 1973. *Manahil al-safa fi ma'athir mawalina al-shurafa*. 'Abd al-Karim Kurayyim ed. Rabat: Matba'at Wizarat.

Garcia-Arenal, M. 2009. *Ahmad al-Mansur: The Beginnings of Modern Morocco*. Oxford: Oneworld Publishers.

Goldenberg, D. 2003. *The Curse of Ham: Race and Slavery in Early Judaism, Christianity and Islam*. Princeton, NY: Princeton University Press.

Gratien, C. 2013. "Race, Slavery and Islamic Law in the Early Modern Atlantic: Ahmad Baba al-Tinbukti's Treatise on Enslavement." *The Journal of North African Studies* 18 (3): 454–468.

Hall, B. 2011. *A History of Race in Muslim West Africa*. Cambridge: Cambridge University Press.

Heath, J. 1998. *A Grammar of Koyra Chiini, the Songhay of Timbuktu*. New York: Mouton de Gruyter.

Hopkins, J., and N. Levtzion. 2000. *Corpus of Early Arabic Sources for West African History*. Princeton: Markus Wiener Publishers.

Hunwick, J. 1964. "A New Source for the Biography of Ahmad Baba al-Tinbukti (1556–1627)." *Bull. SOAS* 27 (3): 568–593.

Hunwick, J. 1985. *Shari'a in Songhay: The Replies of al-Maghili to the Questions of Askia al-Hajj Muhammad*. London: Oxford University Press.

Hunwick, J. 1990. "A Contribution to the Study of Islamic Teaching Traditions in West Africa: The Career of Muhammad Baghayogho, 930/1523-4 to 1001/1594." *Islam et sociétés au sud du Sahara* 4: 149–163.

Hunwick, J. 1999. "Islamic Law and Polemics over Race and Slavery in North and West Africa (16th–19th Century)." In *Slavery in the Islamic Middle East*, edited by S. Marmon, 43–68. Princeton, NJ: Markus Weiner.

Hunwick, J. 2000. "Ahmad Baba on Slavery." *Sudanic Africa* 11: 131–139.

Hunwick, J. 2003. *Timbuktu and the Songhay Empire*. Leiden: Brill.

Hunwick, J., and F. Harrak. 2000. *Mi'raj al-Su'ud: Ahmad Baba's Replies on Slavery*. Rabat: University of Mohammed V.

al-Ifrani, M. 1888. *Nuzhat al-hadi bi akhbar muluk al-qarn al-hadi*. Translated and edited by O. Houdas. Paris: Ernest Leroux.

Isaac, B. 2004. *The Invention of Racism in Classical Antiquity*. Princeton, NY: Princeton University Press.

al-Jarimi, Muhammad al-Sanusi. c. 1898. *Tanbih ahl al-tughayan 'ala hurriyyat al-Sudan*, f. 2, ms. #1575 Centre de Documentation et de Recerces Historiques Ahmed Baba, Timbuktu.

Keenan, J. 1977. *The Tuareg*. London: Allen Lane.

Khaldun, Ibn. 1988. *The Muqaddimah: An Introduction to History by Ibn Khaldun*. Translated by Franz Rosenthal. Princeton, IL: Princeton University Press.

Klein, M. 1983. "Women in Slavery in the Western Sudan." In *Women and Slavery in Africa*, edited by C. Robertson and M. Klein, 68–70. Madison: University of Wisconsin Press.

Levtzion, N. 1986. "Merchants vs. Scholars and Clerics in West Africa." In *Rural and Urban Islam in West Africa*, edited by Nehemia Levtzion and Humphrey J. Fisher, 21–37. Boulder: L. Rienner.

Lliteras, S. 2008. "Ahmad Baba of Timbuktu (1556–1627): Introduction to his Life and Works." In *Timbuktu Scripts and Scholarship: Catalogue of Selected Manuscripts from the Exhibition*, edited by L. Meltzer, L. Hooper and G. Klinghardt, 21–31. Cape Town: Institut des Hautes Etudes et de Recherches Islamiques Ahmed Baba.

Lydon, G. 2009. *On Trans-Saharan Trails: Islamic Law, Trade Networks, and Cross-Cultural Exchange in Nineteenth-Century Western Africa*. Cambridge: Cambridge University Press.

McDougall, E. 1988. "A Topsy-Turvy World: Slaves and Freed Slaves in the Mauritanian Adrar, 1910–1950." In *The End of Slavery in Africa*, edited by S. Miers and R. Roberts, 362–388. Madison: University of Wisconsin Press.

Meillassoux, C. 1982. "The Role of Slavery in the Economic and Social History of Sahelo-Sudanic Africa." In *Forced Migration: The Impact of the Export Slave Trade on African Societies*, edited by J. Inikori, 74–99. London: Hutchinson and Africana.

Meyers, A. 1974. "The Abid 'l'Buhari: Soldiers and Statecraft in Morocco, 1672–1790." PhD diss., Cornell University.

al-Nasiri, A. 1906. *Kitab al-Istiqsa li-Akhbar duwal al-Maghrib al-Aqsa*. Translated by E. Fumey, Paris: E. Leroux.

al-Nasiri, A. 1955. *Kitab al-Istiqsa li-Akhbar duwal al-Maghrib al-Aqsa*. 8 vols. Casablanca: Dar al-Kitab.

al-Nasiri, Muhammad Salih. (d.1854). *Al-Haswa al-baysaniyya fi 'ilm al-ansab al-hassaniyya*. MS 1275, in the Haroun Ould Cheikh Sidia Collection, University of Illinois (Urbana).

Norris, H. 1967. "Sanhaja Scholars of Timbuctoo." *Bull. SOAS* 30 (3): 634–640.

Novo, M. 2011. "Islamic Law and Slavery in Premodern West Africa." *Entremons: UPF Journal of World History*, no. 2: 1–20. http://www.upf.edu/entremons/_pdf/garcia.pdf

al-Qadiri, M. 1977. *Nashr al-mathani li-ahl al-qarn al-hadi 'ashar wa al-thani*. A. Tawfiq and M. Hajji eds., Rabat: Dar al-Ma'arif. Partial English translation by Cigar, N., 1981. *Muhammad al-Qadiri's Nashr al-mathani: The Chronicles*. Oxford: Oxford University Press.

Ruf, U. 1999. *Ending Slavery: Hierarchy, Dependency and Gender in Central Mauritania*. Bielefeld: Transcript Verlag.

Saad, E. 1983. *Social History of Timbuktu: The Role of Muslim Scholars and Notables 1400–1900*. Cambridge: Cambridge University Press.

al-Sa'di, A. 1898, reprint 1964. *Tarikh al-Sudan*. Translated and edited by O. Houdas, Tarikh Es-Soudan. Paris: Adrien-Maisonneuve.

Sanders, E. 1969. "The Hamitic Hypothesis: Its Origins and Function in Time Perspective." *The Journal of African History* 10 (4): 521–532.

al-Tabari. 1986. *The History of al-Tabari: Prophets and Patriarchs*. Translated and annotated by W. Brinner. Albany: State University of New York Press.

Taine-Cheikh, C. 1989a. *Dictionnaire Hassaniyya Francais*, vols. 1–8. Paris: Geuthner.

Taine-Cheikh, C. 1989b. "La Mauritanie en noir et blanc: Petit promenade linguistique en Hassaniya." *Revue du Monde Musulman et de la Méditerranée*, no. 54: 90–105.

Yahya, D. 1981. *Morocco in the Sixteenth Century*. Atlantic Highlands: Humanities Press.

Zaouit, M. 1997. "L'esclavage au Bilad as-Sudan au XVIème siècle à travers deux consultations juridiques d'Ahmad Baba." Thèse de Doctorat. Paris: Université Paris I Sorbonne.

Zouber, M. 1977. *Ahmad Baba de Tombouctou (1556–1627): Sa Vie et Son Oeuvre*. Paris: Maisonneuve et Larose.

A Timbuktu bibliophile between the Mediterranean and the Sahel: Ahmad Bul'arāf and the circulation of books in the first half of the twentieth century

Shamil Jeppie

Institute for Humanities in Africa (Huma), University of Cape Town, Rondebosch, South Africa

This essay focuses on the role of Ahmad Bul'araf in the circulation of books – in their manuscript and their printed forms – from his place of residence in Timbuktu for about 50 years, in the first part of the twentieth century. In this endeavour of a lifetime, he communicated with people involved in the book business in a number of locations across a wide expanse, from Beirut and Cairo in the East, to Algiers and Fes in the North; Dakar in the West, and Kano to his southeast. Here is a case of how a network was kept going and animated through the concern with an object central to the life of learning, the book. His activity is one example of the ways in which contacts and connections were cultivated across spaces in and on the edges of the Sahara.

One legacy of the growth of 'Area Studies' after the Second World War has been the way in which we have come to research on specific regions as if these named regions were hard facts of nature. In a similar fashion, the nation-state in the aftermath of decolonisation has been taken as a unit of study in the non-Western world. In the case of Africa, there is a history of configuration of the continent into separate regions that goes back much further and has a philosophical grounding. This deeper theoretical basis, since it was articulated before the age of the grand colonising schemes of European powers in Africa, may have made it appear to have no political source or consequence. The influential philosopher, G.W.F. Hegel (1770–1831), used the terms 'Mediterranean Africa' and 'European Africa' in his *Lectures on the Philosophy of World History*. This is coastal North Africa he was referring to. While Hegel's 'world history' is really a concept and another way for him to write about Reason, he does bring in empirical detail to make his case. The shoreline region of North Africa as far as the Sahara desert does not belong to Africa but is part of Europe, says Hegel. The further away from the shoreline and southward, the more into 'Africa proper' one moves and away from culture and civilisation. As part of Europe the North has cultures and civilisation and importantly, it has history. The rest of the continent, the large mass of land from the Sahara to the Cape of Good Hope, has no history; it is an 'unhistorical continent, with no movement of development of its own' (Hegel 1975, 190). It is not part of World History; does not share in universal Reason, in other words.

Hegel (1975) presented his first series of lectures on a 'philosophical history of the world' in late 1822. In these lectures, repeated and expanded in 1828 and again just before his death in 1831, he summarised major aspects of his philosophical system and its unfolding in time and space. He classifies ways of approaching the past, gives further elaboration to his idea of the state as the 'realisation of spirit in history', and offers a periodisation and a schema of the world's geography in relation to historical development. For Hegel, history arises in the East and moves westward, and in this passage across time and space it passes over Africa. Hegel easily dismisses Africa because he says that it demonstrates no movement and therefore experiences no temporal change. It is the 'unhistorical continent'. It sometimes appears that very little has changed in terms of perceptions of the continent from where the Sahara starts and southwards towards the tropics.

The dominance of 'Area Studies' approaches to the continent accepts, perhaps even encourages, a good measure of mutual ignorance about histories and historiographies even in overlapping and contiguous 'Areas'. It has meant, in the case relevant to this essay, only rather limited attention to the linkages and movements across the Sahara. An historian of a problem, period or place in 'North Africa' is allowed to ignore or avoid the same problem or period or not have a larger sense of place that would incorporate areas in and beyond the deserts in so-called sub-Saharan Africa. There are, of course, the exceptions. This essay outlines the career of a bibliophile whose pursuit of books meant a long life of communicating and moving books between 'Mediterranean Africa' and 'Africa proper'. The book is, of course, an outstanding example of 'civilisation' and in this one example of commitment to cultivating books we have an aspect of African history that is rather neglected, and it repeatedly breaks down the now accepted configurations of the continent.

Almost two decades before Hegel presented his philosophy of world history lectures and dismissed the regions beyond the southern shores of the Mediterranean an English traveller, Jackson (1809, 257), wrote an account of his long travels in Morocco and has a concluding chapter on the 'city of Timbuctoo', which he never visited but had heard about and seen caravans leaving for it and coming from there. In Morocco he lived in, what Hegel would have considered, part of the European Continent; in Jackson's concern to report about the world deeper into and beyond the Sahara, he was wondering about 'Africa proper' in terms of Hegel's schema. Jackson appears to be quite meticulous in noting items of trade, coming into the port of Mogador (Al-Sawīra, Essaouira) and leaving it; and also the items leaving for Timbuktu. Paper is among the items imported into this region but he does not mention it among the items leaving for Timbuktu. At the end of the century Felix Dubois, a French journalist and traveller, mentions paper as a commodity imported into the French Soudan. He recalled seeing a trade in paper and, on reaching a certain spot on the banks of the Niger River, he says that paper there was sold 'at twenty-five or thirty centimes a sheet' (Dubois 1896, 252).

Jackson may not have seen paper leaving for Timbuktu but he has two rather intriguing lines about libraries. He writes: 'It has been said there is an extensive library at Timbuctoo, consisting of manuscripts in a character differing from Arabic ... ' (Jackson 1809, 257). But he dismisses this report only to add, as if to contradict this sentence: that there is a 'state library' with Arabic, Hebrew, perhaps Chaldic books and probably some translations of works originally in

Greek and Latin! It is revealing that he used the term library consciously and twice here, which is rarely used among travellers.

Other travellers discovered manuscript books and met key scholars but did not use the word overtly or literally to describe encountering libraries filled with books. Leo Africanus (1485–c.1554, [1971]) was the most glowing in his report about the status of books in Timbuktu, making the claim that the book trade was more valuable than any other trade. But a trade in books meant that they were valued and accumulating these items of value, whether for permanent or temporary possession, would of course form a library for somebody. Ahmad Baba (1556–1627), a Timbuktu scholar, reportedly had a collection of works numbering around 1600 when he was captured during the Sa'adian occupation and removed from Timbuktu to live in exile and a form of imprisonment in Marrakech in 1593 (Zouber 1977).

From the time of Leo Africanus' report and Ahmad Baba's scholarship and into the nineteenth and twentieth centuries, we can discern some patterns, points of familiarity – local and regional – in the formation of book collections and libraries. Scholars and collectors like Ahmad Baba and the bibliophile Ahmad Bul'araf (1864–1955), who will be discussed in detail below, are the key figures in the region's long, interconnected, and layered history of handwritten books (Baba 1989; Hunwick 2003; Lydon 2009). This is a history that brings together lives of scholarship, the manuscript book as an object of value, and commerce over short and long distances. In this quiet, persistent, and deliberate activity they forged ties across the vast space between the worlds of the Mediterranean and the Sahel.

Aḥmad bin Mbarak bin Barka bin Muḥammad Bul'arrāf al-Taknī was the full name with genealogical details of Ahmad Bul'araf, or as is the convention in naming him, Bul'araf or Boularaf. His birth year is given as 1864, at Guelmīm in the Sūs region of southwestern Morocco.[1] Around the time he was 30 years old he, along with members of his family, left his birthplace and moved further southward until they crossed the boundaries that separated the Maghrib from the rest of the continent. He went first to the learned town of Shinqīt in Mauritania, then to a location in the French colony of Senegal. His precise itinerary still remains to be confirmed, whether he went first to Shinqīt or then one of the early colonial administrative towns like St Louis or Dakar. These were all then part of the French-occupied territories of West Africa, which the French had divided into separate colonial administrative units.[2] When exactly he left Guelmīm, where and for how long he lived in Senegal and when or why he moved on from there are all still rather vague. In general, we know that due to economic crises there was an outward flow of people from that part of the Maghrib at around the time he and his family left (Abou el-Farah, Akmir, and Beni Azza 1997, 163–169 and Schroeter 1988).

There is one reason why he may have gone to Shinqīt. It is a town recognised for its many distinguished scholars and by going there he could meet many learned men, perhaps people he had heard about, whose works he had some familiarity with, or whose books he had actually read (Hamel 1999, 62–87). Perhaps there were already members of his family or Tikna clan in the town and both factors attracted him there (Lydon 2011, 63–70). Here he developed the habit of sitting with them and, it would appear, in these scholarly circles he was initiated into the more advanced aspects of Mālikī fiqh and other disciplines. It is still unclear at whose feet he sat, whose homes he frequented, or how much time he spent in sessions listening to teachers. There appears to be very few living scholars or their descendants in Shinqit who recall anything about him.[3] He is recorded in a few texts for the hospitality he extended to scholarly visitors to Timbuktu in the late 1920s and his library is remembered as having a rich store of materials relating to the biographies of learned men from Mauritanian families.[4] The exulted status of the larger Bilād al-Shinqīt in Bul'araf's imaginary is confirmed in a compilation of the scholars of his time he completed before his death (discussed below); the vast majority of scholars listed are from that region (Bul'arāf n.d.). But for him the visit made a huge impression. He did not become a 'full-time' scholar and he continued to pursue a life of trade. It was trade that led him further South, to another town with a past reputation for learning, to Timbuktu. There were ways of communicating over land between the towns of the Sūs, Shinqīt, Walata, and Timbuktu, and other settlements. The long-established trans-Saharan trade caravans had taken goods and people back and forth along routes in this vast region for hundreds of years. Camel caravans would over a matter of weeks or months transport items of trade, traders, and scholars as well, over these vast spaces. His steady migration southward from one settlement to another reflects a larger migration in the last quarter of the nineteenth century by people from various parts of the Maghrib to the French-controlled territories of West Africa (Abou el-Farah, Akmir, and Beni Azza 1997).

He arrived in Timbuktu in 1904. This is where he started his book collecting and the trading that generated his livelihood. It is said that three years later, in 1907, his concern with books became an explicit part of his activity (Dadab 1986). It appears that he would never return to visit his birthplace in the southern Maghrib. It can be assumed that he travelled out of the town as a trader but there is as yet no evidence to show how far out of the town or where he went. He appears to have been rather immobile and yet at the same time impressively well connected to people thousands of kilometres away. Timbuktu was then a small, neglected, and rather isolated town and to make such extensive connections from this location with points on the Mediterranean coast and the Sahel is indeed impressive. We may have to speculate about his itinerary until his arrival in Timbuktu but we are on firm ground in saying that he maintained contact with merchants and scholars he had met, and he made new contacts from his location in Timbuktu. Over the years he kept up a regular correspondence with growing numbers of businesses and scholarly contacts in distant places, as we shall show below. His capacity to reach scholars and scribes and then enter into a correspondence with them was his great and enduring skill. This was an important means of developing his manuscript book, and later also his printed book, collection. This distinction is important to keep for it is so easy to forget that the book in its handwritten form did not lose its value or disappear with the appearance and spread of printing on either side of the Mediterranean Sea from the fifteenth century. In most of Africa with writing technologies, printing for long after its introduction sat beside the crafts of making handwritten books. Indeed, even with the appearance of printed books and printing itself from Cairo to Fes, the parallel world of manuscript production remained firmly in place in many places – in the centres and especially the peripheries of these cosmopolitan centres. Developing a network was necessary for his business but it was his passion for books that led him to develop his network of contacts. His life in Timbuktu is a story of the making of a network that in fact linked the Mediterranean coast of the continent with the Sahel. The focus of this essay is on aspects of his book network not on tracing his family, clan, or ethnic networks.

In his book collecting and learning he was clearly interested in Sufism and the major Sufi orders in the area. He collected works of Sufi polemics and what he was concerned to possess gives an indication of his affiliations. However, by the end of his life it appears that he was not a member of any *tariqa* or rather there is little evidence of his participation in the practices of any particular one. It is necessary to mention this here because a good deal of the literature on the movement of ideas and people in this part of Africa has focused on the Sufi brotherhoods, such as the Tijanniyyah, Qadiriyyah, and Muridiyyah (Triaud and Robinson 1997, 2000).

These Sufi orders did indeed spread through the nineteenth and twentieth centuries and their expansion, of course, entailed the production and reproduction of writings and in many cases generous quantities of polemical literature has been the consequence.[5] Even Bul'araf, while not himself explicitly engaged in this does concern himself with these writings and sought to collect and copy some of the polemical writings of the period or of the original Sufi masters in the region.[6]

His network had a tactile, tangible, and material quality. As a bibliophile he accumulated works from great distances away from Timbuktu. He bought works and commissioned copies. He had to concern himself with prices – of paper, of copying, and of the postal service. Content, of course, was important to him; he was not a collector of random materials. He had an interest in specific subjects and books related to these subjects were the object of his pursuit. But here we want to stress the *object* and the network, the *thing* in a network that stretched thousands of kilometres from Timbuktu into every direction. For instance, he wrote to booksellers as far apart as Fes and Tangier, in the distant West, through to Cairo and Beirut, in the East, to acquire works. The manuscript book and the later printed version are the objects that were made and circulated through a network that he actively stimulated and sustained. His network included writers of works, owners of texts, copyists of books, intermediaries between authors and copyists, and middlemen in the movement of the objects from point of origin to him; from point of production to consumption and ultimately conservation. When he encountered the printed book his network embraced booksellers and printers. We cannot say when he first handled printed texts and whether it struck him as very different to manuscript books but for the moment we shall keep this distinction between the handwritten and the printed works. The printing press came to Morocco in the early 1860s and took a number of decades to develop into an independent and full-scale commercial sector. The Sultan and his government were initially opposed to this technical innovation and it took a number of decades for this technology to gain official recognition. Only by the end of the century did acceptance and permission lead to the emergence of printed book publishing (Abdulrazak 1990). However, from quite early on printed books from elsewhere in the Arabic-speaking world, which had state or private commercial printing businesses such as in Cairo, found their way to the Maghrib. The handwritten work or manuscript, however, remained for long after the introduction of printing the fundamental means of producing and reproducing books. Scribal transmission of knowledge remained a highly valued activity. Scholars could write their own books but they would also resort to scribes to copy out texts or to make copies for them. These scribes were both literally the writers of the texts and formed a cohort of copyists (Abdulrazak 1990). How Bul'araf first responded to the printed book is unknown. However, he accepted its appearance and took it alongside the manuscript form of the book as a means of communicating knowledge (Iheri-Ab-T ms 8195).

When Bul'araf arrived in Timbuktu it was already under French administration for a decade. A French military expedition had defeated local resistance and occupied the town at the end of 1893. It was a distant outpost of the expansive Soudan Français.[7] He thus arrived when Timbuktu was under European colonial rule and he appears to have accepted this fact which he must have already encountered elsewhere beyond his homeland and when he entered the larger towns in Senegal. It would have been clear to him then that locals and local powers were subservient to the French rulers. He seems not to have been negatively affected by this reality. It may even have enabled his correspondence and bibliophilic network. Most relevant here is that the colonial administration gradually expanded its modern modes of communication from the Senegalese coasts deep into the interior parts of its newly conquered territories, and thus the operation of the colonial postal service expanded. The postal service in West Africa and across North Africa connected cosmopolitan centres, with many booksellers and printers, and outposts like Timbuktu without a single bookseller or printer. While French territories were separated for administrative purposes the communication networks joined them. The colonial postal service was crucial to the movement of official correspondence, in the first place, but of course, private commercial enterprises run by Frenchmen were also meant to benefit from this system. Communication was the life-blood of effective administration and growing business success in the colonies. Correspondence and goods could circulate in this way. Bul'araf's correspondence and books could come and go. By the time Timbuktu was conquered the French had 14 Bureaux des Postes scattered across the vast space of its Soudan colony. But there were also what the French journalist Felix Dubois called 'second-hand' ones in various places, by which he meant a Petty Officer who ensured the departure and delivery of letters in every town with a French presence. Dubois observed that once a fortnight the French mail was meant to arrive and depart. It apparently travelled at a rate of 35 miles per day (Dubois 1896, 70).

Transport of correspondence and books by writers from the colonised territories would still have been with the trans-Saharan camel caravans they and their predecessors had relied on in earlier times. However, he came to use the colonial postal service, 'al-bustah' as he called it, extensively for his correspondence and for sending and receiving manuscript works and printed books. By the end of the nineteenth century, the postal service was developing steadily in the territories in the areas around Dakar and St Louis. By the start of the Second World War these services had reached the larger settlements of Mali. By this time, telegraphic lines spanned many thousands of kilometres (Direction des archives du Senegal 1911/1950). Various forms of transport were used to move mail internally between the different parts of the colonial territories, including motor vehicle, rail, river, and air transportation, when these forms of transport arrived in the colony and where possible. Delivery by foot and camel were also common. After the First World War telegraphic and telephonic lines were in various stages of planning and implementation for the entire French Soudan colony. There was always the possibility of attacks by bandits in the vast desert – a concern expressed in letters from the period – and the colonial military presence ensured the relative safety of the movement of mail. As a merchant he had many reasons to be concerned about the safety of the region because his goods – such as tea, sugar, leather goods, and perhaps paper – had to come and go.

He would have continued using the older means of transporting books but he was also concerned with the effectiveness of the postal service. He wrote in a letter about postal rates and the length of time it took for items to move between two points by post (Iheri-Ab-T ms 8195). The postal service, in theory, had an elaborate collection and delivery schedule for a number of locations in the colonial territories and Timbuktu was among them. Schedules indicate the routes of certain cycles of collections and delivery. By 1929 Timbuktu was one point in a collection–delivery circuit that ended in Ansongo passing through Kabara and Gao. For instance, collection at Timbuktu Tuesday at 07.00, delivery at Gao Friday at 23.00, until finally arriving at Ansongo the following evening at 20.00 (Archives Nationales – Senegal 1929, 2G 29-52). Mail would have to join other circuits to get to its eventual intended point of arrival. This was rather slow moving it seems. On the other hand, it was regular, predictable, and secure and Bul'araf saw its usefulness.

Another indicator of his acceptance of the reality of political power in his world was his adoption of the Western dating system, alongside the *hijri*, in some of his letters at least. He did interact with the colonial administration. If he wanted to avoid this it would have been hard for they would have picked up that he used the postal service frequently and therefore was a man of some importance. They duly recognised him as a man of substance and potential ally. Among his own papers so far located there only remains correspondence between him and the secretary of the Governor in the early 1950s when the colonial administration was about to withdraw from the region (Iheri-Ab-T ms 6810 and ms 6847).

We are unable to establish when his collecting began to expand and therefore when he initiated his enlarged network. From what remains in the major repository of his material, we learn that during the 1940s his network was active and reached its peak but further work with his material will definitely lead to a more detailed and a more nuanced chronology.

His interest in the written word went seamlessly from manuscript to the printed text. He wrote to Fes, Rabat, Marrakesh, Tunis, Oran, Constantine, Algiers, and Cairo for copies of printed books and magazines. In an undated letter he writes to a Fes bookseller, Ahmad bin Araf Barrāda, requesting a list with prices of the books he sells and asking especially for four titles, including 'the Tarīkh of Ibn Khaldūn' (Iheri-Ab-T ms 8190). His first letters to booksellers and merchants date to 1911 when his correspondence shows him working with a merchant and bookseller in St Louis. In 1922 Bul'araf writes to a merchant in Kano, in the then British-ruled territories of Northern Nigeria seeking some titles. He wrote to Muḥammad al-Sayyid al-Zāhiri al-Wahrānī thanking him for a magazine (*al-Wifāq*) and asking about some books. Another Algerian he wrote to, in 1922, was the editor of the magazine *al-Shihāb* seeking the exchange of books. For 1926 and 1927, there is an exchange with Dār al-Hilāl publishers in Cairo (Abou el-Farah, Akmir, and Beni Azza 1997, 163–174).

Among the correspondence to Bul'araf that has been located are letters from Kano, in British-controlled Northern Nigeria, from Rufisque and Kaolack, (Senegal), Tangier, Marrakech, Casablanca, Rabat, Fes, (Morocco), Algiers, Cairo, Beirut, and Bamako, all dealing solely with book matters or with that and other items of trade. This correspondence spans nearly the five decades of his residence in Timbuktu. The 1920s were years of more correspondence than before or after; there are a few letters from the 1930s and later. All these letters are from just over 100 letters – mostly mailed to him – used some years ago by a team of Moroccan historians who were studying the Moroccan diaspora in the countries to the South of Morocco. There are many more letters spread throughout the region (Abou el-Farah, Akmir, and Beni Azza 1997).

In a letter dated 25 June 1911, a trader in Saint Louis, Ahmed El-Aissaaoui Ben Jelloun, presumably a man of Moroccan origin judging by his name, wrote that he had posted to Bul'araf five parcels containing books, copperware, and silk. The letter also notes that Ben Jelloun had ordered some books from Cairo that had been requested by Bul'araf (Abou el-Farah, Akmir, and Beni Azza 1997). At this point he is relying on a third party to get him books from book dealers in the Mashriq.

In the 1920s his correspondence was extensive, going to and coming from Kano to the South and Tangier and Cairo in the North and northeast. Books feature in all these letters and the names of publishers and bookstores are mentioned in many of these letters. One printed published work that is mentioned is *Le present du Monde Musulman* by Shakib Arslan which Bul'araf, ordered in 1936, but it was apparently banned by the French authorities. This is quite plausible for Arslan was a Druze notable and Lebanese intellectual who had been exiled by French mandate authorities because of his anti-imperialist political activism in the French-controlled Levant. The author of this letter to Bul'araf does say that he will continue to try to obtain a copy of it but also pleads with him to leave Timbuktu for a less isolated town and where his 'immense merits will be truly appreciated'. The writer exaggerates his admiration for Bul'araf by calling him the 'philosophe du Grand Sahara' (Abou el-Farah, Akmir, and Beni Azza 1997). That this book could not reach Bul'araf because of the French authorities had prohibited its circulation makes us wonder whether the parcels of books sent to Bul'araf or to anybody else were the subject of surveillance by the authorities. Were parcels opened? If the books were mostly if not all in Arabic who judged what could pass through or what should be prohibited?

Often amounts of money are noted for the cost of books and postage. In the case of correspondence with Kano northern Nigeria, which was under British rule since 1903 and Stirling was thus the means of exchange, there is one reference to exchange rates in 1924. Kano was a great trading city and had a number of booksellers. Bul'araf had made contact with some Moroccan booksellers there, presumably based in the famous centuries-old Kurmi market of which a section was populated with people concerned with the book trade. Kano–Timbuktu trade and learned connections date back many centuries and the legendary Ahmad Baba's scholarship was known in and around this part of Nigeria (Bivar and Hiskett 1962, 104–148).

Timbuktu has become a symbol of scholarship in pre-colonial African history. There are multiple factors for this association and for the fame of the town. But without a doubt the *Tarikhs* (Chronicles) that were produced in Timbuktu or by writers associated with Timbuktu have played a major role in making the town known as having been a place of scholarship.

Then there is the name of Ahmad Baba, the prolific and famous scholar, who longed for the town of his birth while in captivity in Marrakesh. His ancestral origins were elsewhere and his most productive scholarship happened while he was in exile but Timbuktu held his affections. Traditions of learning were part of the history of the town and they were kept as part of the ethos and mythology of the place even when it was overrun by conquerors and the scholars were few and far between. The learning combined oral transmission of knowledge and reading and writing, so even when book production was low studies continued through speaking and listening. The manuscript tradition has become in the past few decades the pride of the town's intellectual legacy and its collective history (Jeppie and Diagne 2008).

Bul'araf can be placed into this long tradition and he was a kind of transitional figure in it. He was the 'modern' figure and, from all accounts, a pioneer in the town's history because of his work on multiple fronts to both revitalise and conserve the manuscript book arts of the town. His labours, of course, interestingly coincided with the growth of printed books reaching the Sahel. It runs parallel to nearly the entirety of the French colonial period with its postal system and other innovations. The overwhelming weight of handwritten books and other materials today easily lead one to forget more than a century of printing in the region. There was no aversion to print; no fatwa against its use has been found. Bul'araf's manuscript copying project was not a reaction against technological innovation and modernity. We have yet to find a text questioning the permissibility of printing, or on the other hand a text promoting its uses. Bul'araf's library held printed books; among them was *Kitāb al-Sībawayhi,* two volumes, published in Paris in 1885. This was a classic work of Arabic grammar. He also arranged for the printing of local works.[8] He went way beyond the confines of Timbuktu in this pursuit. One claim is that at least ten such works were printed under the patronage of his library (Dedeb, n.d., 6). Tunis is the only place of publication given. The apparent local preference for the manuscript over the printed form, until very recently and even today, deserves further reflection.

When he was 76 years old he completed a work he called '*Izālat al-rayb wa shakk wa al-tafrīt.*[9] It was a biographical dictionary or *tarjamah*, a kind of scholarly *Who's who?* of his time. This type of work is standard in the history and world of Islamic scholarship. It has appeared with various levels of detail for each entry and not only Islamic scholars have had their names captured in such works (Qadi 2006, 23–75). There are biographical dictionaries for other professions and fields of endeavour. Bul'araf's dictionary is considered his major work of original scholarship, and he makes a place for himself in it. Under, 'Aḥmad bin Bul'arāf al-Mūsū Alī al-Taknī' he is, at the time of the composition of the dictionary, 1359 *Hijri* (1940 AD), the compiler of 12 works (Bul'arāf n.d., 81). He writes of himself as a compiler not an author. It seems highly unlikely that the rest of his writing came after this – whether we number them at 150 or in the 1930s.

But when describing his own scholarly efforts in his own *tarjamah* (biographical dictionary) he limits his contribution to scholarship as a *compiler*. He lists his 10 compilations of fatwas of local scholars. He gathered the legal opinions (*fatāwa, nawāzil, ajwiba*) on numerous matters from a host of scholars. He also mentions two commentaries by himself, one on abrogated ḥadīth by Ibn Jawzī, and another on a work by Ibn Ḥajar. He confidently includes himself among the greats of his era and region but merely as a compiler. The entry on himself is of average length (14 lines of printed text), not the shortest but nor long. A number of entries are merely one line noting, for instance, that someone was a writer of poetry or legal opinions. There are around 30 entries that are extensive and one covering 12 pages. This latter, which is the longest entry, is devoted to Muḥammad Yaḥya Salīm al-Wallāti al-Yūnusi (Bul'arāf n.d., 131–141). He was a close friend of the author but died much earlier, in 1936, and we are not told much about his life only given a long list of his works and poems. Most of his writings dealt with the details of law and he made a number of abridgments of classic Maliki law books. A number of his poems were attempts to summarise legal works in poetic metre.

Bul'araf admired men like this al-Wallāti. Later he started to imitate them, probably by first writing out copies of their works. While he was never 'formally' elevated to the status of *'ālim* or a *qāḍī* he did command respect for his learning. In calling his biographical dictionary his only 'original' work we are making too strict a distinction between a work that he started and completed, on the one hand, and others that he had himself copied or the copies he had commissioned. The reality was messier and the record of 'original' and 'copy' rather mixed and intertwined. His hand and mind intervened in the copying process. There is some evidence for this. In a massive text – more than 800 folios – he himself finished copying in August 1937 on the last page he essentially claims that his copy is superior to the copy that he had copied! (Iheri-Ab-T ms 1031) He writes that he had looked far and wide for the original but when he could look no further he fell upon a copy and proceeded himself to work with it to produce a second copy. It was his passion for rare *nawāzil* (juristic opinions) that led him to reproduce it despite his initial reluctance because the copy was so poor – the writing was filled with errors (*fasād*). He writes that his copy is the 'more correct of the two copies as I carefully searched and reflected on it'. Yet he goes on hoping that he may still find the original (Bul'arāf n.d.).

In a letter dated September 1945 to Sayyid Muḥammad, a descendant of the great Mukhtār al-Kuntī (d.1811), he requests a copy of a work by Ahmad al-Bakkā'i (d.1865 [Iheri-Ab-T ms 1145]). He believes that his honourable correspondent has a copy of the work because it is cited in a text by the latter's deceased father. The owner of the work is located somewhere in a desert settlement called Tāku. In the work by Bakkā'i, he responds to another scholar's promulgation of the views of the Tijaniyya sufi order. Bul'araf was not a Tijani; indeed from this correspondence he was interested in the literature that refuted their views. Bul'araf seems to have been more sympathetic to the Qadiriyyah order. Bul'araf says that there used to be copies of this work in the area but they were all consciously destroyed. In his inquiry about this work he asks about the possibility of having it copied and sent to him. He inquires about the cost of copying. He is prepared to pay for the copying and for the paper to be used. It turns out that he has 100 folios of the work but he cannot fathom where they fit; they are random folios. A good part of the letter is his citations of the beginnings and endings of the various sections he owns. Right at the end of the letter he mentions the title: *Fath al-quddūs fi jawāb ibn Abdullah Muḥammad Akansūs*.[10] An intermediary is mentioned, a tailor, who would assist with transferring the completed copy to him. We do not know whether he was successful in this request and got to add this work to his collection. This is however an example of Bul'araf's work on his copying network: owner of a work in another location, request for a copy, offer to pay for copying and paper, identifying intermediaries to transfer item or make sure it enters the rudimentary postal system then operating in the region, take possession and add to collection.

Copying was a way of producing a new work. We can therefore understand the confusion by cataloguers trying to classify his materials. This way of working may not have been unfamiliar in Timbuktu. Copies of the same title fill many catalogues and researchers may be missing originality by passing over them because, we sigh, 'yet another copy'. Timbuktu once had many scholars with their own collections, who were relatively relaxed about lending out their books. A scholar borrowing a copy of a specific work would very often copy it or have a copy made for himself of the borrowed work.

There is one major state-run archive-library named after the town's most famous scholar, Ahmad Baba (1556–1627), originally named the *Centre de Documentation et de Recherches Historiques Ahmad Baba* (Cedrab) and more recently renamed to *L'institut des Hautes Études et des Recherches Islamiques Ahmed Baba de Tombouctou* (Iheri-Ab-T). There are now two famous private collections – *Bibliothèque Mamma Haidara de manuscrits* and the *Fondo Ka'ti* – located in newly constructed buildings supported by donations from overseas; and there are struggling family collections without the means to properly shelf their holdings or prevent the disintegration of paper, parchment, and their leather enclosures (Jeppie and Diagne 2008, 265–329). The Bul'arāf library has been reduced to a modest family collection hardly recognised as a library of significance and barely able to keep going. One estimate is that in 1945 it held 2076 manuscripts, which had dwindled down to 680 by 2002 as the manuscripts were taken by his children for their own collections or given as gifts and possibly sold. Many of the items were donated by his descendants to the state-run archive in Timbuktu and to the university library in Niamey, Niger (Haidara and Taore 2008, 271–275). It is not really known these days except among a few specialists and it is seldom included on the circuit of guided visits to the libraries of the town.

Bul'arāf's network could be reconstructed in fair amount of detail because the names of the people with whom he corresponded are available to us. The vast majority of the correspondence is with men involved in some aspect of the book: writing, copying, selling, and reading it.

Conclusion

Ahmad Bul'araf died in Timbuktu in September 1955. His family and library remained. A small number of items from his library's holdings were sold and can be found in collections in Niamey, Niger but most were kept in Timbuktu. When his library was still functioning it reportedly had a manuscript conservation unit, a place for copyists and for checking copies, and a unit for making covers for the loose leaves of writing (sewn bindings have never been used in Timbuktu [Dabab 1986, 12–13]). It is remembered as an inspiration for other archival ventures and as an example of an indigenous initiative when the UNESCO *General history of Africa* experts visited Timbuktu in the late 1960s.[11] His activities in the first half of the twentieth century are possibly the best recorded in their own terms as to how an archive came to be constituted in the region. Could Bul'araf's work itself be a consequence of an even earlier regional book collecting, archiving, and conservation style? If for him a network was crucial then for his predecessors in Timbuktu it would also have been necessary. In this extensive bibliophilic network he was a generator of material and a medium for their circulation. In many ways, it is useful to think of him as mediator, middleman, and medium in a network.

We have looked at a single learned man who cultivated a network devoted to reproduction of texts and to grow his personal library and his business. His activity was genuinely 'transnational'.

This may not have been unique in the broader narrative of Islamic intellectual or material history but it was significant work over many decades to resuscitate and conserve a way of doing scholarship in a distant Sahelian town. There was originality in it even as it was explicitly concerned with the supposedly unoriginal task of reproduction or copying. Jurisprudence was the field he was keen on, not abstract or classical theories about the subject but the living jurisprudence of Timbuktu and the wider region. This type of jurisprudence was like a living record of his own contemporary society.

The distances his original manuscripts or copies and new books had to move were enormous. The objects of his passion literally had to travel through a network. The modern colonial postal service and linked technical innovations came to serve his network well. These machines of networking and mobility have been neglected but they were indispensable tools of communication especially over the long distances we are considering.

For Africa, studies of book history hardly exist; there is ample material in a number of places on the continent to look at the world and long history of writing and reading into which men like Bul'arāf entered or which they revitalised. His work presents us with an opportunity to work in some detail at the formation of a library and archive. Even though the data are most often fragmentary and partial – chronological gaps and missing materials – many material aspects of manuscript and printed book cultures could be studied: costs of paper, size of paper, handwriting styles used, ink colours, which ones had leather covers, signatures, copying costs, the politics of the colonial postal service, and so on.

As he built his library, he constituted a network between the Mediterranean and the Sahel. Those in it were most probably part of numerous other networks: other business networks, copying circuits, Sufi orders, Islamic reform movements, and family and clan networks. Ahmad Bul'araf's fascination lies in his attention to an object and the activation of a network in the service of that revered thing, the book.

Notes

1. These and other biographical details in this article are from Mahmud bin Muhammad Dadab, *Ma'lūmāt an khizānah usrah Bularrāf limuqayyidihu wa jami'ahu*, unpublished manuscript, 20pp. The author of this ms was a student of Bul'arraf's son and this eulogistic essay was given 'authorisation' by the son.
2. Senegal, Soudan Francais, renamed and conjoined into L'AOF (Afrique Occidental Française).
3. Written information from the Mauritanian historian, Dr. Elemine Mustafa, Nouakchoutt, Mauritania, Email dated March 2014.
4. Information from the historian Dr. Elemine Mustafa.
5. Two major sufi groups, the Qadiriyyah and the Tijaniyyah, had scholarly adherents who produced critiques of one another's sufi teachings. Bul'araf himself was keen to collect critiques of the Tijaniyyah. The catalogues of the Timbuktu libraries reveal several scholars who wrote such works.
6. See entry on Muhammad Salim al-Walati, in *Izalat al-rayb*.
7. Later to be declared part of L'Afrique Occidentale Française (AOF) which was the same administration but under a different name.
8. Dālī, Introduction, '*Izalat al-rayb*, 14. These volumes were possibly from the standard European edition of Sibawyhi, *Le live de Sibawaihi* edited by H. Derenbourg, Paris 1881–89. There is no indication of how he acquired this work.
9. Aḥmad Bul'arāf al-Taknī, '*Izalat al-rayb wa al-shakk wa al-tafrīt fī dhikr al-mu'alafin min ahl al-takrūr wa al-sahrā'a wa ahl shinqīt*, ed. by Al-Hādī al-Mabrūk Al-Dālī (n.d., n.p.; Introduction gives place as Tripoli and year 2000). It is based on three mss: the main ms in from the copy made by Mahmoud Dadab, 176pp.; Ms copy 2, in Iheri-Ab-T collection, , Ms 3, in archives in Libya.

10. Akansus was a well-known scholar himself born in the Sūs in 1796 but went to Fes by the time his was 20 years old where presumably he joined the Tijaniyyah brotherhood. See also Hunwick, *Arabic Literature of Africa*, vol 4, p120, item 6.
11. Oral information from Dr Mahmoud Zouber, first Head of the Cedrab. Bamako, August 2013.

References

Abou el-Farah, Yahia, Abdeluahed Akmir, and Abdelmalek Beni Azza. 1997. *La Présence Marocaine en Afrique de l'Ouest: cas du Sénégal, du Mali et de la Côte d'Ivoire*. Rabat: Institut des Etudes Africaines.

Abdulrazak, F. A. 1990. "The Kingdom of the Book: The History of Printing in Morocco." PhD diss., Boston University.

Africanus, Leo. 1971. *The History and Description of Africa: And of the Notable Things Therein Contained*. Translated by John Pory, 1600 and now edited with an introduction and notes by Robert Brown (Hakluyt Society). New York: Franklin.

Baba, Ahmad. 1989. *Nayl al-ibtihāj bi-tatrīz al-dibāj*. Tripoli: Kulliyah al-dawah al-islamiyyah.

Bivar, A. D. H., and M. Hiskett. 1962. "The Arabic Literature of Nigeria to 1804: A Provisional Account." *Bulletin of the School of Oriental and African Studies* 25 (1/3): 104–148.

Bul'arāf, Aḥmad. n.d. *'Izālat al-rayb wa al-shakk wa al-tafrīt fī dhikr al-mu'alafin min ahl al-takrūr wa al-sahrā'a wa ahl shinqīt*. Edited by Al-Hādī al-Mabrūk Al-Dālī (n.d., n.p. –however, the 'Introduction' cites place as Tripoli, and year as 2000).

Dadab, Mahmud bin Muhmmad, *Ma'lūmāt an khizānah usrah Bularrāf limuqayyidihu wa jami'ahu, unpublished manuscript, written in Timbuktu*, 1986, 20pp.

Dadab, Mahmud, *Kashf al-hā'il, unpublished manuscript*, written in Timbuktu, 338pp.

Dubois, Felix. 1896. *Timbuctoo the Mysterious*. Translated by Diana White. New York: Longmans, Green, and Co.

Haidara, Ismael Diadie, and Haoua Taore. 2008. "The Private Libraries of Timbuktu." In *The Meanings of Timbuktu*, edited by Shamil Jeppie and Souleymane Bachir Diagne, 271–275. Cape Town: HSRC Press.

Hamel, Chouki. 1999. "The Transmission of Islamic Knowledge in Moorish Society from the Rise of the Almoravids to the 19th Century." *Journal of Religion in Africa* 29 (1): 62–87.

Hegel, Georg Wilhelm Friedrich. 1975. *Lectures on the Philosophy of World History – Introduction: Reason in History*. Translated by H.B. Nisbet. Cambridge: Cambridge University Press.

Hunwick, John. 2003. *Arabic Literature of Africa: The Writings of Western Sudanic Africa*. Volume IV. Leiden: Brill.

Jackson, James Grey. 1809. *An Account of the Empire of Morocco, and the District of Suse: Compiled from Miscellaneous Observations Made During a Long Residence in, and Various Journeys Through, Those Countries. To Which is Added an Account of Timbuctoo, The Great Emporium of Central Africa*. London: Francis Nichols, Fry and Kammerer.

Jeppie, Shamil, and Souleymane Bachir Diagne, eds. 2008. *The Meanings of Timbuktu*. Cape Town: HSRC Press.

Lydon, Ghislaine. 2009. *On Trans-Saharan Trails: Islamic Law, Trade Networks, and Cultural Exchange in Nineteenth-Century West Africa*. New York: Cambridge University Press.

Lydon, Ghislaine. 2011. "The Thirst for Knowledge: Arabic Literacy, Writing Paper and Saharan Bibliophiles in the Southwestern Sahara." In *The Trans-Saharan Book Trade: Manuscript Culture, Arabic Literacy and Intellectual History in Muslim Africa*, edited by Graziano Kratli and Ghislaine Lydon, 35–72. Leiden: Brill.

Qadi, Wadad. 2006. "Biographical Dictionaries as the Scholars' Alternative History of the Muslim Community." In *Organizing Knowledge: Encyclopaedic Activities in the Pre-Eighteenth Century Islamic World*, edited by Gerhard Endress, 23–75. Leiden: Brill.

Schroeter, Daniel J. 1988. *Merchants of Essaouira: Urban Society and Imperialism in Southwestern Morocco, 1844–1886*. Cambridge: Cambridge University Press.

Triaud, Jean-Louis, and David Robinson, eds. 1997. *Le temps des marabouts: Itineraires et strategies islamiques en AFrique occidentale francaise v. 1880–1960*. Paris: Karthala.

Triaud, Jean-Louis, and David Robinson, eds. 2000. *La Tijâniyya: une confrérie musulmane à la conquête de l'Afrique*. Paris: Karthala.

Zouber, Mahmoud. 1977. *Ahmed Bābā de Tombouctou (1556–1627): sa vie et son oeuvre*. Paris: G.-P. Maisonneuve et Larose.

Archival sources
Archives Nationales – Senegal:
Serie J. *Postes et telecommunications; versement no.3* 1911/1950.
Sous Serie 2 G. Soudan Francais. 1929: 2G 29-52. *Postes et Telegraphies. Annee 1929. Rapport ensemble*.

Manuscripts

L'institut des Hautes Études et des Recherches Islamiques Ahmed Baba de Tombouctou (Iheri-Ab-T); it was previously called Centre de Documentation et de Recherches Historiques Ahmad Baba (Cedrab), Timbuktu, letters conserved as ms 6810 and ms 6847.

Iheri-Ab-T, Timbuktu, letter, ms 8190.

Iheri-Ab-T, *Timbuktu, ms 1031 Al-'amal al-mashkūr fī jam' nawāzil al-Takrūr.*

Iheri-Ab-T, Timbuktu, ms 1145.

Full circle: Muslim women's education from the Maghrib to America and back

Beverly Mack

Department of African and African American Studies, The University of Kansas, Lawrence, USA

This study examines the relevance of nineteenth-century Maghrib scholarship models to the transmission of Islamic knowledge and information among communities of American Muslims in the twentieth and twenty-first centuries. Nana Asma'u 'dan Fodio (1793–1864) – scholar, teacher, poet, and activist – was actively involved in the trials and itinerancy of the Sokoto Jihad (1804–30), in which she was principally involved. Although she never travelled beyond her region (now known as northwestern Nigeria), her scholarly reputation extended throughout the Maghrib during her lifetime. This paper explains how Asma'u's reputation and work was spread from the Maghrib to the USA by American Qadiriyya groups that purposively modelled their own communities on that of the nineteenth-century Fodio family network, developing women's study groups based on Asma'u's model, the *'Yan Taru* (The Associates), and using her educational materials in twentieth- and twenty-first-century-technological contexts.

Introduction

In the long historic stretch of pre-colonial times, Islamic scholars in the region of the Mediterranean travelled extensively in the pursuit of knowledge, acquiring, disseminating, and cross-fertilising the spread of knowledge in the region. Although Western historians have focused almost exclusively on male scholars in the Mediterranean and Maghrib, recent translations of pre-colonial documents have demonstrated unequivocally that such scholarship regularly was produced by Muslim women as well as by men. A prime example of the historic and geographic pervasiveness of women's scholarship is evident in Mohammed Nadwi's rich study of women scholars of the hadith from about the tenth century CE to the seventeenth. (Nadwi 2007) The detailed complexity of Nadwi's study conveys incontrovertible evidence of Muslim women's authority since the establishment of Islam, in keeping with the Qur'an's consistent command that religious devotion includes the necessity of the pursuit of knowledge.

Similar to the examples offered in Nadwi's study, this discussion focuses on the transmission of a model of women's scholarship across geographic regions and historical periods. The nineteenth-century scholarly legacy of the Fodio family was the context for Nana Asma'u bint Shehu Usman 'dan Fodio's (1793–1864) establishment of the *'Yan Taru* (Associates) model of women's education. The *'Yan Taru* model has continued locally since her death, has been developed in the twentieth century in the USA, and in the twenty-first century it is being transmitted internationally among Qadiriyya Muslim women. This study explains its origins, its transmission from the Maghrib to the USA, and changes in its curriculum in that process.

Nana Asma'u's *'Yan Taru* model of women's education

Prior to the nineteenth century, Asma'u's Fulani antecedents had moved eastward over several generations from the Futa Jalon region of West Africa, following either a pastoralist or clerical mode of subsistence. Her father's family settled in the village of Degel, located in what is now known as northwestern Nigeria. Asma'u's father, Shehu Usman 'dan Fodio, carried in his patronym the intellectual inclination of his lineage: he was a sheikh named Usman, the son of 'Fodio', the Fulfulde term for 'learned'. His daughter Nana Asma'u is just one of a long line of women scholars in her family. Although her accomplishments are exceptional, she was not an exception; her sisters were also scholars, and generations of women in the Fodio family before and after her lifetime also have been notable scholars. Asma'u's entire family was dedicated to the pursuit of knowledge; each child was instructed by his or her mother at an early age. The local village of Degel, and later the town the Fodios founded, Sokoto, now seem far from the Maghrib and even farther removed from the southern shores of the Mediterranean, but in pre-colonial times, the region called 'the Maghrib' extended well beyond present day Moroccan borders into Mali and Mauretania. The present political divide did not exist between the pre-colonial 'Maghrib' region and what is now known as Nigeria. Although she never travelled beyond her region, Asma'u's scholarly reputation extended into the Maghrib during her lifetime. Among Asma'u's collected works is a letter from someone identified only as a 'Maghribi scholar' named Shinqiti, who praises her erudition. The reputation of the Fodio family of intellectuals had spread so extensively in the region that scholars in late twentieth-century Rabat and Fez needed no explanation to identify the Fodio family (Personal communication in Rabat and Fez, circa 2003). Thus, it is not inaccurate to discuss the scholarly influence of Nana Asma'u bint Usman 'dan Fodio in the context of the Maghrib, extremely south of the shores of the Mediterranean.

The Fodio family's involvement in the Sokoto Jihad (1804–30) overshadows their accomplishments as scholars in most recent historical accounts. Throughout the itinerancy of the war years, manuscripts were loaded on camels and moved as the clan fled enemy pursuit, and books were the sole precious commodities that were not jettisoned in flight. In addition to the classic works, some by authors dating to the twelfth century, were numerous works by members of the family. The Shehu is known to have written over 300 treatises. His son Bello, Bello's friend Gidado, and Asma'u all wrote extensively, composing both singly and in collaboration with one another (Boyd 1989; Boyd and Mack 1997; Mack and Boyd 2000; Boyd and Mack 2013).

Asma'u was very close to her brother Bello. She was 11 when the warfare began, and married his friend Gidado a few years after that, at an age that was customary for the time. However, her classical education had begun years earlier, as was the tradition in her family. Among the classical manuscripts available to her, Asma'u also studied the written works produced by her father and brother Bello, and eventually contributed her own written works to the canon of Fodio family manuscripts. Together Bello, Gidado, and Asma'u worked seamlessly to strategise warfare tactics and establish approaches to reconstructing a fractured social order at the jihad's end. Much of this reconstruction depended on written texts that were used in the re-education of the masses. The written works that evolved from this collaborative triumvirate focused on ethics, social responsibility, and histories of the period. Following the template of classical works they had studied in the Islamic historical canon, the works of the Shehu, Bello, Asma'u, and Gidado constitute a formidable window into the intellectual history of their time. Their manuscripts, housed in the family holdings, continue to be studied by scholars in contemporary times.

Asma'u's post-jihad social activism focused on the establishment of a model of women's education in which a cadre of women first studied with her to learn her poetic works, and then used these works as the basis for lessons when they travelled to rural areas to teach women there. The women Asma'u trained acquired a name known to the Hausa majority as 'the Associates' – 'Yan Taru – indicating both their association with one another as teachers and their association with Nana Asma'u, whose erudition was legendary. The 'Yan Taru women travelled to villages to stay with local women (who were unable to leave their family obligations) for extended periods of time, teaching them about the Qur'an, and honing their social skills in the newly reformed Qadiriyya mode of Islam promoted by the post-jihad leaders. 'Yan Taru teachers would then return to Asma'u to report on their accomplishments, gain further knowledge, and subsequently return to the rural areas to give more lessons. Following Asma'u's death in 1864, the 'Yan Taru model of women's education continued in the region, even as the twentieth century brought British colonial rule to the newly designated country called Nigeria. British ideas about Western education overshadowed the structure of the Islamic curriculum as it had developed prior to the arrival of the British in 1903, but local scholars continued to study the Fodio family manuscripts in the traditional way nevertheless. The 'Yan Taru model of educating women to educate other women continued throughout 60 years of British colonial presence in the region, quite off the radar of British officers, whose lip service to promoting women's education was belied by their focus on boys' schools (Boyd and Mack 2013).

Northern Nigeria moved through the period of colonial over-rule (1903–60) accommodating British pressures to teach English, create schools for boys, and establish a tenuous balance of ethnic competition for jobs in newly created public institutions like banks and businesses. The 'Yan Taru practice seemed to have disappeared only because no administrator acknowledged women's own education activities; it appears that no one could conceive of women's self-motivated education programmes. Only gradually, begrudgingly, were women allowed to pursue educations in the new, Western-focused, colonial schools. Between Independence in 1960 and the 1980s, two decades of political and economic turmoil took its toll on Nigeria, and women's traditional educational roles were all but forgotten by those in power, although a few northern scholars continued to speak out in support of opportunities for the education of women. Many of these advised a return to the example of women's education in the Sokoto Caliphate (Boyd and Mack 2013, Chapter 5).

By the last decades of the twentieth century, Nigerian women began to organise themselves in associations that echoed the aims of the nineteenth century 'Yan Taru: education and community activism. In the early 1980s an organisation called Women in Nigeria (WIN) held two conferences, and eventually formed the Federation of Muslim Women's Associations in Nigeria (FOMWAN), a women's organisation unlimited by religious or ethnic affiliations. FOMWAN remains active in the twenty-first century, complete with its own website and platform to advocate for women's rights in Nigeria.[1] Journalist and activist Hajiya Bilkisu Yusuf's column on a FOMWAN conference drew a distinct connection between FOMWAN and the example of the Sokoto Caliphate's concern for women's participation in society and politics.[2] Throughout each of the two annual WIN conferences, and in discussions concerning the establishment of FOMWAN, the activist example of Nana Asma'u was the recurrent rationale for these efforts.[3] During this time, a public education system operated in tandem with Islamic schools; both of these overshadowed the *'Yan Taru* model, which appeared to be moribund, although it has continued, quietly, in the Sokoto region.

Twenty-first-century American *'Yan Taru* (Boyd and Mack 2013, Chapter 6)

The *'Yan Taru* model appeared in the USA through Malcolm X's interest in Qadiriyya Sufism. In New York in 1964, disillusioned with the Nation of Islam (NOI), Malcolm X established the Muslim Mosque Inc. (M.M.I.), along with a School of Islamic and Arab Studies, and then, in April 1964, departed for Makkah on hajj, where he became el-hajj Malek el-Shabazz. After his hajj, el-Shabazz visited several sites in Africa, including Sokoto, Nigeria, where he spoke with members of the Fodio family, talked with scholars, examined written documents, and decided that this Sunni interpretation of Islam was the one to which he should dedicate his energies; he was photographed wearing the traditional turban and long white robes favoured by Qadiriyya Sufi men in Sokoto. In the months between his disassociation from the NOI and his assassination (21 February 1965), el-Shabazz promoted Sunni Islam to serve the needs of African-American Muslims who shared his interest in this West African-derived Qadiriyya Sufi affiliation.[4]

Inspired by el-Shabazz's interest in Qadiriyya Islam, several American Muslims travelled to places they felt to be their heritage sites, seeking knowledge about and training in authentic traditional approaches to Islamic studies. They became affiliated with a *shaykh* of a West African Qadiriyya community,[5] sought guidance from Fodio family scholars in Sokoto, Nigeria, and in the Fodio family home of exile in Maiwurno, Sudan, spending years studying Arabic and working with descendants of the Shehu to study his writings. Among these were American Muslim scholars whose families had initially been NOI adherents, and then converted to Sunni Islam as the face of American Islam began to change through Malcolm X's influence. They established the Sankore Institute in Timbuktu as an organisation to facilitate the restoration of cultural ties between African-Americans and Africans. The physical home of the Sankore Institute originally was in Sudan, and now re-established in Mali, the American Muslim scholars affiliated with it returned to the USA and continued their work translating the Shehu's writings into English, and promoting the values of the Sokoto Qadiriyya community. The website for this Institute explained its origins in 1985 as an institution to promote Islamic African heritage through the formality of the partnership established between West African scholars and their students in the USA.[6]

Education was a central focus of this twentieth-century North American community, as it had been for the nineteenth-century Sokoto community. In the nineteenth century, the Shehu's reputation was wide-spread in the West African region, and his written works were not only housed in his Sokoto family compound, but also distributed throughout the Maghrib, as far away as Timbuktu and the Sudan, having been disseminated by other scholars. At the end of the twentieth century, the African-American Muslims were focused on translating Fodio family manuscripts with scholars in the Sudan and preserving these works digitally on their website, for international dissemination.

By the late twentieth century, American Muslims who had spent time studying Islam in West Africa and in Sudan, settled in Pittsburgh, PA, the site of the first American Muslim community (established in 1930). This Pittsburgh community became the home of American Muslims affiliated with the Qadiriyya Sufi teachings of the historic Fodio family. The men of the community in Pittsburgh favoured attire that symbolised their cultural and religious affiliation: white robes and turbans of the Qadiriyya brotherhood. They regularly used Islamic rosaries, the *tasbeeh*, for prayer. The women of this community also adopted modified forms of West African attire, wearing the hijab (instead of more cultural tradition head ties), long skirts, and long sleeves. Thus, at the end of the twentieth century, a community of African-American Muslims in Pittsburgh had modelled itself in action and appearance on an African Muslim community they believed to represent their heritage. The community was not ethnically exclusive; in keeping with Islamic precepts of equality, it also welcomed the membership of anyone who adhered to the Qadiriyya Sunni Sufi precepts of the Fodio family. The membership of Latino and Caucasian converts/reverts is demographically significant in Pittsburgh and in other chapters throughout the USA.

Familiar with the Fodio family and their accomplishments, the Pittsburgh community's leaders suggested that the women of this umma might consider establishing a 'Yan Taru network of women scholars, following the model begun by Asma'u. Thus, the first North American chapter of Asma'u's 'Yan Taru began in Pittsburgh in the 1990s, using published English translations of Asma'u's works as their lesson plans, exactly as Nana Asma'u had done a hundred and fifty years earlier. Jean Boyd's biography of Asma'u had been published in 1989, so the women of this contemporary Pittsburgh umma knew something about Asma'u's role in the community.[7] With the publication of Asma'u's poetry in 1997, followed by a volume explaining more about the 'Yan Taru organisation in 2000, they had available to them both material that they could use in the same way that it had originally been implemented and a model for women's involvement in education and community development (Boyd and Mack 1997; Mack and Boyd 2000).

This time, however, the Internet was available for the dissemination of Asma'u's poetic lessons plans. With this in mind, they procured permission to post Asma'u's works on a website for their own 'Yan Taru organisation. In 2005, the American 'Yan Taru organisation, a part of the Qadiriyya-affiliated umma in Pittsburgh, launched an electronic newsletter (called 'Yan Taru) website; new issues appeared every two months (Mack 2011). Their mission statement explained that by highlighting Asma'u's material and methods they aimed 'To provide services to women and children through establishing an organisation that facilitates Education, Entrepreneurship, Social Welfare and Community Outreach in accordance with the Koran, the Sunnah, and the methodology of Shaykh Uthman ibn Fuduye (1754–1817 CE).'[8] The site included commentary on the organisation itself, notices about local fundraising events, a column on health issues, business advice, recipes, childcare information, religious education lessons, community service announcements focused on orphans, business advice, and outreach to minority ethnic groups. One of its prominent columns was the poetry corner, in which Nana Asma'u's works were featured as educational tools.[9] Asma'u's poem 'So Verily' was featured to recommend perseverance in the face of misfortune;[10] her poem 'The Qur'an' was used as a means of memorising all the names of the Qur'an's 114 chapters, in keeping with its original purpose. The website's structure reflected the concerns of the organisation: women were inspired by Asma'u's example as much as by her poetry, but the poems were valued for underscoring her ethical perspective, which they shared. The organisation and its site were created around the image of Nana Asma'u as a teacher and social activist, and both operated as resources for women learning in and working for the entire community. These contemporary 'Yan Taru found in Nana Asma'u a role model who provided a means of helping Muslim women to benefit themselves and their communities. The Pittsburgh 'Yan Taru organisation was a women's organisation, but its activities benefited everyone in the community.

This website's connection to its local community – a natural outgrowth of Asma'u's intentions for the 'Yan Taru – also was impressive. One issue summarised the group's social welfare accomplishments, which included delivering clothing, shoes, and bedding to Somali refugees in nearby towns, partnering with refugee families, participating in the distribution of clothing at the Muslim Community Centre of Greater Pittsburgh, and developing a method of providing for the food pantry and for anonymous assistance for needy families in Northside Pittsburgh. These are exactly the kinds of social welfare efforts that Asma'u's works would have encouraged among rural women students in the nineteenth century, because her poems were all about teaching ethics and right behaviour towards others. Thus, the 2005 inaugural issues of the 'Yan Taru website presented a chronicle of contemporary women's activities based on Asma'u's nineteenth-century example.

The Pittsburgh congregation, however, was not allowed to grow as it had planned. It was subject to US governmental scrutiny, and in 2005 it already was under surveillance. In the next few years, it was disrupted by an FBI raid that led to the dispersal of many of its families.[11] Although the reason for the raid was never clarified, it is likely that FBI surveillance of Muslim communities in America is part of the fallout of the 9/11 tragedy. So the women who began the American 'Yan Taru movement in Pittsburgh did not stay in one place. As families moved away to ensure their safety, the irony of technology's weakness became evident: although it took only one person to make materials available to thousands via a website, conversely, the absence of that one web-meister left a vibrant 'Yan Taru website inoperative.

Meanwhile, the idea of an American 'Yan Taru organisation had spread wherever affiliation to the West African Sokoto Fodio community had taken hold. Interest in and affiliation with the Fodio-affiliated Qadiriyya order spread, and with it, sister organisations appeared in Hartford, CT, Atlanta, GA, Houston, TX, and Oakland and San Diego, CA.[12] These were small groups, comprising the women of each local *umma*. In San Diego the Latina membership was significant; Qur'anic classes increasingly were held in Spanish. An online In Focus article (3 March 2007) ran the headline: 'Traditional Islam for the Hip-Hop Generation' (by Zaid Shakur, staff writer):

SAN DIEGO – In the heart of San Diego's inner-city, just blocks away from 'the Four Corners of Death' (an intersection so nick-named by locals in the 1980s because of its notoriety for gang violence), nestled unceremoniously between a martial arts dojo and a neighbourhood grocery store is the Logan Islamic Community Centre (LICC). Situated in a working-class neighbourhood that is overwhelmingly Latino, LICC serves a Muslim congregation that is small yet incredibly diverse. Within its 27 founding members there are Filipinos, Africans, African-Americans, Caucasians, and of course, Latinos. The most striking characteristics of this up-and-coming community is the fact that it is made up entirely of reverts to Islam – and though some regular attendees are anywhere from 40 years of age well into their 70s, the average age of LICC's members is a tender 26 years old. It is precisely this youthful energy that one feels pulsating through the masjid and fuelling its impressive list of programs, activities, and services. Presently the sisters sponsor each other to attend "Deen intensives" around the country and hold classes for the other sisters when they come home. The women of LICC also perform charitable work for the community, recently holding a community sponsored rummage sale with the proceeds going to buy food vouchers that were given to the needy.

Inspired by Nana Asma'u's accomplishments and activism, the 'Yan Taru in San Diego worked to resolve problems unique to their community in the manner demonstrated by Nana Asma'u, that is, through thoughtful attention to problems, and positive action. Wherever the 'Yan Taru meet, they establish study groups and organise community charity projects whose benefits extend beyond the Muslim community. As was true in the nineteenth century, twenty-first century 'Yan Taru are concerned with a holistic approach to education.

It may appear that the nineteenth century 'Yan Taru were solely about the oral transmission of poems, while twenty-first-century American 'Yan Taru are all about literacy; neither literacy nor morality is the point. The focus of 'Yan Taru groups is instruction by whatever means is suitable to the audience. A Hadith notes that the Prophet advised that one should teach to the level of the student; for the nineteenth-century woman in rural West Africa, this meant oral transmission of information, while for the contemporary North American Muslimah, this means material transmitted electronically, through the written word. But the means of transmission is irrelevant; the information conveyed is the same, offering an ethical foundation based on Islamic values of service to the community and the family, in addition to Qur'anic instruction. When we discuss the original students of the *'Yan Taru*, the focus on Asma'u's poetry should not blind us to the point of the poem's messages: the point of each work is its content, not its literary style. Thus, what the contemporary website emphasises – community service, health care, childcare – are issues that would have been major topics of instruction in the course of discussing Asma'u's poems one hundred and fifty years ago. The delivery may be different, but the product is the same.

As in nineteenth-century Africa, the role of the local American twenty-first century *Jaji* (teacher) is to orchestrate women's efforts; contemporary women are hard-pressed to balance their domestic and childcare obligations with their spiritual interests. More often, in the twenty-first century, these women have the additional economic burden of needing to work outside the home. This leaves little discretionary time for *'Yan Taru* work. Nevertheless, these women are inspired in contemporary North America by their nineteenth-century West African mentor. It may be that Asma'u's most useful contribution to them is as a model of respectability: she was a woman whose intellect and contribution to the betterment of society was revered and appreciated, and because of that model, contemporary American Muslim women are confident that this can also be their role.

In 2010, when a new website for the Sankore Institute was established, the ''*Yan Taru* Women's Educational and Charitable Foundation' link was featured on its home page. This new *'Yan Taru* site picked up where the earlier one left off, featuring discussions of health as understood in the Shehu's writings, environmental concerns as discussed in the Qur'an, a library section with a brief piece, 'The Essential Nana Asma'u' by Jean Boyd (2005); a synopsis of the *'Yan Taru* origins in the 'about us' section, and a business section that was being developed. As of mid-2011, the *'Yan Taru* site was not available on the Sankore page, while they are being reconstructed. But it is expected that the site will develop, reflecting the features of previous *'Yan Taru* sites: an outline of the organisation's history, examples of the services the modern *'Yan Taru* provide for communities, advice on childcare, health issues, and charity work, and guidance on scholarly and religious activities. The earliest *'Yan Taru* website focused on a particular local community, so it was able to include weekly notices about charitable projects and calls for assistance for families in particular neighbourhoods. How a new website will unite *'Yan Taru* groups across America remains to be seen. The religious scholarship, leadership, and activism of these organisations and the extent to which they are youth-focused suggests that the voices of the young Muslimahs who comprise contemporary *'Yan Taru* communities will have significant impact on the evolution of American Islam in the twenty-first century.

In 2010, Dylia bint Hamadi Camara, a Malian raised in Houston, Texas, was named the national *Jaji* of US *'Yan Taru* groups. She trains and oversees *Jaji*s in North America and their *'Yan Taru* in urban centres, including Los Angeles, CA; Hartford, CT; Springfield, MA; Pittsburgh, PA. She recruits and helps in the formation of new *'Yan Taru* groups, such as those beginning to be active in Oakland, Sacramento, and San Diego, CA. *Jaji* Dylia has developed rigorous training programmes for both *Jaji*s and *'Yan Taru*, in consultation with Shaykh Muhammad Sharif, whose knowledge of Fodio family scholarship is extensive. The *Jaji* training programme includes eight core texts[13] and four areas of focused study.[14] Of the eight texts, two are works by the Shehu, and one each is by Bello and Abdullahi. The eight foci of study include jurisprudence, social etiquette, and astronomy. The four areas of study include Arabic language and grammar; Asma'u's works; Qur'anic recitation; and media training. It is significant that the entire body of nineteenth-century Asma'u's known works – over 64 long poetic compositions – comprise a quarter of the *Jaji* training. It is also interesting that they balance another, distinctly twenty-first-century concern – media training – to accomplish what Asma'u would heartily endorse, that is, communication with one's audience according to their needs. *Jaji* Dylia's practical attention to these means of communication is fully in keeping with the *modus operandi* of Nana Asma'u.

The *'Yan Taru* programme is the more complex of the two because it is the foundation on which *Jaji* scholarship is built. It involves three levels of education, broken into multiple sub-levels. Level I (7 parts and 25 texts) includes two sections on creed using the Shehu's and Bello's works as texts, a section each on Sufi science, Arabic grammar, Nana Asma'u, women in Islamic history, and explanation of the Qur'an.[15] Two of these sections include attention to women in Islam: one part includes the full complement of all of Asma'u's known works and writings about her life, while another part involves commentary about women in the early Islamic community. Clearly, a focus on women's history of involvement in Islamic scholarship and social activism is a powerful message in this curriculum. Level II (5 parts and 26 texts) includes texts by the Shehu and Abdullahi on creed, social sciences, Sufism, advanced Arabic grammar, and Qur'anic exegesis.[16] Level III (9 parts and 31 texts) involves works on the sources of jurisprudence, worship, diplomacy/government, Prophetic medicine, Sufism, advice to the community, brotherhood history, and advanced Arabic.[17] Most texts are classical Arabic works in translation, Arabic texts as part of the language/grammar curriculum, and the Qur'an in Arabic. The curriculum is organised to produce women scholars who are well trained in the same topics studied by their male counterparts, as well as providing a thorough grounding in the works produced by Muslim women scholars in history. There can be no doubt about the twenty-first-century *'Yan Taru* connection to Nana Asma'u's programme.

Jaji Dylia travels extensively, conferring with and training women in regional centres. At the same time, she is planning recruitment internationally, in South Africa, Senegal, and other African countries. The American *'Yan Taru* organisation is a work in progress. The *'Yan Taru* model may prove to operate organically, spreading geographically through universal electronic access to materials on this website and then to expand the website as local examples of activities and new study documents are fed back into it. But that possibility rests in large part on the extent to which the African-American Muslim community embraces the model, and integrates it into their own Muslim communities throughout North America. Such action may or may not involve dependence on electronic media.

This raises another problematic issue, that of racial-ethnic affiliations among Muslims in America. African-American Muslims have struggled through successive generations of change, from African-American-affiliated NOI origins in the philosophy of Noble Drew Ali and then Elijah Muhammad, to Warith Deen Muhammad's dissolution of the NOI and affiliation with mainstream universal Sunni Islam on the one hand, and Louis Farrakhan's reinstitution of the NOI on the other. In addition, since the mid-twentieth century, a wave of Muslim immigrants into the USA has resulted in a wide variety in North American Islamic communities. Added to these are the vast numbers of converts/reverts who affiliate themselves with Islamic communities depending on denominational preferences. Thus far, *'Yan Taru* groups are found among African-American Muslims who identify with the particular Qadiriyya Sufi brotherhood and heritage of the Fodio family of West Africa.[18] Even so, the racial and ethnic identity of some *'Yan Taru* chapters is changing as they reflect the Latina identity of some new converts/reverts in the communities. There is one new Latina convert in the Hartford, CT *'Yan Taru* organisation, and several Latinas in the Pittsburgh, PA *'Yan Taru* group. As the news item about San Diego indicated above, the numbers of Latinas in that *'Yan Taru* group appear to be higher still. Some of the nineteenth-century Fodio manuscripts posted on the Sankore website are translated into Spanish.

Asma'u wrote her works in Fulfulde, or Hausa, or Arabic, depending on the audience she wanted to reach, and her *Jaji* leaders and *'Yan Taru* teachers used Hausa, the language of the masses, for their lessons; serving diverse populations would seem to be in keeping with the approaches undertaken by the Fodio family in the nineteenth century. Even as the racial and ethnic profiles of *'Yan Taru* communities change, whether the *'Yan Taru* concept will remain within these communities of Muslims or grow beyond the limits of Qadiriyya-affiliated groups remains to be seen.

On the other hand, while these *'Yan Taru* chapters may appear to be growing with the increase of their respective communities, the truth is that the vitality of *'Yan Taru* organisations is threatened by the pace and distractedness of twenty-first-century life, in which economic pressures often require every adult in a household to work outside the home. Added to a schedule of adult jobs and children's educational and activity schedules is the need to observe daily prayer times, and to accomplish all this without the benefit of extended families in residence to relieve daily pressures. This leaves little time, energy, or opportunity for undertaking the perpetuation of discretionary educational meetings like those which the *'Yan Taru* organisation involves. Wherever a *'Yan Taru* chapter exists, the women who seek to orchestrate it struggle to find the time and opportunity to fit educational and social welfare work meetings into their busy lives.

Meanwhile, the nineteenth-century *'Yan Taru* tradition remains intact and active in its place of origin, Sokoto, Nigeria, but lacks a direct connection to the American *'Yan Taru* movement. It is too expensive and time-consuming for American *'Yan Taru* women to be able to easily visit Sokoto, and electronic communication with Nigeria is inconsistent, so there has been little communication among them. However, with the publication of another volume on Nana Asma'u, in which the American *'Yan Taru* story is told, it is possible that women involved in *'Yan Taru* groups on both continents will have the chance to know about one another and perhaps eventually work together.

It is significant that Nana Asma'u's written works have given substance to her legacy internationally. The written materials contained in her collected works provide the blueprint for social action. They are preserved as written documents, and used in oral form. What cannot be easily quantified is the use to which they are put, since these are not literature lessons, but social and ethical directives. Even when the poems are merely referenced and not actively used, they represent their author symbolically. Nana Asma'u constitutes a model of intellectual engagement, ethical values, productivity, and activism for women of another age and culture, whose only certain shared circumstance is that of being Muslimahs, and being connected by heritage to the Fodio family legacy. Through Asma'u's nineteenth-century example, twenty-first-century women in both West Africa and North America confirm their Islamic right to pursue education and engage in social welfare work in the community (Badawi 1995; Wadud 1999; Barlas 2002). They teach Asma'u's poems as a means of organising their students to be actively involved in social welfare projects, which is the foundational message of these works. The preservation and dissemination of Asma'u's works explain Asma'u's and her community's ethos to women of another age and place, who receive these words in a mode of transmission unimagined in Asma'u's time, bringing the best of nineteenth-century into a twenty-first-century context that can benefit from a traditional canon.

Conclusion

Asma'u's works and the model of her education programme have been discussed extensively in Boyd's and Mack's single and joint publications; the current study examines the ways in which Asma'u's nineteenth-century model and materials have been relevant to Islamic American communities in the twentieth century, and expectations about the international dissemination of Asma'u's model of women's education well beyond both the Maghrib/Mediterranean and the USA. The mission statement of the American *'Yan Taru* in Pittsburgh explains their aim:

> To provide services to women and children through establishing an organisation that facilitates Education, Entrepreneurship, Social Welfare, and Community Outreach in accordance with the Koran, the Sunnah, and the methodology of Shaykh Uthman ibn Fuduye [Shehu Usman 'dan Fodio] (1754–1817 CE).

As they note on their website, the Pittsburgh women viewed Nana Asma'u as a role model who provided a means of helping Muslim women to benefit themselves and their communities 'without compromising [their] religion or dignity'. Their male counterparts also chose to follow the Fodio family approach to Islam, in which women's active involvement was advocated. By adhering to the Fodio family's ethos, these American Muslims re-established their historical identity in a new dynamic of cultural ties to West Africa.

The American women who established the *'Yan Taru* movement in Pittsburgh, and its sister organisations in urban centres like Los Angeles, CA, Hartford, CT, and Springfield, MA,[19] seek to follow the example of Nana Asma'u even as they strive to balance the demands of life in the twenty-first century. They are focused on religious scholarship, leadership, and activism – values that are shaping the evolution of American Islam in the twenty-first century. The Pittsburgh Islamic community (*umma*) and its *'Yan Taru* women demonstrate Islam's ability to adapt flexibly to new cultural conditions while retaining its spiritual core. They contrast markedly with the misogynistic criminal *Boko Haram* movement, which also claims Fodio inspiration. While the Pittsburgh *umma* relies on a pre-colonial, pre-industrial nineteenth-century West African model of Islam, it focuses on the Fodio clan's ethical practices and enthusiasm for intellectual pursuits as these resonate in contemporary life. It seeks to provide its community with social welfare benefits, including advice on childcare, health issues, and charity work. When I was invited to speak to the Hartford, CT *umma* about Nana Asma'u in 2003, I met and spent a few days with the women who were then just beginning to organise their *'Yan Taru* group. Since 2003, the women have continued to meet in classes that study Asma'u's texts and discuss social welfare issues, childcare concerns, entrepreneurial advice, and prayer.

The American *'Yan Taru* phenomenon is one of several significant movements in twenty-first-century North American Islam that demonstrates how African-American Muslims define their own cultural and spiritual identities based on Islam by looking to West African models, yet neither this development in African-American Islamic history in general nor the American *'Yan Taru* specifically has received broad academic scrutiny. Leonard (2003) addresses the history of the NOI and the influx of immigrants from Africa, but includes nothing about African-Americans who travel to Africa to study. McCloud (1995) and GhaneaBassiri (2010) discuss Islam in America, while Last (1967) and Hiskett (1973) discuss the Fodio family in Sokoto, but none of these addresses the relevance of the Fodios for Islam in America. Following the Immigration Act of 1965 immigrants have diversified American Islam, adding Sunni and Shi'a practices to the spectrum of Islamic practices in North America. Islam in America now includes communities that range from liberal Sufi to conservative Salafi approaches. In the midst of such diversity, many African-American Muslims have moved away from the NOI to embrace an approach to Islam in which they create their own history, as in the case of followers of the Fodio brand of Qadiriyya Islam.

Each of the Fodio-related communities I have studied has a group of *'Yan Taru* women educators: this is the lens through which I examine the nature of these communities. Islam's transnational identity in a Western political democracy is exemplified clearly in the Americanisation of the *Yan Taru* movement. This study provides insight into ways in which Muslim African-Americans are establishing a cultural history that slavery denied them; in these communities, women's educational activities are central to the establishment of a line of spiritual communication spanning historical time and geographic displacement, from pre-colonial West Africa to twenty-first-century North America. One man explained the sense of heritage this West African tradition has given him when I visited his small community in Hartford, Connecticut: 'Because of slavery, we were like dots, floating, without roots. Now we are connected to a particular culture through Islam. Now we have a history instead of just a past'.

Disclosure statement

No potential conflict of interest was reported by the author.

Notes

1. Its website explains: The FOMWAN was established in October 1985 and registered with the Corporate Affairs Commission the same year. With a consultative status with the United Nations, FOMWAN is a non-profit and non-governmental civil society umbrella body for Muslim women associations in Nigeria. Today FOMWAN is in 34 states of the federation and has over 500 affiliate groups. FOMWAN National headquarters, Utako Abuja is under construction. The multi-million-naira project includes an administrative building, a hostel block, conference hall, and a mosque. FOMWAN is a network of Muslim Women organisations nationally. It is emerging and growing as a national faith-based, non-governmental organisation with emphasis on promoting and protecting the interest, welfare, and aspirations of its members in line with Islamic injunctions. The impetus for the establishment and existence of FOMWAN is the provision of social service especially to its members and the desire to contribute to national development. In particular, FOMWAN seeks to contribute to the overall health, literacy, and economic empowerment of its members and promotion of positive social behaviour of Muslim girls for responsible living and adulthood in Nigeria. Recently, FOMWAN reviewed and adopted a new strategic plan redefining its vision, mission, value statements, goals, and strategic objectives. http://www.fomwan.org/index. php.
2. The FOMWAN held its 23rd Annual National Conference from 21 to 24 August 2008 in Sokoto, the seat of the caliphate. The conference was attended by over 1000 delegates from all the states of the federation. Since it was established in 1985, the federation has been organising these conferences and workshops which rotate between the Northern and Southern parts of the country. The event is a grassroots affair with delegates drawn from various states and local governments. The conference papers, although delivered in English, are always translated into Hausa and Yoruba. All the members from the South East branches speak English which eased the task of translating into Igbo for the conference organisers. The activities began on Thursday with a spiritual and social night that featured a Quranic recitation competition in which award-winning female reciters participated. This year the theme of the conference was Revival and Reform in the Sokoto Caliphate and Its relevance to Present Time. The opening ceremony which was held at the Trade Fair Complex was attended by the delegates and dignitaries from state and federal levels. The Sokoto State Governor Alhaji Aliyu Magatakarda Wamakko was represented by the Commissioner, Ministry for Religious Affairs, His eminence, the Sultan of Sokoto; Alhaji Muhammad Sa'ad Abubakar was the royal father of the day while the former President, Alhaji Shehu Shagari, who was out of the country for an important affair, was the Chairman of the occasion. He was represented by Professor Abubakar Gwandu, former Vice Chancellor of Usman Danfodio University Sokoto and also the former chairman of the National Pilgrims Commission. The First Lady, Hajiya Turai Yar'Adua, was represented by the Minister, Federal Ministry of Women Affairs and Social Development, Hajiya Saudatu Usman Bungudu. The wives of the Governors of Adamawa and Kaduna States, Hajiya Asmau Nyako and Hajiya Amina Namadi Sambo, also attended, while the wife of the Zamfara State Governor, Hajiya Aisha Mahmud Shinkafi, presented an address.
3. I attended these conferences, and heard these discussions.
4. The origins of the Qadiriyya Sufi brotherhood, of course, predate its West African appearance, having begun with the preaching of Baghdad ascetic 'Abd al-Qadir al-Jilani (470/1077-561/1166). It is known as the first major order of many Sufi brotherhoods, and has branches and subgroups throughout the world.

5. Lately, these connections have been with individuals from the Sudan, where the Fodio family fled during the British colonial period and established another Qadiriyya community in Maiwurno, Sudan.

6. The Sankore Institute of Islamic-African Studies International (S.I.I.A.S.I) is a non-profit, non-political educational institution founded (in 1985) for the sole purpose of researching into the educational, political, cultural, and religious heritage of Islamic Africa. The primary area of concern is that part of Black Africa traditionally known as the Bilad's-Sudan (The Lands of the Blacks). These lands include all the regions located south of the Sahara desert and north of the tropical jungles, between the Atlantic Ocean and the Red Sea. The purpose of the S.I.I.A.S.I is to elucidate and evidence the Islamic traditions which were born out of African nations such as Takrur, Songhay, Mali, Ghana, Kanem-Bornu, Wodai, Fur, Funj, Sokoto, Segu, Massina, and the Mahdist kingdom of the Nile valley. http://www.siiasi.org/. (Its website is under reconstruction.)

7. Shaykh Muhammad Sharif, the Imam in the late 1990s, learned about the *'Yan Taru* model and recommended to the women of the community that they investigate and pursue the kinds of educational goals inherent in it.

8. Owing to variations in transliteration from the Fulfulde in Ajami (i.e. Fulfulde language in Arabic script), the family name Fodio is spelled variously: Fodio, Fodiyo, and Fuduye. Each is correct.

9. Organizers contacted Jean Boyd and me to procure permission to post translations of Asma'u's works from the *Collected Works* volume.

10. This poem was one written in response to her brother Bello's distressed poem on the eve of a jihad battle, when the enemy's drums were heard over the hill.

11. For an account of this see the DVD 'New Muslim Cool' (Specific Pictures), narrated by Hamza Perez.

12. In September 2010, I visited the *'Yan Taru* group in Hartford, CT, whose membership is drawn from a wide region of the state. The group was small, about 10, and included a Latina who was a new Muslimah.

13. These include *Umdat al Muta'abeeden wa l Muhtarafeen* (The Suppport of Worshippers and Professionals) by Shehu Uthman 'dan Fodio; *Risalat li Amrad* (Epistle that Cures Sicknesses, Containing Advice that Meets the Goals) by Sultan Muhammad Bello; *Taleem al Anam* (The Education of Humanity) by Sultan Muhammad Bello, the *Khabair* (major sins or enormities) text to be announced, *Adab al Muashirat* (Manual of Social Etiquette) by Shaykh Abdullahi 'dan Fodio, the laws of Marriage, the laws of Trade, and *Ilm Al falak* (Islamic Astronomy to Determine the New Moon, Times of Prayer).

14. The first level includes studies of Arabic letters (pronunciation and reading), basic grammar, vocabulary, introduction to *Tajweed* (pronunciation), rules of *tajweed, tajweed* for the entire Qur'an, and calligraphy. The second level includes attention to the collected works of Sayyida Nana Asmau, a reading of Usman Bugaje's A Revolution in History, and *Zamaan an Nasara* (Time of the Christians). The third level focuses on memoration, using *Hifz al Qu'ran* (Memorization of the Qur'an), and *Hifz al Hadith, wal mutun* (Memorization of the Qu'ran, Prophetic traditions and our texts). The fourth level discusses media training, with a focus on how to explain Islam to the world using the methodology of the Shehu and family; modern media such as movies, radio, and documentaries; and the dos and don'ts in the media.

15. Level I includes (1) *Aqeedah Usul ul din* (Foundation of the Religion-Introduction to *'Aqeedah* or the Muslim creed), *Kifaya Al-Muhtadeen* (The Sufficiency of the Rightly Guided) – Introduction to *'Aqeedah* by Shaykh Uthman dan Fodio), and *Mi'raj ila Al-Awwam sam'i ilm Al-Kalaam* (*Aqeedah*) ((Ladder of the Common to the Hearing of the Sciences of Desputation). Level II includes *Aqeedah, Fiqh, Tasawwuf* (Science of social behaviour), *Taqrib ad-daruri* (The Essentials of the Sciences of the Religion – Overview of *aqeedah, fiqh and tasawwuf*) by Shaykh Abdullahi dan Fodio, *Ruh as Salah* (The Essence of Prayer by Shaykh Abdullahi 'dan Fodio), *Risalah lil-Amraad Shafiyah* (Seven Socio-spiritual Remedies for Individuals and Communities by Shaykh Muhammad Bello), *al-Sullam ila al-huda, ma'rifat arkan al-salat* (Ladder to the Right Path, Knowing the Pillars of Prayer) (*fiqh of salaah*), *'Ulum Al-Mu'amilah* (*fard Al-ayn* – Individual obligation – *Aqeedah, fiqh* and *tasawwuf*), and *Masaa'il al Insan Nayl'l-Maram* (The Obtainment of the Goal from Habits of Nobility). The third level includes *Tasawwuf* (Spiritual purification), *Akhlaq al Mustapha* (The Character of the Chosen One by Shaykh Abdullahi 'dan Fodio), *Tariq 'l jannah* (The Path of Paradise by Shaykh Uthman 'dan Fodio), *Usul at-Tariqah* (Foundations of the Spiritual Path by Shaykh Uthman 'dan Fodio), *Sabil Najah* (The path to Success: Protecting the Heart and the Seven Members of the Body), and *at-Tanbeehaat' l-Waadihaat* (The Clear Warnings). The fourth level includes study of Arabic letters, basic grammar, introduction to *Tajweed* (pronunciation), and rules of *Tajweed*. The fifth level includes an introduction to *Sayyida* Nana Asma'u, reading: 'The Essential Nana Asma'u' (Boyd), The Caliph's Sister (Boyd), One Woman's Jihad (Mack and Boyd), and The Collected Works of Nana Asma'u (Boyd and Mack). The sixth level includes history readings: the women around the Messenger (*salallahu alayhi wa salaam*) – *seerah*, female scholars of Islam past and present. The seventh level includes *Tafsir* and *Tajweed* of *Juz Amma* (Part 30 of the Qur'an, chapter 78 to the end) and *Kifaayat*

du'afa al-Sudan fi bayan tafsir al-Qur'an (The Satisfaction of the Poor/Weak of the Sudan in the Explanation on How to Comment on the Qur'an by Abdullahi 'dan Fodio).

16. The first level involves attention to *Aqeedah-Umdat al Bayan* (The Supporting Explanation of the Sciences Obligatory Sciences) and *Umdat al Muta'bedeen wa Mu'tarefeen* (The Support of the Devout Successful Worshiper). The second level focuses on behavioural social sciences: *Sawq Al-ummah* (Mobilisation of the *ummah*- hadiths teaching the foundation *'aqida, fiqh* and *tasawwuf*), *Diya 'Uluum 'd-Deen* (The Light of the Sciences of the Religion), *'Umdat Al-'Ubbad* (The Support of the Servant of Allah-the Essential Supergatory Worship), *Nazm (al-Aqida) al-wusta* (Verse of the Middle One), *Daah 'z-Zaad Ila 'l-Mìaadl* (Making or Garnering Provision for the Hereafter), *Tanbeeh as-Saahib* (Advice to a Friend by Sultan Muhammad Bello), and *At-Tarjumaan 'An Kiyfayat'l-Wàdh* (The Interpreter on How to Preach). The third level is about Sufism (*Tasawwuf*), including *Sawq as-Siddiqeen* (The Mobilisation of the Champions of Truth), *Riyaadh as-Saalikeen* (The Garden of the Travellers), *Tabsheer Ummat al-Ahmadiyya* (Good News to the Community of Ahmad), *Shukhr 'l-Insaan 'Ala Manan'l-Manaan* (The Gratitude of Spiritual Excellence), *Niyat Fi'l-'Amaal* (The Intention in Action), *Tareeq as Saliheen* (The Path of the Pious), *Tahtheeb Al-Insaan* (The Training of Humanity Against the Traits of *Shaytan-tasawwuf*-about the art of governing the soul and body) by Shaykh Abdullahi 'dan Fodio, and *Nasihah Al-Wadi'ah* (About the Evil of Loving this World). The fourth level focuses on intensive Arabic grammar (*nahu*) and linguistics (*lugha*), including: Al-Ajurumiyya (grammar) of Muhammad ibn Muhammad as-Sanhaji, *Al-Alfiyat* (A Poem of 1000 Verses) of Ibn Malik, *khat* (calligraphy), *Qira'at wal Hifz* of *juz Amma* (reading and memorisation), *Hifz* of *ahadith* (memorisation of hadith), and 40 hadiths of Imam an-Nawawi, *Hifz* of texts of the *Jama'at* (memorisation of texts of the people). Level V is about Qur'anic exegesis (*Tafsir al Qur'an*), including *Diya't-Ta'weel Fi Màana at-Tanzeel Kifaayat 'd-Dùafa* (The Sufficiency of the Non Scholarly Blacks Regarding the Commentary of the Qur'an).

17. Level I includes *usul* (principles, or legal methodology), focusing on *Mirat at-Tullab* (The Reflection of the Student- Qur'anic and Prophetic Intellectual Proofs of *aqida, fiqh* and *tasawwuf* by Shaykh Uthman 'dan Fodio, *Ihya as-Sunnah* (Revival of the *sunnah* and the Destruction of Heretical Innovation-Explication of the *Sunnah* and the innovations concerning *aqida, fiqh* and *tasawwuf*), *Tawfeeq l' Muslimeen* (The Success of the Muslims by Shehu Usman 'dan Fodio), *Tarweeh 'l-Umma* (The Reassuring of the Community -Shaykh 'Uthman's methodology regarding *aqida* and *fiqh* by the Shehu), *Umdat Al-'Ulama* (The Support of the Scholars -the Qur'anic and Prophetic foundations in *aqida, fiqh* and *tasawwuf*), *Lubaab 'l-Madhkhal* (The Essence of the Introduction into the courtesies of the people of the *deen* (religion) and erudition) by Shaykh Abdullahi 'dan Fodio, *Kifaya ad-Doua'fa as-Sudan fi Bayan tafsir al- Qur'an* (The Indispensable Interpretation), and *Diya as-Sanad* (The Sixty-three Golden Chains of Authority). Level II is *mou'amalat* (transactions between people). Level III includes the study of *dawah* (social welfare work and preaching), including *Amr bil-Ma'ruf wa nahy anil munkar* (Enjoining the Good and Forbidding Evil), *Diya ahl Al-ihtisab* (The Establishment of Social Uprightness), *Udad ad-Da'ee* (The Principles for Those People Invited to Allah the Exalted), and *Tarjuman fi kayfiya wa'th Shaykh Uthman* (Shaykh Uthman's methodology in *da'wah*). The fourth level is the science of diplomacy and government, including *Usul As-Siyasah* (The Principles of Politics), *Masaa'il Al-Muhimmah* (*da'wah* and the government), and *Ghayth Al-Wabl* (The Rights and Duties of Leaders). The fifth level concerns prophetic medicine, including *Masalih bil-adyaan Al-Muta'alliqah Al-Insaan wa'l-abdaan* (The Essential Knowledge of the Religion and Prophetic Medicine) and *Ujaalatir-Rakib* (Prophetic Medicine) by Muhammad Bello. The sixth level concerns sufism, including *Usul Al-Wilayah* (Foundations of Sainthood), *Shukr Al-Ihsan* (A Complete Overview of *tasawwuf* and the Branches of Faith), *Sabil ahl-salah ila Al-falah* (Sufism and News of the Hereafter), *Diya Ulum Ad-Diin* (The Light of the Sciences of Relgion- *aqida, fiqh, awraad, adaab*, and *tasawwuf*), and *Diya Al-Qawa'id* (The Light of Rules – sufism and *athkaar*). The seventh level focuses on the sciences of the conditions of the Signs of the End of Time, and includes *Tanbeeh'l-Umma* (Admonishing the Musleem Community). The eighth level is about Sufi brother hoods, and includes *Salasil ath-Thahabiyyah* (The Golden Chain of the Qadirriyyah Brotherhood), *Tabshir Al-Ummah* (Concerning the Virtues of Shaykh Abdul-Qadir Al-Jilani, may Allah be pleased with him), and *at-Tafriqa Bayna at-Tasawwuf* (Differentiation Between Sufism … [incomplete title]). The ninth level focuses on advanced Arabic, and includes: *An-Naadhim* of Abu Mugra' regarding rhetoric (*mantiq*) and eloquence (*balaagha*), *Ar-Rajaaz* [metric poetry] of Abd'l-Karim al-Maghili concerning poetry (*shìr*) and rhyme (*qawaafi*), *Al-Ajurumiyya* of Muhammad ibn Dawud concerning grammar, syntax, and inflection, and *Al-Alfiyat* of Ibn Malik concerning grammar, syntax, inflection, and verbal conjugation. I am grateful for the assistance of Professor Yacine Daddi Addoun in translations of the Arabic in notes 13–17.

18. This historical connection is so strong that there are families in Georgia who have assumed the dan-Fodio surname in honour of the illustrious West African family, without any evidence of lineal connections.

19. This is not an extensive list of 'Yan Taru groups in the USA. There are currently about a dozen chapters in various stages of development and activity, all located in major urban centres.

References

Badawi, Jamal. 1995. *Gender Equity in Islam*. Plainfield, IN: American Trust Publications.

Barlas, Asma. 2002. *Believing Women in Islam*. Austin: University of Texas Press.

Boyd, Jean. 1989. *The Caliph's Sister*. London: Frank Cass.

Boyd, Jean. 2005. *The Essential Nana Asma'u*. http://www.yantaru.com/books/The%20Essential%20Nana%20Asma'u.pdf

Boyd, Jean, and Beverly Mack. 1997. *The Collected Works of Nana Asma'u, Daughter of Usman 'dan Fodio 1793–1864*. East Lansing: Michigan State University Press.

Boyd, Jean, and Beverly Mack. 2013. *Educating Muslim Women: The West African Legacy of Nana Asma'u 1793–1864*. Oxford: Interface Publications.

FOMWAN. "Federation of Muslim Women's Associations in Nigeria." http://www.fomwan.org/index.php

GhaneaBassiri, Kambiz. 2010. *A History of Islam in America: From the New World to the New World Order*. New York: Cambridge University Press.

Hiskett, Mervyn. 1973. *The Sword of Truth: The Life and Times Shehu Usuman dan Fodio*. New York: Oxford University Press.

Last, Murray. 1967. *The Sokoto Caliphate*. London: Longman.

Leonard, Karen Isaksen. 2003. *Muslims in the United States: The State of Research*. New York: Russell Sage Foundation.

Mack, Beverly. 2011. "Nana Asma'u's Instruction and Poetry for Present-day American Muslimahs." *History in Africa* 38: 1–16.

Mack, Beverly, and Jean Boyd. 2000. *One Woman's Jihad: Nana Asma'u, Scholar and Scribe*. Bloomington, IN: Indiana University Press.

McCloud, Aminah Beverly. 1995. *African American Islam*. New York: Routledge.

Nadwi, Mohammad Akram. 2007. *al-Muhaddithat: The Women Scholars in Islam*. London: Interface Publications.

"New Muslim Cool". 2009. DVD (Specific Pictures), narrated by Hamza Perez, Producer Jennifer Maytorena Taylor.

Wadud, Amina. 1999. *Qur'an and Woman*. Oxford: Oxford University Press.

The diaspora and the cemetery: emigration and social transformation in a Moroccan oasis community

Paul A. Silverstein

Department of Anthropology, Reed College, Portland, USA

This essay explores the history and social consequences of emigration from the southeastern oases of Morocco, which since the 1940s have functioned as a veritable demographic pump, sending streams of labour migrants to northern cities and across the Mediterranean. It examines the close symbolic and material relations between physical and social mobility, as migrant remittances transform embedded hierarchies based on property ownership, irrigation rights, and economic independence. The essay situates these micro-level dynamics in the larger political tensions around 'harrag' (overseas undocumented migration), Berber (Amazigh) ethnic activism, tribal land rights, and racialised violence that have recently struck rural Morocco – tensions that have made Amazigh militants, often based in the diaspora, particularly concerned about the cultural fate of their homeland oases communities. In underlining these political frictions and ambivalences, the essay critically intervenes in a larger literature that has too often, and without qualification, characterised emigration as cultural uprooting and an inevitable harbinger of social death.

Dear Ghérissois of the Diaspora
Tamazirt suffered greatly to give you birth,
She nourished you, cradled you, raised you, embraced you ...
Afterwards, you left her, abandoned her, forgot her ...
The city bewitched you, absorbed you, dehumanised you,
Decultured you, exploited you, enslaved you ...
Makes you build cities in the city,
Engorges you with steak and grilled meat [*méchoui*]
While your parents and brothers
Continue to breathe the dust
Trudge through the mud
And boil up stones to eat.
The young people only learn of your existence
When you return to be buried.
They don't mourn you.

Only those of the diaspora come to take part.
As such you attend your own funeral.
So, dear Ghérissois of the diaspora,
Tamazirt calls out to you:
'My dear, dear sons, have pity on me!
Don't turn me into a mere cemetery.
You give my fruits to others,
And they only return your remains.
I need you, I need to feel you,
I need your children, your money, your blood,
Your effort and your sweat;
I need strong, living men
Not dead ones.
My dear sons, do not be mad at me
If one day I refuse to accept your bodies
I cannot bear to be the mother of coffins and tombs.'

The above poem – penned in 1991 in French and anonymously distributed under the name 'Ilayt-mas' (He who has brothers) by Ali Harcherras, a Berber (or Amazigh) cultural activist from the southeastern Moroccan oasis town of Goulmima – figures the relationship between the diaspora and the homeland (*tamazirt*) as one of life and death.[1] Written as an open letter to emigrants from the local Ghéris valley, the poem constitutes a plea and a warning. Tamazirt cannot survive on dead bodies alone; the cradle of cultural life and material sustenance risks becoming little more than a sterile cemetery. The symbolic attachment that the diaspora maintains with the homeland is simply not enough; a real investment of labour, time, and money is required.

On the one hand, there is nothing particularly surprising about such a discourse of social abandonment and cultural death. Indigenous activists across much of the global South have lamented the role played by out-migration, and globalisation more generally, in endangering local cultures if not abetting wholesale cultural genocide. In Morocco, the large-scale 'rural exodus' (*l'exode rural*) from southern Berber-speaking regions to northern cities and northern Europe that followed the Second World War has provoked periodic fears among academic observers, international advocates, and local militants about the loss of Berber culture through the modernisation of habits and the Arabisation of language; the abandonment of traditional habitations, in particular the adobe, multifamily, walled granaries known as *ksour* or *ighremen*; and the feminisation and ageing of the oasis populations caused by the semi-permanent departure of working men. The mushrooming of new cement homes built from emigrant remittances outside of the *ksour* walls or in the modern centres of oasis boomtowns such as Goulmima has been generally taken, by local populations and scholars alike, as a concrete sign that the oases' death knells have sounded (Bencherifa 1993, 5; Bencherifa and Popp 1990, 37; Bisson and Jarir 1986, 344–345; Naciri 1986).

On the other hand, as most rural Moroccans will reluctantly admit, emigration has functioned as the condition of possibility for the survival of oasis communities challenged by overpopulation, periodic droughts, the date palm *bayoud* disease, environmental degradation (the lowering of aquifers, salination of the soil, and eventual desertification caused in large part from over-pumping), and the normative practice of partible inheritance whereby parcels of arable land are divided among heirs into smaller and smaller plots eventually impossible for subsistence. Emigrant remittances balance budgets, pay off store credits, allow for economic diversification, and provide the wealth necessary to contract marriages and begin new households (see de Haas 2006). Nearly every person I have interviewed in the Ghéris valley over the past five years has a sibling or parent working abroad, and many themselves had spent earlier years working in construction, agriculture, or domestic service in large cities such as Tangiers, Casablanca, or Agadir. If for the many remaining behind emigration is but a necessary evil, for those migrating it is increasingly a practice of personal and social emancipation – for individual young men and women seeking to escape their fathers' tutelage, as well as for those landless segments of oases populations previously stagnated at the bottom of stratified ethnic hierarchies. For such groups, emigration breathes new life into a stultified social structure, transforming what was a cemetery of stillborn ambition into a vibrant space of personal development and cultural renewal. From their perspective, it is not the oases that risk becoming graveyards, but rather the distant cities where young men and women without expansive kin networks risk falling victim to temptation or employer predations.[2] Alternately, death is associated with the act of clandestine migration (*harrag*), where trans-Mediterranean migrants literally tempt fate in precarious fishing vessels crossing what are colloquially called the 'straits of death' (cf. Fall 2004).[3]

In what follows, I explore the history and social consequences of emigration from the southeastern oases of Morocco, which since the 1940s have functioned as a veritable demographic pump, sending streams of labour migrants to northern cities and across the Mediterranean. I examine the close symbolic and material relations between physical and social mobility, as migrant remittances transform embedded hierarchies based on property ownership, irrigation rights, and economic independence. The essay situates these micro-level dynamics in the larger political tensions around *harrag*, Amazigh ethnic activism, tribal land rights, and racialised violence that have recently struck rural Morocco – tensions that have made Amazigh militants, often based in the diaspora, particularly concerned about the cultural fate of their homeland oases communities. In underlining these political frictions and ambivalences, I want to critically intervene in a larger literature that – like the poem quoted earlier – has too often and without qualification characterised emigration as cultural uprooting and an inevitable harbinger of social death.

Mobility and social structure

Freedom of mobility and freedom *from* mobility are intimately connected attributes of authority, prestige, and social standing in Morocco. In general, those Moroccans with the resources to travel freely abroad and send their children for education overseas are among the least likely to emigrate; *harrag* – the willingness to 'burn' one's identity papers as well as potentially one's ties to the 'homeland' – if unaffordable to the most desperate, tends to be the province of the educated unemployed (*les diplomés chomeurs*) or underemployed who find their social mobility in Morocco blocked.[4] At the pinnacle of society, the King – as his Sultan forebears – reinvigorates his own authority through the ritual movement (*harka*) of the royal court and army across the national landscape, originally as an assertion of military might, but today more generally to bless the faithful he commands and inaugurate new public works projects – all accompanied by an entourage of reporters who rebroadcast his every act on the nightly news (see Geertz 2000, 134–142; Hammoudi 1997, 62). The ritual efficacy of the *harka* is premised on a radical disjuncture between the monarch's mastery over the spatial and spiritual landscape, and the relative immobility of his subjects. The King's own genealogy as an 'Alawi *sharif* (pl. *shurfa*) and thus a descendent of the Prophet not only entrenches his authority as Commander of the Faithful and primary node of *baraka* (blessing), but also indelibly links his person to an elsewhere, to Arabia through the Tafilalet southeastern oases.[5]

In the oases themselves, shurfa deploy similar genealogical capital to accumulate local prestige and found great households based on gifts of land and irrigation rights from the local laity, as well as on their ongoing commercial relations originally linked to the trans-Saharan caravan trade. Their spiritual and economic wealth is paralleled by the local political power of the 'freemen' Berber tribes (*ahrar* or *Imazighen*) who historically exchanged their armed protection of the sedentary oasis populations for the latter's agricultural produce. Over the last few centuries, these formerly transhumant tribes settled in the oasis valleys, treating the areas as territories of occupation and conquest, and arrogating to themselves preferential landholdings and irrigation channels. Although the French Protectorate and post-independence Moroccan state authorities forced the sedentarisation of transhumant peoples, Imazighen still uphold their pastoral ancestry (*asl*) as central to their family honour and local prestige and point to those few remaining nomadic groups as the bearers of authentic Berber culture.[6] Mobility remains central to oasis residents' self-conception as autonomous from the control of the central state (*makhzen*).

In particular, southeastern Moroccan oasis Imazighen (particularly Ait 'Atta and Ait Merghad) contrast their historical mobility to the relative immobility of the darker-skinned *Haratin* (locally known as *Iqeblin*, *Assouqin*, or *Drawa*), the demographic majority of agricultural, artisanal, and ritual specialists who formerly sharecropped the lands of their Amazigh and sharif patrons. Among the other racialised prejudices that associate black bodies with animality to which they are subject, *Haratin* are reviled for their lack of *asl*, for being tied to the land in dependent relations, and for lacking an independent, honourable genealogy (Aouad-Badoual 2004, 340) constituted through war, religious study, pilgrimage, or other recordable deeds generally associated with travel.[7] At the same time, the Haratin's relative lack of arable land and irrigation made them particularly vulnerable to the periodic droughts and inter-tribal wars that racked the region. Haratin often had little choice but to respond to such upheavals with self-imposed exile, seeking refuge in a more stable ksour where they could ply their crafts and ritual specialties or where they could enter into a sharecropping relationship (*khamass*) with new landowners, working for daily meals and generally one-fifth of the annual harvest. This deracinated state of being tied to the land but not *of* the land – of lacking both freedom *of* and freedom *from* mobility – reinforced the Haratin's historical position at the bottom of the oasis ethnic hierarchy.[8]

Rural exodus

When the French military finally occupied the pre-Saharan oases of Morocco in the 1930s (a full 20 years after the establishment of the Protectorate in Rabat), they established a regime of 'control' (*contrôle*) according to a primary imperative of stability, if not fixity. They worked to 'pacify' the 'dissidence' (*siba'*) existing between the larger Ait 'Atta and Ait Yafelman tribal confederations that for three centuries had shifted ownership of the oases, displaced various peoples, and periodically threatened the makhzen. French Indigenous Affairs (AI) officers signed pacts with the Imazighen and shurfa recognising their local authority, officialising their land tenure, and appointing certain notables to permanent administrative functions as caïds (see Ensel 1999, 76; Herzenni 1990, 18).[9] In spite of their post-revolutionary ideology of republican equality and their subtle encouragement that Haratin should have some representation in the *jma'a*, the French administrators, prioritising local order, did not attempt to reform the oasis system of dependent sharecropping or challenge existing social hierarchies, thus effectively maintaining the subordinate status of the Harratin.[10] More generally, as Hammoudi (1970, 43) and Herzenni (1990, 18) have argued, these new modes of 'modern' governance had the overarching effect of 'individualising' or 'territorialising' each *ksar*, and of erecting administrative barriers to the various inter-regional migrations, commercial transactions, and matrimonial exchanges that had previously linked the various oasis valleys, mountain villages, and market towns across southeastern Morocco.

Yet, the French Protectorate simultaneously ushered in an unprecedented wave of mobility: the out-migration of oasis dwellers to the cities of northern Morocco and later to northern Europe that was ultimately glossed as a 'rural exodus'. As much as the Protectorate worked to settle oasis communities in their place, they also faced an increasingly desperate lack of available workforce in the factory farms, mines, industries, and expanding northern cities – a deficit which by the early 1930s, according to Salahdine (1986, 203–204), had become a 'nightmare' and 'psychotic obsession' for the colonial administration. This need was paralleled by, and sometimes in tension with, similar manpower shortages in the metropole before and after the Second World War, which was made all the more urgent by calls to replace foreign workers with subjects of the French Empire (Devillars 1952, 4; Salahdine 1986, 210).[11] Thus began a concerted effort of labour recruitment from the rural south, often through the intermediary of local AI officers and caïds, followed by the wartime requisitions of soldiers for the allied forces' Armée de l'Afrique. Recruiters particularly targeted Berber-speaking populations, as colonial ethnologists had consistently presented 'the Berbers' as more dependably laborious and more martially skilful than their 'Arab' neighbours (Lorcin 1995; Silverstein 2002).[12]

Charged with mobilising emigrant populations in their rural oasis districts (cercles), AI officers complained in their weekly reports and exit testimonies (consignes de poste) about their initial difficulties in convincing residents to embark on such expeditions. Imazighen and shurfa, in particular, were disinclined to engage in manual labour of any kind, and were further reluctant to leave for extended periods of time communities where they lived in relative comfort overseeing their agricultural patrimony. Furthermore, rumours circulated about poor labour and transport conditions, as well as about the use of North African troops as cannon fodder on the European front in the fight for a country that had so recently (and sometimes brutally) conquered them.[13]

Yet, by the mid-1940s these hesitations had been largely overcome, and Protectorate officials were congratulating themselves on their recruitment success. Writing in 1947, Capitaine Ruef, chief officer of the Bureau du Cercle des Ait-Morrhad based in Goulmima, praised his Berber charges for their 'loyalty' during the war: 'although having only laid down their arms [to the Protectorate] a short time before, [they] supplied a strong contingent of regular and supplementary forces and contributed spontaneously, and sometimes touchingly, to the financing of our national defense' (25). Ruef (1947, 16) similarly noted that, given recent droughts and outbreaks of bayoud, residents were increasingly seeking to supplement their household resources with seasonal labour migration to northern Morocco and French Algeria. Indeed, 'veritable colonies' of Ghérissois (Ahl Rheris) had formed in the Middle Atlas cities of Azrou, Khenifra, and Meknès, maintaining ties to the oasis through monetary remittances.[14] Baul (1944) made similar observations in the neighbouring Ferkla oasis where drought conditions (in large part due to over-pumping of aquifers) were more worrisome, estimating that 600–700 Ait Merghad migrated seasonally each year. After 1947, others from the region were recruited through the National Office of Immigration to work in the mines of northern France, joining the Sousi Berbers (Chleuhs) who had already established an overseas 'colony' there (Devillars 1952, 7–8, 29).[15] By 1960, the French traveller Joly (1960, 409) could describe the oasis countryside as a 'land of emigration'.

A second wave of migration from the region occurred in the 1960s and 1970s, bringing oasis residents to construction and mining jobs in northern Europe and the northern Moroccan boomtowns of the Rif. During this period, scholars commented that emigration from the region had 'reached such an extent that it is rare to find an oasis household that does not have at least one member working overseas sending back more or less substantial revenues' (Bencherifa 1993, 10). If most of Western Europe closed its doors to subsequent labour migration in the mid-1970s, clandestine migration continued apace, as did the more general movement to Moroccan cities given repeated drought conditions in the 1980s. Indeed, in that decade alone, emigration from the southeastern province of Errachidia doubled in scale (Azzi 1993, 127). Largely as a consequence of such a history of mobility, between 1936 and 1952 the urban population of Morocco doubled as a percentage of the total population (Salahdine 1986, 207). It further tripled between 1960 and 1982 (Fadloullah 1990, 77).

This radical acceleration of the scale of the 'exodus' derives in large part from a transformation in oasis habitus, as Sayad (1977) has beautifully demonstrated in the case of rural Algeria. The first generation of emigrants were effectively sent as representatives – as the 'delegated emissary' (Salahdine 1986, 221) – of their community (*qbila* or *taqbilt*), selected by their lineages for their unimpeachable moral uprightness. Their displacement was conceptualised as a pure pragmatic necessity and utterly temporary in duration; the expectation was that they would return to the oasis as soon as possible and resume their roles in the local generational and ethnic division of labour. Migration thus served as a means to reproduce the local community.[16]

But the experience abroad entailed a number of unintended consequences, including the spread of a new set of desires around consumption and living standards. Emigrants directed remittance monies to build new houses based in urban architectural styles outside of the walled ksour, often in emerging oasis town centres supplied with electricity and running water, or, alternately, in their fields or gardens that were increasingly less important for their daily subsistence. The resulting spatial dispersion contributed to the valorisation of migration among the younger generation, who viewed such movement as a means of household, rather than lineage, development.[17] For them, urban modernity was a desired good, not a moral pollutant – an attitude that perfectly dove-tailed with an emerging state development discourse that privileged the city as the locus *par excellence* for forging the new Moroccan nation. Male labour migrants in the 1960s and 1970s often left with their wives and children and thus had a much more attenuated relation with their natal villages.

In the contemporary period, this separation has continued apace and has motivated fears of the oases' cultural death. With high unemployment across Morocco and most international borders closed to labour migration, the new exodus is one of *harrag*, of a desperate individual flight towards a better life overseas, even at the expense of 'burning' one's connections to the 'home-land'.[18] Even those with relatively stable positions in their oasis communities are tempted by opportunities abroad, seeking some mythical 'Eldorado' elsewhere. In the early 2000s, two separate close acquaintances of mine in Goulmima – one Merghadi man, one Hartania woman – gave up permanent jobs as schoolteachers and broke off local marriage arrangements to take advantage of windfall US green cards they won in the lottery. However disrupting their departures were to their local kin networks, it was the rare residents like Ilaytmas/Harcherras who criticised their emigration. Indeed, one young man even recounted to me with some surprise that even *his own mother* was encouraging his *harrag*. Given such instances, it would be difficult to dispute the conclusion reached by Salahdine (1986, 221), three decades ago: 'From an agent of conservation of the *qbila* community, the Moroccan labour migrant was transformed into an agent of decomposition and dislocation'.

Nevertheless, the aforementioned modernisation narrative – of a teleological evolution from homeland tradition to diasporic modernity – fails to account for the varied ways differently situated ethnic communities in the oasis approached and conceptualised mobility, and the divergent effects such mobility had on their relative social standing. In general, the Haratin initially took greater advantage of the new opportunities arising from labour migration than either shurfa or Imazighen. Lacking in property and accustomed to manual labour, Haratin sharecroppers were the first to welcome the possibility of earning wages abroad (see Bisson and Jarir 1986, 341; Ilahiane 2001; Naciri 1986, 359; Pascon and Ennaji 1986, 71). As Petit and the Castet-Baron concluded in their 1954 intelligence report on the *exode rural*,

> It is obviously the non-owners, the economically weak, the agricultural workers without title, the *khamass* who supplied the greatest part of the rural exodus. One can even say that in certain regions with a high percentage of emigration ... the *khamass* are disappearing (22).

Working in occupations that paralleled their labour specialisations in the oases – as water-carriers, tanners, butchers, cultivators, and construction workers – Haratin men moved in large numbers throughout the 1940s, particularly to Casablanca where they established a semi-permanent community.[19] Although subject to a certain amount of racism, they nonetheless enjoyed a relative social equality not present in the oases, no longer having to defer to either the shurfa or their former Imazighen patrons (Ensel 1999, 76–78, 157–159). To a great extent, it was the visible financial and social gains of these early migrants that encouraged other local ethnic groups to subsequently follow suit.

Moreover, the emigration of Haratine, Imazighen, and shurfa diverged not only in timing, but also in trajectory. If shurfa primarily re-traced the commercial routes of their forebears, the Imazighen's increasing mobility in the 1960s and 1970s was largely mediated by opportunities for advancement in the post-independence Moroccan military, state administration, and national education system. Already the privileged targets for recruitment into French army (because of their presumed martial character) and benefiting disproportionately from colonial educational opportunities (because of their superior social status in the oasis), Imazighen were well situated for postings and advancement in the Moroccan state services.[20] Indeed, throughout this period the children of Berber notables in the region achieved remarkable success in the national high school examination and gained admission to top university programmes in engineering, public administration, and other technocratic fields. They were subsequently posted to administrative centres in Rabat or Casablanca – or army bases also primarily in the north of the country – where they settled and raised their families. While many did continue to provide financial aid to family members remaining in the oases, their relationship – as Ilaytmas/Harcherras bemoaned in his poetic open letter to diasporic Ghérissois – often became largely symbolic, returning infrequently for holiday vacations, family occasions, or their own burial.

In contrast, Haratin emigrants across generations maintained closer ties to the oasis and were able to translate their accumulation of migrant economic capital into local social and political capital – what many have characterised as a veritable 'emancipation' (Herzenni 1990, 14). Ilahiane (2001) has ethnographically described this process in some detail for the Ziz valley, showing how Haratin used emigrant remittances to purchase land from Imazighen and shurfa elites and, in doing so, established both symbolic asl and local prestige. Others have described a similar trajectory for the Tafilalelt (Bisson and Jarir 1986) and the surrounding valleys of the Dra'a (Bahani 1994; Hammoudi 1970), the Ferkla (Naciri 1986), the Todrha (Büchner 1990), and in Tata (Herzenni 1990). They note that while these land purchases permitted the construction of new houses outside the overpopulated and deteriorating ksour, they did not necessarily entail the fragmentation of Haratin social cohesion as a modernisation narrative would predict. Indeed, if anything, these developments actually helped produce a Haratin 'sense of community' and 'ethnic consciousness' (Ilahiane 2001, 383–384). Overall, Haratin social mobility constituted an 'overturning' (*bouleversement*) of traditional hierarchies inscribed in spatial, agricultural, and irrigation structures and premised on Haratin marginalisation (Aït Hamza 1999, 153), with a new oasis social organisation based in class coming to replace that previously based in ethnicity (Büchner 1990, 31).

In Goulmima where I have pursued anthropological research on and off for the past decade, this transformation in the local political ecology is manifest. Already in 1947 the local AI officer Ruef predicted that the times were changing and that the dominance of the Ait Merghad was approaching its term limit. 'The harder-working Haratine are bit by bit buying back the lands that the Ait-Morrhad [*sic*] had usurped from them, and they will end up constituting an aristocracy of money that will replace the aristocracy of race' (6). By 1950 this situation had emboldened Haratin to make increasing demands for political representation. An AI officer based in the provincial capital of Ksar-es-Souk noted that, 'the Haratine are returning from Algeria and the Gharb [the northern Moroccan plains] with a more apparent spirit of resistance (*esprit revendicateur*) than previously. Increasingly they express the need to break off the shackles of their former masters'.[21] In April of that year Haratin gained direct political representation in the jma'a of the Igoulmimin ighrem – the central ksar where Ait Merghad and Haratin cohabited in Goulmima – and in the ensuing months they demanded a similar reform in the ksour in the adjacent Ferkla valley. Finally, with the 1962 Moroccan constitution, the Haratin were finally granted full political rights as citizens of the independent Moroccan state.

In subsequent years, the return of Haratin (Iqeblin) emigrants and the continued out-migration of Ait Merghad men and women further tipped the demographic balance in the Ghéris valley in favour of the Iqeblin, with Ait Merghad never constituting more than 20% of the local population. Increasingly, local politics has become a 'black' and 'white' affair, with elections contested by candidates and populations that are racially defined, and Ait Merghad and Iqeblin occupying parallel positions in all matters of local authority. The state-appointed position of *moqaddem*, formerly reserved for the Ait Merghad, now has been doubled to include both an Aqebli and a Merghadi, as has the position of irrigation overseer (*amghar n wemman*), previously the exclusive province of the Iqeblin. Iqeblin are likewise increasingly elected to important positions in the local administration. In the late 1990s, a returned emigrant from Holland – who had lost his hand in an industrial accident and continued to collect compensation from his former employer – further enriched himself through land speculation and began to achieve political influence in the region. He was subsequently elected vice-president of Goulmima's municipal council, unseating a long-time Merghadi politician from a large landowning, notable family.[22] In this capacity, he directed public works projects that Merghadi critics condemned as advancing sectarian Iqeblin interests, including projects which challenged the Ait Merghad's exclusive claim to large sections of tribal land on the outskirts of Goulmima.[23]

This political transformation of the Ghéris has provoked widespread resentment among the local Ait Merghad. Many Ait Merghad, like the Ait 'Atta in the neighbouring Ziz valley (Ilahiane 2001, 386–389), are nostalgic for an 'old order' of pastoral honour and moral rectitude. Hamed, a Merghadi interviewee who bemoaned what he saw as an increasing number of thefts in the oasis, which he attributed to Iqeblin youth, recounted the former social control exerted by Ait Merghad elders, and particularly by his own father who had been *shaykh* of the lower valley under the French Protectorate. In Hamed's retelling, his father spent his days sitting in the plaza in front of the entrance to the ighrem, surveying the various comings and goings of its inhabitants. In one instance, he saw a woman entering the ksar carrying a water jug, stopped her, and interrogated its contents. Upon further inspection, he discovered that, as he had suspected – as he had not seen any water spill over when the woman had been walking – the jug contained not water, but recently picked dates. In so far as he knew that the woman's household did not own sufficient palm trees to fill such a jug, he immediately recognised that they had been stolen, confiscated them, and reported her to the jma'a for judgement. Such instances earned the shaykh a feared reputation of incorruptibility, if not omniscience, and, according to Hamed, kept the oasis community safe and secure – a state Hamed now fears is absent with the most talented and trusted Ait Merghad young men leaving the community to Iqeblin oversight.[24]

While the older generation of Iqeblin respect the memory of former Ait Merghad notables and warmly greet Hamed across the oasis, younger Iqeblin are more than happy to have escaped what they see as the petty tyranny of Ait Merghad 'big men'. They further distrust Hamed, Harcherras, and other Amazigh activists whom they accuse of trafficking in Berber culture to support narrow Ait Merghad tribalism. 'You can't trust them, Paul', one Aqebli woman, Latifa, who worked for a local non-governmental organisation (NGO) providing literacy education to impoverished women, explained to me. 'They are foxes (uccen). They talk about culture and community, but they only care about themselves. It is they who walk in a zigzag, saying one thing, doing another.' Other educated Aqebli women like Latifa were active in grassroots development efforts, and still other Iqeblin had become adepts of new Islamic piety movements that had spread across the oasis. They took the increase in the number and public presence of mosques in the oasis as a sign of a new democratic morality, and in general they were optimistic about the future.[25]

In contrast, some Ait Merghad interlocutors view such new equality as little more than social disorganisation. They deride Iqeblin for betraying their cultural heritage, for neglecting their maternal language Tamazight for the Arabic colloquial (darija) picked up on city streets, and for importing a foreign Islamist political ideology to an oasis traditionally marked by various non-orthodox – even pagan – religious practices, if not by an incipient secularism.[26] Drawing on a racist discourse, some compare Iqeblin to flies (izzen) and resent them for over-reproducing, for filling the oasis with black bodies. One Merghadi, Moha, even projected a dystopian future: 'Paul, if you were to return to Goulmima in 100 years, you wouldn't find a single Merghadi. Only Iqeblin. It's a fact of nature. The blacks are simply more suited to this climate'. For Ait Merghad like Moha, it is not simply a Merghadi presence that is dying in the Ghéris valley, but the Berber culture as a whole.

It is in this context of racialised tensions that one needs to interpret Ilaytmas/Harcherras's poetic jeremiad. For, at first blush, it would appear ludicrous to project the Ghéris tamazirt as a 'cemetery'. The valley's overall population has continued to expand in spite of a seemingly endless stream of emigration. Agriculture has prospered since independence, with the palm forest growing in both density and expanse, both intensively and extensively. Even the left bank of the Ghéris arroyo (asif), formerly cultivated only in times of extensive winter rainfall, has greened with an intricate irrigation canal system of its own. And more and more of the surrounding desert steppe is now gridded with electrified homes – veritable mini-boomtowns built on the ksour's parcelled collective lands and financed primarily with emigrant remittances. Emigration, rather than leading to social death, has been the very motor of the oasis marked fecundity. As Bencherifa and Popp (1990, 47) have similarly noted regarding Figuig:

> [Migration] does not lead automatically to the decline and degradation of an irrigation-based agricultural economy. Curiously, one could even claim that external resources have created the conditions for the persistence of the oasis and today contribute directly to its resuscitation and renewal.

Indeed, the only place in the Ghéris where such renewal is not as evident is in the Ait Merghad dominated Igoumimin sector. There, in spite of the investment of disproportionate state and NGO monies to transform the ighrem into a tourist destination, development appears to have stagnated. Unlike other local ksour, political infighting in the Igoulmimin jma'a has precluded any segmentation of its collective land, and, as a result, new homes have been built in the surrounding fields and gardens. Other parcels of cultivatable land have been sold (mostly to Iqeblin, but also to new immigrants from the surrounding mountain villages) to finance marriage or emigration projects, and still others have been abandoned by emigrants without resident kin to tend them. And more and more Ait Merghad leave every year to work or marry abroad, often on a seemingly permanent basis. Indeed, very few of the Ait Merghad I first met in Goulmima in 2001 continue to reside there; I am more likely to meet them in Ouarzazate, Rabat, Paris, Roubaix, or New York. It is to this specifically Merghadi diaspora that Ilaytmas/Harcherras' poem is addressed; the tamazirt in question is predefined as a Berber homeland, with the Igoulmimin ighrem experience taken as a synecdoche for the fate of the Ghéris valley as a whole. In this poetic logic, the mobility of the Ait Merghad is equated with the immobility, if not death, of local Berber culture more broadly.

Diasporic politics

Beyond its clear ethnic slant, there is something similarly deceptive about the poem's apocalyptic imagery. The very projection of tamazirt, and Berber culture more broadly, as an endangered good is neither self-evident nor historically given. In the past, the fertility of tamazirt as soil did always require hard labour, ritual intervention, and a certain amount of God-given luck; and the defence of tamazirt as patrimonial property did always necessitate armed vigilance, tribal alliances, legal contracts, and matrimonial strategies. In each of these cases, the loss of able-bodied men did indeed risk the durability and productivity of tamazirt as a material resource. Yet, at least until the arrival of the French, drought and displacement were frequent occurrences in the region, and neither necessarily resulted in wider social death. At most, people feared for the reproduction of a given patrilineage or tribal segment; more often, concerns were for a single household.

However, in the present condition of mass 'rural exodus', linguistic and cultural Arabisation, and global communication, tamazirt has taken on wider significance, standing in for a wider set of intangible cultural values and ways of life. Hoffman (2002, 940) has discussed the role of urban migrants in nostalgically objectifying the village land, 'turning tamazirt into a discursive construction as much as a geographical location'. Furthermore, university-educated Amazigh activists such as Harcherras now link their nostalgia for the cultivation of a tamazirt past to a larger transnational discourse on the rights of autochthonous peoples, and defend Berber language, culture, and *territory* as endangered global goods. In recent years they have founded autonomy movements across peripheral regions of the country that advocate for local (read Amazigh) control over land, water, and other natural resources. In demonstrations, marches, and sit-ins across the southeastern oases, the militants have declared that 'Tamazight = Tamazirt', that Berber language/culture and land are commensurable and fungible attributes for which they must struggle. In this larger ethno-nationalist struggle, the diaspora takes on unprecedented importance as a source of a material and symbolic support, a wellspring of ideas, and an intermediary to key supranational institutions such as UNESCO and the European Parliament.

The diaspora's role in the development of nationalism in North Africa is well known. Some of the earliest Algerian independence movements arose among Algerian immigrants in France, and throughout the 1954–62 war of national liberation the diaspora remained an important site for recruitment, fundraising, and lobbying (Haroun 1992; Stora 1991). Moroccan nationalist ideology, if vastly different in its content, followed a similar trajectory, flowing from circles of 'evolved' students and urban elites (*les évolués*) in Fez and Paris to the rural margins of the country where the wars of resistance to the French 'pacification' campaigns were a living memory and open wound. AI officers stationed in the southeastern oases remarked that the spread of nationalism to the area in the 1950s was mediated in large part by seasonal workers to urban areas in the north of the country.[27] Ait Merghad in Goulmima, for instance, came under suspicion because of their close ties to the diaspora in Azrou and Khenifra.[28] Battalion Commander Jouandon (1954, 3) tried to defend his Ghéris charges, but similarly noted the diaspora as a hotbed of political activism.

> If in the Ghéris ... nationalism does not seem to have an audience, it is no less true that it is from within the numerous colonies of Ait Ghéris ... that the principal leaders of the Middle Atlas [nationalist] cells are recruited.

He further feared the potential influence that repatriated political prisoners from the diaspora might have in the oases. Although the oasis populations only ended up contributing minimally to the nationalist movement, the Ait Merghad 'resistance' remains the source of great nostalgia for local Amazigh activists, as was the later role of Ghérissois in the post-independence Addi ou Bihi revolt of 1956 and the attempted coup d'état of 1973.[29]

This continued self-identification of the southeastern oases with their prior status as a *bled essiba'* (land of dissidence) has likewise underwritten the expansion of the institutions of civil society in the region over the past thirty years. In the early 2000s, Goulmima hosted two grassroots development organisations, two human rights associations, one women's group, and one large Berber cultural association.[30] Surrounding towns and villages, if not perhaps as well endowed, each have minimally one Amazigh and one development association. Goulmima's Amazigh cultural association, Tilelli, is one of the oldest and most outspoken in the country, existing since 1991 at a time when public expressions of Berber language and culture were subject to heavy state surveillance. In 1994, seven members of the association were arrested and imprisoned for up to one month for having unfurled a banner written in the Berbero-Libyan script Tifinagh at a May Day march in neighbouring Errachidia. Their detention provoked international outcry that forced the hand of the Moroccan state to take steps towards officially recognising Berber culture as part of its national patrimony. In 1997, four of the fifteen members of the Moroccan delegation to the first World Amazigh Congress held in the Canary Islands originated from Goulmima. Because of this history of militancy, Goulmima has become a veritable site of pilgrimage for Amazigh activists from around the world.

Yet, the Berber cultural movement did not spring fully formed from the oasis tamazirt. If Ait Merghad activists have played an important role in Amazigh militancy at the national and transnational scales, this role has been largely mediated by their experiences outside of the Ghéris. As in the history of Moroccan nationalism, university students and urban cultural elites were at the forefront of the development of a Berber culturalist ideology. In the late 1960s, groups of Rabat-based students from the southeastern oases and the Sous valley founded cultural associations dedicated to collecting Berber oral folk tales, music, and poetry and transcribing them in Arabic and Latin scripts. They also worked to standardise Berber's orthography and syntax, creating a standard Tamazight from the three major dialects and multiple local variants.[31] This work paralleled similar efforts occurring within the Algerian diaspora in France, where expatriate Kabyle intellectuals and immigrant workers united in the promotion of Berber culture (Dirèche-Slimani 1997; Silverstein 2003). In the meantime, the younger brothers and sisters of these initial Moroccan Berber activists were being politicised as student unionists in the Marxist Qa'idiyyin movement, advocating democratic reforms and fighting a nascent Islamism on university campuses in Fez, Meknès, and Marrakech throughout the 1970s and 1980s.

It was among the Qa'idiyyin that the Amazigh question was first explicitly politicised, and those activists later returned to their hometowns to found local associations such as Tilelli. Subsequently, Berber student activists broke from the Qa'idiyyin and founded their own Amazigh Cultural Movement (MCA) union, lambasting their former comrades for being 'Arab nationalists' and 'Ba'athists'. The leadership of the MCA has been consistently from the southeastern oases. In 2003 and again in 2007, the MCA and the Qa'idiyyin battled for control of southern university campuses, leaving at least one militant dead and many seriously injured. Veterans of these struggles have been at the forefront of new calls for regional autonomy in the pre-Sahara.[32]

In other words, the very premise of tamazirt as Berber cultural patrimony at risk that motivates Ilaytmas/Harcherras' jeremiad was developed in diasporic settings and urban university campuses, in dialogue with transnational movements that united Berber speakers across the world to various other indigenous peoples' advocacy groups. Ironically, emigration is thus, in Amazigh discourse, both a primary cause of cultural deracination and the condition of possibility for realising that cultural deracination is a problem in the first place. Moreover, the diaspora is clearly part of the solution. Beyond the investments of money and bodies that Ilaytmas/Harcherras call for, the diaspora is a vital resource of social connectivity upon which Ghéris activists frequently call. In addition to posting messages on international Internet forums such as www. mondeberbere.com and www.kabyle.com, they promote local causes by sending communiqués to national newspapers, calling upon personal connections to oasis natives working as journalists in Rabat – journalists who sometimes double as Internet site managers and bloggers.

Likewise, oasis activists call on similar diasporic connections for the occasional political fix. In 2004, five local Ait Merghad activists in Goulmima were threatened with prosecution for staging an illegal sit-in on a parcel of collective land that the provincial governor had hoped to offer as compensation to a service station owner whose business had been threatened by a recent public works project (see Silverstein 2010). At first the activists used the prosecution as a forum to publicise their demands, but they soon realised that the prosecutors had compiled an extensive dossier of past violations that, at least in the case of one militant, would have resulted in a lengthy prison term. The activists contacted a former Goulmima comrade living in Rabat who worked for a very powerful and well-connected politician who was a native of the same southeastern oasis where the prosecuting governor was based, and next in line to become the *wali* of the larger region that included the governor's province. Drawing on such connections and a history of favours made and received, the politician (at least in the activists' recounting) imposed on the governor to drop the case and to find another means to compensate the service station owner. In this case at least, the diaspora arguably proved to be the saviour of tamazirt as local Berber (read Ait Merghad) patrimony. The diasporic sons of the Ghéris had performed their filial duty.

Conclusion: Tamazirt, the Diaspora, and the nation

None of which should minimise the urgency or evocative force of Ilaytmas/Harcherras' plea. The majority of Ghérissois – at least the majority of Ait Merghad from the Ghéris – in the diaspora have not expended economic or political capital for the betterment of tamazirt in any collective sense. The erosion of fields, desertification of public spaces, and mushrooming of cheaply constructed cement houses in what were once verdant gardens around the Igoulmimin ighrem do remind one of a cemetery, especially when contrasted with the prosperity of the oasis palm forest around other neighbouring ksour. But Berber culture cannot be equated with some Ait Merghad pastoral past; the genius of Amazigh activists today is their recognition that Berber culture crosses tribal and even national lines. These young men and women rediscover lines of migration, interaction, and exchange that for centuries connected darker-skinned Touareg desert nomads with the red-haired Kabyle seafarers on the Mediterranean coast via the pre-Saharan oases and various Berber mountain villages. This mobility was productive of a richness of language, craft, music, and religious practices, different versions of which are shared by Imazighen, shurfa, and Haratin alike. And today's diasporic experience only widens the richness of oasis culture, bringing Arab, French, and even North American elements into the mix. Some qualities of unity are lost, surely, but many others are gained, and the tamazirt is arguably the better for it.

While the aforementioned narrative has focused exclusively on a narrow band of one region of Morocco, the story is by no means unique. There is likely an Ilaytmas for every area that has experienced a pronounced 'rural exodus' and a 'globalisation' of its local culture, whether in Morocco or elsewhere. Indeed, Morocco as a national whole seems to be in a similar predicament as the Ghéris. With skyrocketing unemployment, overpopulated cities, and environmental neglect, harrag has become popularly decried as a national problem of epidemic proportions. While for decades emigration functioned as a propitious economic and political safety valve to siphon off the disaffected, regulate the domestic labour market, and balance trade deficits with remittances (Brand 2006, 59–69), now Morocco is called upon by the European Union to police its borders and keep potential emigrants at home. Fearing a deluge not only of Moroccans but also of sub-Saharan Africans transmigrating through Morocco, the EU has effectively sought to offshore its immigration controls to North Africa in exchange for development euros and preferential trade pacts. With African asylum seekers now blocked at the Mediterranean shore, Morocco has become a country of immigration, not just of emigration (de Haas 2005; Lahlou 2004, 115). Certain neighbourhoods in Rabat, such as Ettakdoum and Youssoufia, have become increasingly populated by immigrants from sub-Saharan Africa, and, like in the Ghéris, one now hears expressed apocalyptic racist fears of the blackening of Morocco.

In this context, the Moroccan state has explicitly reached out to its diaspora. After many hesitant attempts to grant overseas Moroccans some direct mode of political participation (Brand 2006, 74–80), the state has recently created a ministry devoted to the Moroccan Community Abroad (MCE), as well as a council of notable Moroccan emigrants from across the world designed to represent the community's interests. The government additionally sponsors foundations and associations to provide consular services, language education, religious training, and cultural programming for the diaspora.[33] These ties were enshrined in the new 2011 national constitution that explicitly promised to reinforce the MCE's 'contribution to the development of their homeland (*patrie*)' (Articles 16–18). To a certain extent, this explicit outreach derives from security concerns over the growth of Islamist militancy in the Moroccan diaspora at a time when Morocco's geopolitical status is dependent on its identity as a moderate Muslim country. But there is a larger concern about the future of the nation as a viable economic and cultural space. Much as in the Ghéris, the national *tamazirt* needs the diaspora, just as the diaspora needs the nation. Notwithstanding the EU's fantasies of constructing a hermetic border on the southern shore of the Mediterranean, Europe and Morocco are already interpenetrated by a history of migratory, ideological, and economic exchanges. It is Europe, as much as Ilaytmas, that ultimately fears Morocco becoming a cemetery.

Acknowledgements

Earlier versions of this article were presented at research workshops at the University of Florida and the University of Minnesota. The author wishes to particularly thank Hakim Abderrezak, Aomar Boum, Greg

Feldman, Patricia Lorcin, Laurie McIntosh, Ayse Parla, Esther Romeyn, Daniel Schroeter, and Maria Stoilkova for their generous welcome, engagement, and comments.

Funding

This work was supported by research grants from the United States Institute of Peace, the Fulbright-Hays Faculty Research Abroad Program, and the Carnegie Corporation of New York.

Notes

1. For an ethnographically nuanced discussion of the gendered construction of the *tamazirt* in the Moroccan Anti-Atlas through men's migration and nostalgia, and women's dwelling and hard labour, see Hoffman (2002). In this essay, I complement her important work by exploring how the dialectical production of homeland and diaspora as interdependently moral places operates in and through ethnic stratification and conflict.
2. In High Atlas villages from which young women are regularly sent to Marrakech or Agadir to work as domestic servants (*petites bonnes*) for bourgeois families, the city is popularly referenced as a 'cemetery' (*lmedint*) (Crawford 2008, 174).
3. The Moroccan and Spanish media regularly report on migrant bodies that wash up on the beaches.
4. For ethnographic discussions of *harrag*, see Fernandez (1999) and Pandolfo (2007).
5. The intimate relationship between travel, religious education, and sainthood in North Africa has been much studied. See Clancy-Smith (1990), Evans-Pritchard (1949), and Gellner (1969) for the history of development of several important *zawiyat* in relation to learned migration. See also Eickelman (1985) for a discussion of Moroccan notable education in relation to rural–urban movement.
6. See Skounti (1995) on questions of transhumance and Berber identity.
7. Ilahiane (2001, 382) lists five negative attributes imputed to Haratine in the southeastern Zis valley: dark skin colour, landlessness, obtuseness, clientage, and laboriousness.
8. See Aouad-Badoual (2004, 352) and Ensel (1999, 25–26) for discussions of Drawi deracination and dependence.
9. The caïd function contrasted directly with a previous system of local authority based in a village assembly (*jma'a* or *taqbilt*) of lineage elders who elected an annual leader (*amghar*), a position that rotated among the tribal fractions represented in the ksar.
10. The legitimacy of Haratin property ownership in the oases was gradually recognised by the dominant tribal groups, as was their eventual representation in the *jma'at* of the various ksour where they resided. Yet, as Salahdine (1986, 225–226) has emphasised, citing official texts from the Résidence Générale in Rabat, the Protectorate supported the khmass system in the name of stability (cf. Petit and Castet-Baron 1954, 22–23). Indeed, the French rural administration continued to forcibly extract Haratine corvée labour for public works projects (Ilahiane 2001, 389).
11. A royal decree (*dahir*) of 27 October 1931, enacted in the midst of an economic crisis, eugenic anxieties over the weakening of the French race, and fears of Protectorate officials losing its workforce to the metropole, required overseas emigration candidates to compile a dossier of six forms obtained from five different administrations: a passport, work contract, identity card, anthropometric data card, medical certificate, and a deposit receipt to the cover the costs of the emigrant's repatriation. Attempts to reform this *dahir* and simplify the process failed, and as a result the vast majority of emigration to France during the Protectorate occurred without authorisation (Devillars 1952, 3–4).
12. Indeed, the original North African immigrants to France were recruited from Berber-speaking regions, particularly Algerian Kabylia and the Moroccan Sous valley, and these populations still remain over-represented in the metropole. Of the approximately 19,000 Moroccans in France in 1952, as many as 13,000 were from the Sous (Devillars 1952, 19). See Dirèche-Slimani (1997), Khellil (1979), Sayad (1977, 1994), and Silverstein (2004) for more recent histories of this immigration. The 2006 film *Indigènes* (*Days of Glory*) includes a felicitous sequence where Berber Ait Segrouchen tribesmen are recruited on the basis of the fact that they were the 'fiercest' fighters during the recently concluded wars of 'pacification'.
13. Rapport Trimestriel, Bureau Régional de Territoire de Tafilalet, 4e trimester, 1939 (No. 256 A.I.T.), 2 (unsigned). CADN Meknès, 215.
14. These 'colonies' notably included shurfa who left to become shopkeepers (Jouandon 1954, 10).

15. The first recruitments of temporary workers for France in the southeastern oases actually began in 1938 and met with some success in Goulmima and Erfoud, where 'the numbers of volunteers exceeded expectations.' Bertot, Rapport Trimestriel, Bureau Regional de Territoire du Tafilalet, 2e trimester, 1938, 1. CADN Meknès 215. However, such labour recruitment was quickly interrupted by the war.

16. Crawford (2008, 145–174) makes a similar point in his nuanced discussion of the role of urban labour migration in the maintenance of 'articulated' household economies in a Berber High Atlas village.

17. For a parallel discussion of this process in the anti-Atlas, see Alahyane (1990).

18. In 2003, the most popular song on the Moroccan airwaves was entitled '[Give me a] Visa or Passport' by chaâbi singer Abdelaziz Stati.

19. By 1950, 13% of the total number of immigrants to Casablanca were Haratin from the southeastern oasis (Aouad-Badoual 2004, 352), a figure massively out of proportion with their general representation in the Moroccan population.

20. On the colonial education of rural Berber notables, see Benhlal (2005), Bidwell (1973, 237–257), Eickelman (1985), and Leveau (1985, 172–193).

21. Bulletin de Renseignements Poliqtiques (Tafilalet), 20 nov. – 5 déc. 1950 (No. 893 AITC/2). CADN Meknès, 217.

22. The Merghadi's father had previously served as caïd from 1946 until the end of the Protectorate.

23. See Silverstein (2010) for a discussion of one such project involving the sale of 5 hectares of arid collective land to a non-Merghadi for the construction of a tourist complex.

24. The shaykh also established the equivalent of a lost-and-found box in the ighrem where even the smallest piece of firewood dropped in public spaces would be deposited. Compare to Ensel (1999, 187–190), his discussion of the Shurfa discourse of *adab* (civility) and their judgement of the Drawa's contrasting 'zigzag behaviour.'

25. For parallel Haratin future-oriented narratives, see Ilahiane (2001, 391).

26. On the Amazigh discourse on Berber traditional religiosity and secularism, see Ben Layashi (2007) and Silverstein (2012).

27. See 'Bulletin fin d'année du Territoire du Tafilalet' (signed Parlance), 25 Feb. 1955, 2. CADN Meknès, 108.

28. Communiqué from Général de Division Miguel, Chef de Meknès, No. 104, 6 Dec. 1954. CADN Meknès, 286bis.

29. On the political situation in the southeastern oases in the immediate wake of independence, see Leveau (1985). On the role of Goulmima in the 1973 coup attempt, see Bennouna (2002). For a beautiful, fictionalised account of the ambivalent reception of nationalism in the southeastern oases (Ferkla), see Layid (1992).

30. Goulmima is also the site of a disproportionate number of security installations, including a municipal police force, a large gendarmerie, a battalion of rapid response troops (*groupes mobiles*), a (now largely abandoned) army base, and a hilltop radar station.

31. For a history of the Berber cultural movement in Morocco, see Aourid (1999), Maddy-Weitzman (2012), and Pouessel (2010).

32. For a more detailed history of Amazigh activism in Goulmima, in all its scalar dimensions, see Silverstein (2013).

33. For an overview of these various institutions and services, see the website of the Moroccan ministry, 'Moroccans of the World,' http://www.marocainsdumonde.gov.ma/index.php?option=com_frontpage&Itemid=52

References

CADN = Centre des Archives Diplomatiques de Nantes.

Aït Hamza, Mohamed. 1999. "Migration et dynamique de l'espace local: Bouteghrar (versant Sud du Haut Atlas central)." In *Migrations internationales entre le Maghreb et l'Europe*, edited by Mohamed Berriane and Herbert Popp, 147–158. Série: Colloques et Seminaires 75. Rabat: Université Mohamed V.

Alahyane, Mohamed. 1990. "Le processus de mutation à Lakhsas, Anti-Atlas occidental." In *La Culture populaire*, 37–48. Rabat: Manshur al-'Ukaz.

Aouad-Badoual, Rita. 2004. "'Esclavage' et situation des 'noirs' au Maroc dans la première moitié du XXe siècle." In *Les Relations transsahariennes à l'époque contemporaine*, edited by Laurence Marfaing and Steffen Wippel, 337–360. Paris: Karthala.

Aourid, Hassan. 1999. "Le Substrat culturel des mouvements de contestation au Maroc. Analyse des discours islamiste et amazighe." PhD diss., Université Mohamed V (Rabat-Agdal).

Azzi, Hrou. 1993. "Enclavement et developpement dans la province d'Errachadia." In *Espace et société dans les oasis marocaines*, Série Colloques 6, 117–133. Meknès: Université Moulay Ismail.

Bahani, Abdelkbir. 1994. "La crise des structures socio-économiques dans les palmeraies du Drâa – Maroc." In *Mutations socio-spatiales dans les campagnes marocaines*, edited by Abdellatif Bencherifa and Mohamed Aït Hamza, 37–51. Série: Colloques et Seminaires 28. Rabat: Université Mohamed V.

Baul, Capt. 1944. Tribus des Ait Morrhad de Ferkla, June 1. CADN Meknès, 75.

Bencherifa, Abdellatif. 1993. "Notes sur les systèmes hydroagricoles oasiens et leurs changements récents." In *Espace et société dans les oasis marocaines*. Série Colloques 6, 5–19. Meknès: Université Moulay Ismail.

Bencherifa, Abdellatif, and Herbert Popp. 1990. "L'économie oasienne de Figuig entre la tradition et le changement." In *Le Maroc: espace et société*, edited by Abdellatif Bencherifa and Herbert Popp, 37–48. Passau: Passavia Universitäts-verlag.

Benhlal, Mohamed. 2005. *Le Collège d'Azrou: Une élite berbère civile et militaire au Maroc (1927–1959)*. Paris: Karthala.

Ben Layashi, Samir. 2007. "Secularism in Moroccan Amazigh Discourse." *Journal of North African Studies* 12 (2): 153–171.

Bennouna, Mehdi. 2002. *Héros sans gloire. Echec d'une révolution, 1963–1973*. Casablanca: Tarik Editions.

Bidwell, Robin. 1973. *Morocco under Colonial Rule: French Administration of Tribal Areas, 1912–1956*. London: Frank Cass.

Bisson, Jean, and Mohamed Jarir. 1986. "Ksour du Gourara et du Tafilelt. De l'ouverture de la société oasienne à la fermeture de la maison." *Annuaire de l'Afrique du Nord* 25: 331–345.

Brand, Laurie. 2006. *Citizens Abroad: Emigration and the State in the Middle East and North Africa*. Cambridge: Cambridge University Press.

Büchner, Hans-Joachim. 1990. "Types récents d'habitat oasien en remplacent du qsar. Observations sur les modalités de constitution spontanée des nouveaux villages chez les Ahl Todrha (Sud marocain)." In *Le Maroc: espace et société*, edited by Abdellatif Bencherifa and Herbert Popp, 23–36. Passau: Passavia Universitätsverlag.

Clancy-Smith, Julia. 1990. "Between Cairo and the Algerian Kabylia: The Rahmaniyya *Tariqa*, 1715–1800." In *Muslim Travellers: Pilgrimage, Migration, and the Religious Imagination*, edited by Dale Eickelman and James Piscatori, 200–216. Berkeley: University of California Press.

Crawford, David. 2008. *Moroccan Household in the World Economy: Labor and Inequality in a Berber Village*. Baton Rouge: LSU Press.

Devillars, Commandant Pierre. 1952. *L'Immigration Marocaine en France*. Mission Report to the Direction des Offices du Maroc, Rabat. CADN DAI 448.

Dirèche-Slimani, Karima. 1997. *Histoire de l'émigration kabyle en France au XXe siècle*. Paris: Harmattan.

Eickelman, Dale. 1985. *Knowledge and Power in Morocco: The Education of a Twentieth-Century Notable*. Princeton, NJ: Princeton University Press.

Ensel, Remco. 1999. *Saints and Servants in Southern Morocco*. Leiden: Brill.

Evans-Pritchard, E. E. 1949. *The Sanusi of Cyrenaica*. Oxford: Clarendon Press.

Fadloullah, Abdellatif. 1990. "Evolution récente de la population et du peuplement au Maroc." In *Le Maroc: espace et société*, edited by Abdellatif Bencherifa and Herbert Popp, 75–84. Passau: Passavia Universitätsverlag.

Fall, Papa Demba. 2004. "Les Sénégalais au Maroc: histoire et anthropologie d'un espace migratoire." In *Les Relations transsahariennes à l'époque contemporaine*, edited by Laurence Marfaing and Steffen Wippel, 277–292. Paris: Karthala.

Fernandez, Jean. 1999. "Passages à Tanger." *Revue de Socio-Anthropologie* 6: 65–78.

Geertz, Clifford. 2000. *Local Knowledge*. New York: Basic Books.

Gellner, Ernest. 1969. *Saints of the Atlas*. London: Weidenfeld and Nicolson.

de Haas, Hein. 2005. "Morocco: From Emigration Country to Africa's Migration Passage to Europe." Country Profile Morocco. *Migration Information Source*, October. http://www.imi.ox.ac.uk/about-us/people/hein-de-haas#sthash.EMEwONg4.dpuf.

de Haas, Hein. 2006. "Migration, Remittances, and Regional Development in Morocco." *Geoforum* 37 (4): 565–580.

Hammoudi, Abdellah. 1970. "L'évolution de l'habitat dans la vallée du Draa." *Revue de Géographie du Maroc* 18: 33–45.

Hammoudi, Abdellah. 1997. *Master and Disciple: The Cultural Foundations of Moroccan Authoritarianism*. Chicago: University of Chicago Press.

Haroun, Ali. 1992. *Le Septième wilaya*. Paris: Seuil.

Herzenni, Abdellah. 1990. "Eléments de stratification sociale dans une oasis du Sud: Angherif, region de Tata." In *Le Maroc: espace et société*, edited by Abdellatif Bencherifa and Herbert Popp, 11–22. Passau: Passavia Universitätsverlag.

Hoffman, Katherine. 2002. "Moving and Dwelling: Building the Moroccan Ashelhi Homeland." *American Ethnologist* 29 (4): 928–962.

Ilahiane, Hsain. 2001. "The Social Mobility of the Haratine and the Re-Working of Bourdieu's *Habitus* on the Saharan Frontier, Morocco." *American Anthropologist* 103 (2): 380–394.

Joly, F. 1960. "Promenade dans les palmeraies et les oasis." *Confluent* 8 (June–July): 406–410.

Jouandon, Chef de Battalion. 1954. Consigne du Bureau de Cercle de Goulmima. June 17. CADN Meknès, 107.

Khellil, Mohand. 1979. *L'Exil kabyle*. Paris: Harmattan.

Lahlou, Mehdi. 2004. "Filières migratoires subsahariens vers l'Europe (via le Maghreb)." In *Les Relations transsahariennes à l'époque contemporaine*, edited by Laurence Marfaing and Steffen Wippel, 113–140. Paris: Karthala.

Layid, Moha. 1992. *Le Sacrifice des vaches noires*. Casablanca: Eddif.

Leveau, Rémy. 1985. *Le Fellah marocain, défenseur du trône*. 2nd ed. Paris: Presses de la Fondation Nationale des Sciences Politiques.

Lorcin, Patricia. 1995. *Imperial Identities. Stereotyping, Prejudice and Race in Colonial Algeria*. London: I.B. Tauris.

Maddy-Weitzman, Bruce. 2012. *The Berber Identity Movement and the Challenge to North African States*. Austin: University of Texas Press.

Naciri, Mohamed. 1986. "Les ksouriens sur la route. Emigration et mutation spatiale de l'habitat dans l'oasis de Tinjdad." *Annuaire de l'Afrique du Nord* 25: 347–364.

Pandolfo, Stefania. 2007. "'The Burning': Finitude and the Politico-theological Imagination of Illegal Migration." *Anthropological Theory* 7 (3): 329–363.

Pascon, Paul, and Mohammed Ennaji. 1986. *Les Paysans sans terre au Maroc*. Casablanca: Editions Toubkal.

Petit, J. C., and Commandant Castet-Baron. 1954. *Contribution à l'étude des mouvements de la population marocaine musulmane et de l'exode rural*. Secrétariat Permanent du Comité Central des Perimètres Irrigués. CADN DIA 448.

Pouessel, Stéphanie. 2010. *Les Identités amazighes au Maroc*. Paris: Editions Non Lieu.

Ruef, Capt. P. 1947. Fiche de Tribu du Bureau de Goulmima. December. CADN Meknès, 107.

Salahdine, Mohamed. 1986. *Maroc: tribus, makhzen, colons*. Paris: Harmattan.

Sayad, Abdelmalek. 1977. "Les trois 'âges' de l'émigration algéreienne en France." *Actes de la Recherche en Sciences Sociales* 15: 59–79.

Sayad, Abdelmalek. 1994. "Aux origines de l'émigration kabyle ou montagnarde." *Hommes et Migrations* 1179: 6–11.

Silverstein, Paul A. 2002. "The Kabyle Myth: The Production of Ethnicity in Colonial Algeria." In *From the Margins: Historical Anthropology and Its Futures*, edited by Brian Keith Axel, 122–155. Durham: Duke University Press.

Silverstein, Paul A. 2003. "Martyrs and Patriots: Ethnic, National, and Transnational Dimensions of Kabyle Politics." *Journal of North African Studies* 8 (1): 87–111.

Silverstein, Paul A. 2004. *Algeria in France: Transpolitics, Race, and Nation*. Bloomington: Indiana University Press.

Silverstein, Paul A. 2010. "The Local Dimensions of Transnational Berberism: Racial Politics, Land Rights, and Cultural Activism in Southeastern Morocco." In *Berbers and Others: Shifting Parameters of Ethnicity in North Africa*, edited by Katherine Hoffman and Susan Gilson Miller, 83–102. Bloomington: Indiana University Press.

Silverstein, Paul A. 2012. "In the Name of Culture: Berber Activism and the Material Politics of 'Popular Islam' in Southeastern Morocco." *Material Religion: The Journal of Objects, Art and Belief* 8 (3): 330–353.

Silverstein, Paul A. 2013. "The Pitfalls of Transnational Consciousness: Amazigh Activism as a Scalar Dilemma." *Journal of North African Studies* 18 (5): 768–778.

Skounti, Ahmed. 1995. "Le Sang et le Sol. Les implications socioculturelles de la sédenterisation. Cas des nomads Ayt Merghad, Maroc." PhD diss., Ecole des Hautes Etudes en Sciences Sociales (Paris).

Stora, Benjamin. 1991. *La Gangrène et l'oubli. La Mémoire de la guerre d'Algérie*. Paris: La Découverte.

Beur/Maghribi musical interventions in France: rai and rap

Ted Swedenburg

Department of Anthropology, University of Arkansas, Fayetteville, USA

The article examines three songs from the rai and rap domains which have all, to varying degrees, been hits in France: 'Partir Loin' by 113 with Reda Taliani, 'Don't Panik' by Médine, and 'Même Pas Fatigué' by Khaled with Magic System. The songs raise a number of critical concerns for young North Africans and Muslims living in France and the Maghreb, including: Islamophobic and racist media representations, migration, police violence and social discrimination against banlieue youth, intolerant French secularism, and multi-culturalism. It is through creative interventions such as these that Maghrebis in France are bringing their culture and their socio-political issues to a wider French public.

Over the past two decades, both rai and rap music have come to occupy important positions within France's cultural mainstream. Musicians working in both genres have also done a great deal to bring the culture and the issues of concern to France's citizens and residents of North African origin into the centre of French life. Of all arts France's Arabs engage in, popular music is the domain in which they are by far the most numerous (Daoudi and Miliani 2002, 11). Although Maghribis have lived and laboured in the metropole since at least 1890, only recently has their music moved out of the ethnic margins. Previously, it was ghettoised, performed in 'ethnic' cafés or bars and at family celebrations, and available on recordings marketed almost exclusively to Maghribis. Besides the persistent subject of love, Maghribi music produced in France mostly dealt with questions of exile and expressed strong emotions of nostalgia for the homeland (Daoudi and Miliani 2002, 29–30; Miliani 2002). While Maghribi artists sang of the racism and hardships encountered in the metropole, they typically understood these as matters of destiny or bad luck, as problems to be solved by return to North Africa (Miliani 2002).

The emergence of rai, originally from Algeria, as a mainstream vehicle of Maghribi expression in and about France is closely connected to the early to mid-1980s' mobilisations of the 'Beurs', the French-born children of North African immigrants. The chief demands of the 'Beur generation' focused on full citizenship rights, but culture was an important dimension of their struggles

109

(Daoudi and Miliani 2002; Gastaut 2006, 115; Gross, McMurray, and Swedenburg 1996). Rai began to gain popularity in France in 1986 (Daoudi and Miliani 2002, 95), at first chiefly within the 'world music' scene, and in part due to Beur mobilisation.

Rap in France began to develop at roughly the same time, in a somewhat different context. Whereas rai is produced in France primarily by Algerian immigrants or visitors, plus some Beurs, rap is, for the most part, created by youth from France's multi-ethnic *banlieues*, the urban periphery of 'bleak peripheral estate[s]' (George 2007, 111). Due to the banlieues' demographic character and the fact that youth there do not self-segregate by ethnicity, French rap is not associated with a specific national group. Nonetheless, Arabs are an important and distinctive part of the *banlieue* scene and played a leading role in the development and proliferation of French hip-hop. Although young Arab rappers frequently belong to multi-ethnic groups, they often rap about issues of special concern to Arabs.

Both rai and rap first appeared on the French charts in the early 1990s.[1] Ever since, both genres have been commercially successful, although rap is by far the biggest seller. But while both raise topics pertaining to Franco-Maghribi interests, they are consumed and regarded in very different ways. The *banlieue* from which French rap emanates is typically seen as dangerous, home to so-called immigrant populations, and the domain of a youthful population considered congenitally inclined to criminality, extremism, and Islamism.[2] In October–November 2005, three weeks of country-wide clashes between young *banlieuesards* and French police erupted after two teens from Clichy-sous-Bois (a commune in Paris' eastern suburbs) seeking to avoid arrest were electrocuted. In the unrest's wake, nearly a quarter of the French parliament signed a petition addressed to Justice Minister, Pascal Clément, accusing seven French rap outfits of provoking the 'riots' through their lyrics, which, the MPs asserted, promoted 'incivility, if not terrorism' among the country's 'deracinated, de-cultured youth'. Clément promptly launched an investigation into the artists who, the petition's initiator claimed, were guilty of endorsing 'anti-white racism' and 'hatred for France'. Although ultimately no charges were filed, other French rappers have been charged and fined, for similar reasons (Prévos 1998, 2001). The 2005 hysteria was symptomatic of official views of rap, particularly at moments of moral or political panic. Such sentiments are fed in part by the fact that French rap's dominant trend is hardcore or 'gangsta'. Yet, as in the case of US gangsta rap (NWA, Ice Cube, Tupac, and Snoop Doggy Dog), French rappers' projection of danger both incites fear and sells massively.[3] Therefore as, over two decades, the *banlieues* have been progressively militarised and stigmatised, *banlieue* rap has conquered the centres of French popular culture. This is in part due to the state's cultural protectionist policies, which since 1996 require radio stations to devote a minimum of 40% of musical programming to French artists (Silverstein 2012a). The policy fuelled French rap production and prompted major labels to sign up rap artists, as commercial radio stations increasingly favoured hip-hop. Furthermore, since the mid-1990s, the government has targeted the *banlieues* for neo-liberal 'development', creating tax-free zones for commercial ventures and thus benefitting many multinational music production companies. The massive commodification of young *banlieuesards'* antagonism towards state policies and mainstream culture is therefore a product of this complex mix of state protectionism, neo-liberal corporate penetration, and intensive securitisation.

Rai is regarded quite differently. Although since the early 1980s its core audience has been France's Maghribi population, both young Beurs and older immigrants, the general public tends to consume it as an exotic genre categorised as 'world music'. Rai is thus acceptable, hip even, for the discriminating French middle class. Since the late 1980s, the media has typically represented rai as Algerian 'rebel' youth music, analogous to rock'n'roll, as a cultural practice resistant to Algerian conservative values or Islamist extremism (Gross, McMurray, and Sweden-burg 1996; Schade-Poulsen 1999). Mahmoud Zemmouri's 1997 film *100% Arabica* is an instance of how mainstream discourse works to make rai acceptable. Its plot revolves around a struggle for youth leadership in a mostly Arab, impoverished, Paris neighbourhood, pitting a gang of intoler-ant and corrupt Islamists against a bunch of fun-loving, tolerant, rai musicians (played by rai stars Cheb Mami and Khaled), and their friends. The rai musicians win over not just young Maghribis but also 'native' French. Rai's foreign attractiveness seemed to increase in the wake of the 2005 'riots'. A *New York Times* article, appearing in the travel section shortly after the uprising, described how North African fashion, cuisine, and music had become chic and trendy in Paris, particularly among middle and upper middle-class sophisticates (Sherwood 2005). Of all North African musical genres marketed in France, it is rai that has made the most inroads into the non-Arab public, becoming virtually mainstream during the 1990s. Artists like Khaled, Cheb Mami, and Faudel, as well as rocker Rachid Taha, who occasionally performs rai numbers, are well-known 'French' stars and winners of numerous major music awards. Yet, if rai has 'crossed over', it is still often viewed and represented as appealingly alien, representative of an 'authentic' elsewhere. Rai stands for a colourful, benign, and entirely acceptable 'other', in sharp contrast to the much more threatening 'other' of the *banlieues*.[4]

The songs discussed below emerge out of this complex political/cultural mix, where rai is stereotypically exotic and friendly while rap is forbidding and potentially terroristic. The artists performing these songs are products of the prevailing atmosphere and their work is scripted by normative expectations and mainstream stereotypes. Yet at the same time that they work within musical/generic conventions, which they help reproduce, they deploy these formulae to bring issues of concern to young North Africans, in both France and the Maghrib, to a wider French public. In practice, especially of late, the two genres do not operate in separate domains but often intersect. I focus on three songs from the rai and rap domains, all, to varying degrees, successful with non-Arab French audiences; they provide keen insights into the diverse and complicated impact that North Africans and their culture(s) and socio-political concerns have on contemporary France.

To go far away

Although regarded as two very different genres, rai–rap collaborations became increasingly common by the early 2000s and produced a number of hits, in France and Algeria.[5] One of the first was 'Oran/Marseille', from raiman Khaled's 1997 album *Sahra*, featuring Khaled's singing and raps from IAM, one of France's premier hip-hop groups. 'Parisien du Nord', 1999's collaboration between Cheb Mami and rapper K-Mel, reached number five on the French singles charts, with lyrics expressing the kind of alienation that generated the 2005 upris-ing.[6] In 2004, the collaborative practice received a genre name, 'Raï'n'B', with the release of the first in a series of collections called *Raï N'B Fever*. The album was certified double gold in France and it was also a success in Algeria.[7] Some observers (Davet 2004) claimed that Raï'n'B gave a much-needed jolt to a flagging rap scene, the world's second largest hip-hop market, one that was in need of 'a breath of fresh air'. At the same time, the genre brought rai music to a much larger French audience (Merzouk 2004). The hybrid genre has also been a sensation in Algeria, where major concerts have been organised bringing together rai and rap stars from both countries (Z.M. 2005). Algerian rap artists, in an effort to break through rai's near monopoly of the country's soundwaves, often include on their albums a duo with a rai singer (Boumedini and Hadria 2013, 277).

'Partir Loin' (To Go Far Away) is from rap group 113's certified-gold 2005 album, *113 Degrès*.[8] One of seven rap outfits charged by French MP's with inciting the 2005 'riots', 113's three members are of Algerian, Malian, and Guadeloupean heritage and hail from the Paris *banlieue* of Vitry-sur-Seine. 'Partir Loin' pairs 113's leader, Algerian-born Rim'K,[9] with Algerian rai singer Reda Taliani, who is now based in Marseille.[10] Rim'K raps mostly in French with a bit of Algerian dialect, while Taliani uses French extensively in his Arabic vocals. The track commences with sounds of traditional Algerian percussion and electronic keyboards playing typical rai riffs that imitate the trumpet, chief instrument of Algeria's 'pop rai' from the late 1970s, and the *gasba* (reed flute), 'folk' rai's lead instrument. The drumming and simulated *gasba* and trumpet sounds serve to guarantee the track's rai 'authenticity'. The dominant rhythm is 'Western' dance style, typical of much contemporary rai, but the bass is more restrained than on other typical rai–rap tracks with their deep funk beats. Taliani's vocals are auto-tuned, making his voice sound slightly synthesised and ratcheting up its expressiveness and emotionality.[11]

After the instrumental introduction, Reda Taliani sings verses from the song 'Ya l'babour' (O Steamboat), originally written and recorded by Cheb Bouâa, a rai artist from Anvers, Belgium. The first verse goes:

*Y'al-bābūr yā mon **amour*** (O steamboat O my love)
*Kherjnī min **la misère*** (Take me away from misery)
Fī bledī rānī maḥgūr (I'm despised in my homeland)
*'Ayit 'ayit ū **j'en ai marre*** (I'm tired, tired and fed up with it)
*Ma nrāṭīsh **l'occasion*** (Don't want to miss this chance)
*Fī bālī **ça fait longtemps*** (It's been on my mind for so long)
*Hādā nssātnī **qui je suis*** (It [migration] has made me forget who I am)
*Nekhdem 'alīhā **jour et nuit*** (I work on it day and night)
*Y'al-bābūr yā **mon amour** / kherjnī min **al-misère***
Évasion spéciale (Special escape)
*Min **l'Algérie** à **l'occidental*** (From Algeria to the West)

The number is a kind of love song to a tramp steamer (*bābūr* is from the Italian *vapore,* steamboat) with a simple, clever, and amusing lyric. Until the last quarter of the twentieth century, the aeroplane was too expensive for Maghribis of modest income who travelled back and forth to Europe, and so the ship was *the* mode of transport (Daoudi and Miliani 2002, 43). The sentiment is also tragic, for the young Algerian man's love song should be addressed to a young woman. (Love is the chief theme of modern rai songs [Boumedini and Hadria 2013; Schade-Poulsen 1999].) But because this song's subject finds conditions in the homeland so miserable, he is obsessed not with a beautiful girl but with dreams of escape, *évasion spéciale*, to the West. So 'Partir Loin' is at once love song and lament. The chorus vocals, 'Special escape from Algeria to the West', are more heavily auto-tuned than the verses, lending the statement a heightened emotive resonance.

The code-switching and borrowings from French (in bold) are typical of rai, and of contemporary urban Algerian speech (as well as of many Arabs in France).[12] Taliani, for instance, when using the French verb 'rater' (to miss) in *Ma nrāṭīsh l'occasion,* conjugates it as an Arabic verb (Caubet 2002, 125). All but one line (ending with *maḥgūr,* 'despised') begin in Arabic and conclude with French, so the rhyme scheme is mostly in French. According to Boumedini and Hadria (2013, 224), it is very common for rai singers to use French expressions in love songs, in order to legitimise sexual desire by making it seem more civilised and to serve as a means of euphemisation.

After Rim'K's rapped verse, Taliani expresses fondness for the homeland: *Yā blādī ntī fīk lkhīr* (O my country, you're full of treasures). But, only 'the one with connections' (*llī 'indu lktāf*) will succeed there, and only the one with luck (*al-zahr*) will benefit from those national resources. So, he sings, 'let's go, let's go' (*rwāḥ rwāḥ*), let's board the *babour*. Once abroad, Taliani vocalises, 'I'll sacrifice' (*nsākrīfī*, conjugating the French *sacrifier* as an Arabic verb), I'll build a home and 'I'll become a rich man' (*nwllī rīshār*, from *richard*, French for 'moneybags'). The aspirations and dreams expressed are typical of the would-be migrant.

When Rim'K versifies, instrumental backing turns sparer, appropriate for a rap song, and rai keyboard frills mostly drop out. Rim'K and 113 are among the best-known French rappers who have fostered a hardcore or 'gangsta' reputation, in French, *caillera* or 'riffraff'.[13] 113 also express social concerns, especially of *banlieue* youth.[14] Rim'K's 'Partir Loin' raps are more 'message' than gangsta. He begins by stating that he is from 'Kabylifornie', and has smoked '350 benji' (hashish[15]) along the Corniche, either Marseille and/or Algiers (both cities are shown in the 'Partir Loin' video). Although of Kabyle (Berber) background,[16] Rim'K claims a hybrid identity, rooted in an imaginative space whose name refers simultaneously to the homeland (*bled*) and to the place of eternal sunshine and cradle of gangsta rap (South Compton). Rim'K adds, regarding the 350 benji, so what if I do something illegal? Go ahead, 'arrest me, who cares?' (*ḥabsīnī ma 'līsh,* Arabic*).* Rim'K underscores his hard life and dangerous state of mind: 'Nothing to lose, Rim'K mentally ill'; 'I consider myself lucky to be alive'; 'I grew up only with thieves'. His plaints sometimes echo Taliani's: 'take me far away from my misery', but the tough conditions he alludes to are doubtless those of the *banlieues*. Rim'K also highlights his Algerian background and traditions. He wants to 'decorate his beloved with henna', for marriage. *Comme Cheb Hasni j'suis sentimental,* he says: he's 'sentimental' like the celebrated singer of romantic 'love rai', assassinated in 1994, probably by the extremist GIA (Armed Islamic Group). At heart, Rim'K asserts, he remains a *bledard*, a country boy, and ululations (*youyous*) always echo in his head.[17]

For Taliani, escape (*évasion*) is from Algeria, and misery (*la misère*) lies in the homeland (*bled*). For Rim'K, *la misère* is in France. 'As soon as the airplane lands I clapped', he raps, but clearly, since disembarkation, the migration experience has not been happy. If there is any escape for Rim'K, it seems to lie in *benjis*, in nostalgic recollections of the *bled* and its culture (but not a desire to return), in 'Kabylifornie', and in music and dance. 'A moment of escape' (*Un moment d'évasion*), he raps, 'c'mon donkey (*yā ḥmār*, Arabic, used affectionately), get up and dance'.

Taliani's verses speak to how migration and the goal of reaching Europe function in the imaginations of many Maghribi youth. Migration has been a constant theme in Algerian rai since the early 1990s (Miliani 2005, 119). Desires to leave are very strong. A recent poll showed that 72% of Moroccans dreamed of expatriating (Abderrazzak 2011), while in 2009 *The Economist* reported a canvas of Algerian men between 15 and 34 years that found half would probably or definitely attempt to get to Europe in the near future (Mundy 2009). Algerian journalist Benachour (2007) asserts that Taliani's 'Ya l'babour' showed him to be one of the singers who had 'best captured the concerns of the new young generation for whom the dream of illegal sea crossing is the only hope for which they live'.[18] Those who leave Algeria are known colloquially as *harraga,* those who burn (from *ḥaraqa,* 'to burn'). The term refers to the fact that many migrants torch their papers before departure, to make it difficult for receiving countries to repatriate them. This document incineration is a remarkable act: a literal destruction of one's 'identity' before leave-taking, and a desperate measure given how essential 'papers' are in everyday Algerian life. Among the reasons so many seek emigration are: severe lack of adequate employment,[19] tensions and fears created by the violence of Algeria's civil war (1991–2005) and ensuing state of emergency (2005–2011), social controls exercised by an authoritarian State and Islamist forces, a severe housing crisis that particularly impacts young people wanting to start families. Despite its racism towards Arabs, Muslims and illegals, Europe remains an attractive destination for young Algerians, due to the availability of work, even if menial. Algerian columnist Daoud (2011) argues that migration has different motivations:

> Our *harraga* don't leave the country because they are poor or jobless or can't find a storefront to rent, even if that's what they say. They leave because here, in this country, their lives are pointless, there's no room to dream, and worst of all, there's no fun, no laughter, no kissing, and no colour.

Rim'K appears to agree when he asserts, at the end of 'Partir Loin', 'Go far away, to escape the problems in our head, dude (*mec*)!'

Harragas, however, do not typically exit Algeria via *babour*, especially not the sort of big ship depicted in the 'Partir Loin' video. If a 'babour' is the vehicle of conveyance for legal migrants and travellers, *harragas* typically venture to what Rim'K calls their 'Eldorado' in rubber dinghies or small, vulnerable, and slow flat-bottomed boats or inflatable rafts. Algerian rai artist Cheb Mansour sings about the *harraga* experience in his 2007 song 'Nekalaa fi chalutier' (Benachour 2007):

> **Chalutier** *nqala' fîh* (I board a trawler)
> *Alméria wala Alicante* (For Alméria or Alicante [Spanish ports])
> *Negla'a galbî* **nrîskî** *'umrî* (I don't listen to my heart, I risk [Arabic conjugation of the French *risquer*] my life)
> *La khidma wālū fīl* **compte** (Because I've no work, nothing in my bank account)

Cheb Mansour is cognizant that *évasion spéciale* is not merely illegal, but dangerous and potentially deadly. Between 2005 and 2008, the number of victims found dead on Algeria's coast more than tripled, from 29 to 98 (Madjid 2009), while the number washing up on the Mediterranean's northern shore grew as well. In 2011, the non-governmental organisation, United for Intercultural Action, reported that nearly 10,000 migrants and refugees had died by drowning in the Mediterranean since 1988, around 6000 of these coming from Morocco or Algeria (Manach 2011; Rekacewicz 2013). The Algerian state, in response to pressures from would-be Fortress Europe's demands to stem the flow, has criminalised undocumented emigration. In 2008, Algeria's coast guard arrested over 1300 potential migrants, aged 21–27 years. Meanwhile, some 67,000 'illegals' arrived in Europe in 2008 (Madjid 2009).

While rai singers have recorded songs about *babour*s, visas, and migration,[20] Algerian's filmmakers have produced some remarkable films on the subject. Tariq Teguia's 2006 *Rome plutôt que vous* (Arabic: *Roma wa la 'touma*) chronicles the desperate efforts of two young Algerians, Kamal and Zina, to obtain forged documents allowing Kamal to travel abroad. Merzak Allouache's 2009 *Harragas* treats the travails of ten passengers departing Mostaganem, in western Algeria, for the Canary Islands. Abderrazzak (2011) observes that in contemporary Maghribi films, the seashore no longer functions, as it once did in, as a space of leisure and vacation but rather, as a place where Maghribis go to gaze at the water and imagine crossing, to a better future elsewhere, in Europe or further afield (Abderrazzak 2009).

'Partir Loin', and particularly the video, presents migration in a lighter tone than these films. The boat, as object of affection, is no insubstantial *chalutier,* but large, sleek, and solid. The song imagines migration and travel as legal, that of a Reda Taliani who can move legally between Marseille, his residence, and Algiers, his birth town. The video shows the ports of both Algiers and Marseille (hard to tell apart), between which Taliani and Rim'K lawfully rotate. French comic film star Julien Courbey (French father, Mauritanian mother), appears as well, adding a touch of levity as he dances around and mugs for the camera.

Although 'Partir Loin' does not depict migration and displacement in particularly bleak terms, it does attempt to bring these issues into mainstream French consciousness. In the absence of research on listener reception, we can only speculate on its effects. Given that those with a rudimentary knowledge of Arabic might understand the opening lines of 'Partir Loin', this love song to a steamboat that will bring deliverance from misery might engender some sympathy regarding the conditions pushing so many young Algerians to leave their homeland. Some native French speakers would understand the line, *khrejni min al-misère*, since *khrej* (synonym for *sortir*) is an Arabic verb that – like the better known *kiffer*, to like or fancy, from *kīf*, pleasure – has been incorporated into French slang, as in 'si tu voulais khrej avec elle' (if you'd like to go out with her) (Caubet 2002, 128). In the banlieues, where youth of various ethnic backgrounds are much more familiar with Arabic than elsewhere, where Arabic music is a part of youth culture, and where rap music's core audience resides, no doubt, a number of non-Arab listeners could grasp the song's meanings.

Don't panik, Je Suis Muslim every day

Rapper Médine's 2008 song 'Don't Panik'[21] confronts head-on the realities of life for young French Arabs and other *banlieue* youth that Rim'K touches on in 'Partir Loin'. Whereas Rim'K belongs to French rap's reigning hardcore tendency, Médine calls his brand 'conscious rap' (Planet Hip Hop 2005).[22] Médine's shaved head, full beard, and football-player build make him look more like a *caillera* than does the rather slight Rim'K, but his lyrics are far from gangsta. Born Mehdi Zaouich, a *cité* ('projects') boy of Algerian heritage from Le Havre in Upper Normandy, Médine is more the tough but progressive, teacherly rapper than the *insoumi* 'gangsta', more Chuck D than Eazy-E.[23] Médine has emerged as a thoughtful, measured spokesperson for rap and the *banlieue* and often engages in public political debates. A sense of his analysis of the position of young *banlieusards* can be gauged from this 2009 statement:

> We are in a social organization that parks us in unsanitary geographic locations, which treats us as rapists, butchers of sheep or chickens, and burners of cars. From our side of the fence, the violence would have a thousand reasons to flare up again. (Fara 2009)

'Don't Panik' is a riposte to mainstream media representations of *banlieue* life, which rarely mention its everyday horrors: gloomy and decrepit housing, dearth of local amenities (parks, sports facilities), quotidian police harassment and abuse, incessant profiling and demands to present identity papers,[24] high unemployment rates, poor job prospects for graduates due to endemic racism,[25] sub-par schooling that tracks students into unskilled labour, absence of political representation,[26] and so on. Instead, for official media discourse, Muslim youths of North African background define the 'terror' of the *banlieues* (Derderian 2004, 148).[27] 'Don't Panik' is a response as well to the pervasive Islamophobic rhetoric of conventional French discourse.

Like most 'hardcore' French rap, the soundtrack of 'Don't Panik' is located within traditions established by US-produced rap, dominated by r'n'b, soul, blues, and jazz, without a trace of Middle Eastern musical trappings. Set in a minor key, the song's beats and synthesised keyboard convey a sense of urgency, as does Médine's tough tone of voice. Yet, the track's theme in some ways cuts across the sonic atmospherics. The core of Médine's message for a French audience prone to prejudice against denizens of France's urban peripheries, is: when you see something 'different', don't panic, don't get hysterical, and don't worry. And Médine's advice for all the named stigmatised social categories in France, for the devout Muslim, the bearded one or *boulé-hia de ta barbe*,[28] for the veiled woman, for the *banlieuesard*, for the proletarian, for the African, is the same: tell 'them' (*dis-leur*), 'don't panik!' Médine repeats the phrase in English, rather than using the French, *ne paniquez pas*, positioning himself within the hip-hop trans-nation.[29]

Médine proceeds to give his 'chronicle' (*chronique*) of the decayed (*effritée*) republic, one whose values he is in truth much invested in. Muslim philosophy, he insists, favours the emancipation of women, and does not, contrary to popular belief, support female circumcision or embrace the 'Afghan' (Taliban) way. Nor does it advocate equal work for men and women but unequal pay for the latter. Such gendered economic practice, as well as giving respect to the 'sisters' only on the International Day of Women (8 March), he asserts, is the hypocritical act of a patriarchal society. The act of a society that has turned injustice into a Patriot Act (*patriote acte*), one that imposes the values of 'Libertine, Laïcité, et Liberticide' (libertinism, secularism, and liberticide), values that 'rape (*viole*) our civil rights without a condom'. Here, Médine calls attention to what he considers a degradation of the ideals of French Republicanism (*Liberté, Égalité, Fraternité*), and protests the impositions of a dogmatic and intolerant secularism, the property of the French left as much as the right, which targets Muslims and regards them as unassimilable.[30] Many Muslims view as a particularly repressive secularist initiative the 2004 law, passed with the support of all political parties, that bans the wearing of 'conspicuous' religious symbols in public schools, in particular the headscarves of Muslim girls. At the same time, official discourse touts bikinis and miniskirts as signs of female liberation.[31]

Médine uses the term Patriot Act, the US security response to 9/11, as a metaphor for the West's broader response to the Islamist 'terrorist' threat and specifically France's securitisation moves, which predate 9/11. During the 1990s, motivated by both generalised Islamophobia and responding to a perceived growth in local extremist Islamist tendencies,[32] the French state played a central part in the rearticulation of the mainstream image of the *banlieue* as a special threat and object of fear. It did so through an array of new policies (such as creating a special 'Cities and Banlieues' section of the Intelligence Service [RG] specialising in 'urban violence'), repressive laws, and statements (producing new sorts of statistics on 'urban violence' and so on) (Dikeç 2004, 195, 199). The militarisation and stigmatisation of the *banlieues* were ratcheted up even further during Nicolas Sarkozy's tenure as Minister of the Interior from 2002–04, immediately before Médine released 'Don't Panik'.

Médine next inventories, and lampoons, all the insulting and simplistic ways mainstream France depicts and views *banlieuesards* (Derville 1997), employing plenty of *verlan* (the back-slang that is a badge of identity for *cité* youth [Sekaninová 2012, 21]), clever internal rhymes, linguistic borrowings, and sharp images. He begins by saying it is commonly believed that *banlieue* youth share a great deal with Abu Hamza, the Egyptian jihadist based in London, extradited to the USA in 2012. *Banlieuesards*, he says, are typically represented as having: one foot in the demonstrations (*manifs*), one foot with the rioters (*casseurs*); one with the sportsmen, one with the dealers (*dealeurs*, an anglicism); one foot in the mosque, the other with the gang rapists (*tournantes*); one in the mire (*bourbier*), one in the turmoil (*tourmente*); one in the *minibar*, the other in the *minbar* (mosque pulpit); one foot with the barbarians (*barbares*), the other with the bearded ones (*bu-bar*, verlan for *barbus*); one in the stickups (*cage-bra*, verlan for *braquage*), one in brawls (*gar-ba*, verlan for *bagarre*); one foot in custody (*gard'av*, for *garde à vue),* the other toward the Kaaba (in Mecca, in whose direction Muslims pray); one foot in the riots (*émeutes*), one with the dropouts (*zonards*); one foot with the imams, the other with the zidanes (a reference to soccer star, Zinedine Zidane); one with the Arabs, the other with the gypsies. By writing his list, Médine says, he'll have revenge against the journalists, à la

Mesrine – a reference to France's most notorious twentieth-century criminal, Jacques Mesrine, who French rappers often refer to as the archetypal gangster.[33] Médine's catalogue of how the public, media, police, and state officials typically regard young *banlieusards* calls attention to the dual and deeply contradictory nature of the 'panicked' mainstream imagination: on the one hand, they are seen as violent criminals, rapists, thugs, boozers, and drug dealers, and on the other, as fanatical, bearded, Muslim terrorists. The widespread tendency is to lump together *banlieues*, immigrants, Muslims, rappers, gangs, Arab citizens, dealers, 'fundamentalists', youthful lawbreakers and so on; to view each category as more or less equivalent to the others; and single them out as the chief sources of France's social 'problems'. Conflicts involving *banlieue* youth responses to police violence are typically labelled 'riots', as though caused by spontaneous hooligan outbursts.[34] The only 'positive' association in this otherwise relentlessly negative mix is with athletics, and specifically Zinedine Zidane, regarded as one of the greatest French soccer players of all time. But even this reference is not entirely positive, as it consigns Arabs to the realm of the physical as opposed to the refined domain of the mental; meanwhile, Zidane's star had fallen after the 2006 World Cup finals' infamous head-butting incident.

Médine contrasts the press' negative views and its chiefs' 'gloomy faces' with his own, a religious person with a sense of entertainment (*Je suis un religieux avec le sens de l'entertainment*), using the English word instead of the French *divertissement*. He concludes his call for no panic with an assertion of Muslim identity. Having begun the song with '*Don't panik, je suis* [I am] *Muslim every day*', as if to say his religion is a way of life, not (as for secularists) a weekend affair, he ends it stating, 'Every day the bull's eye (*au centre de la cible*)/Because every day I'm Muslim': every day my religion puts me under heavy suspicion. He concludes by repeating several times, in English, 'Every day I'm Muslim! Every every every day I'm Muslim, every day I'm Muslim Muslim Muslim'. In an electronically distorted voice, Médine pronounces Muslim as *mu-si-lam,* using three syllables. Here he samples Rick Ross' five-times platinum 2006 hit, 'Hustlin'', a paean to cocaine dealing, whose chorus goes 'Everyday I'm hustlin'', pronounced 'hus-tle-in'. Médine converts 'hus-tle-in' to 'mu-si-lam'. Citing Rick Ross, Médine connects to global rap and channels Ross' tough streetwise aura, but also underlines that he is a Muslim, not a dope dealer.

The 'Don't Panick' video reinforces the messages in interesting ways. The opening sequence shows Médine in a t-shirt emblazoned with the English slogan I'm Muslim Don't Panik, as if to say, 'I'm fiercely proud of my religious heritage and beliefs, but don't let it worry you'. In the video, Médine vocalises on stage, fist in the air, in front of a banner reading Don't Panik, and before a multi-ethnic throng in black t-shirts like Médine's and pumping fists along with him. The event is as much combative political rally as concert. Médine also paces around his hometown of Le Havre. The video's attitude and atmosphere are militant and hard-hitting, as though designed to mobilise and unite the despised social categories his song name-checks. But one wonders whether scenes of crowds of fist-pounding *banlieue* youths convey the intended message to a suspicious public. Might not the clip in fact make some viewers 'panic'? Interestingly, no women in the video, in the crowds or in Médine's female posse, wear anything that might pass as 'Islamic dress'. Women with covered hair sport hoodies, baseball caps or scarves, accessories coded as 'hip-hop' rather than Islamic.

Although Médine does not enjoy anything like Rim'K's star or best-selling status, he is well respected and has a decent audience for an 'underground' musician.[35] As of late July 2014, the 'official' Youtube 'Don't Panik' video had over 729,000 views. 'Don't Panik' has become Médine's signature, his motto,[36] and he has spread the song's message through other means. He co-authored a book of the same title with French academic Pascal Boniface (Boniface and Médine 2012), and he appears in Keira Maameri's 2011 documentary, *Don't Panik*, discussing, along with five other rappers, what it means to be a Muslim in hip-hop. In the film, Médine states that the song 'Don't Panik' was intended to bring together France's diverse underprivileged communities and to denounce discrimination against them. But, he complains, all anyone seems to remember is that the track is about Muslims. Perhaps he should not be surprised, and not simply because he ends the song by repeating, 'Every day I'm Muslim'. For while all young residents of the *banlieues*, no matter what ethnic or national background, face similar problems, makers of public meaning in France tend to single out Muslim North Africans as the 'problem' and as *the* representatives of the *banlieues*, a synecdochic process that besmirches, taints and in a sense, 'Islamizes', *all* youth of the *cités* (De Koning 2006). The residential 'apartheid' dividing the *banlieues* from the zones of privilege reinforces that 'spatial stigmatization' (Dikeç 2004, 203).

'Don't Panik' is of a piece with Médine's other work, which also advocates not the refusal of essential French values but instead a strong desire for France to live up precisely to its traditional republican standards, the Declaration of the Rights of Man and Citizen. Médine is relentless in exposing of French double standards, in unmasking the official hypocrisies and intolerances of a self-declared broad-minded society, and he can do so because of his deep familiarity with mainstream mores. He is much less interested in trumpeting his personal piety or in proselytising than in arguing for Muslims' rights to practise their beliefs without interference and in correcting mainstream misconceptions about Islam (Jouili 2013, 70). On his 2005 album *Jihad: le plus grand combat est contre soi-même* (Jihad: the greatest struggle is against the self), Médine attempts to recast dominant Western notions of *jihad* as simply holy war. He instead highlights *jihad al-nafs,* the individual Muslim's struggle to control his/her lesser instincts, what the orthodox regard as the 'greater jihad'. Another of Médine's chief targets is what he considers illiberal secularism. On 'Anéanti' ('Annihilated'), from *Jihad*, he complains that 'they' want him to abandon his beard at France's gates, that 'they' wish his religion would come down simply to a *couscous merguez*, a dish made with spicy Maghribi sausage. That is, hegemonic secularists would that he gave up his masculine sign of piety (a 'conspicuous' religious symbol), preferring that his religion be little more than an exotic, tasty, and easily digested tradition. Yet, Médine's concerns are in no ways exclusively 'Muslim', for he is devoted to making connections and affiliations between marginalised peoples, by linking the struggles of Muslims to those of others in a similar position, by supporting mobilisations against racial and class discrimination, and by exposing the legacies of colonialism. His positions seem to reflect the tendency, post-2005, of the formation of new coalitions in France that are not circumscribed by ancestral ethnicities (Hargreaves 2009, 311).

There's no problem (in the country of the poor)

'Même pas fatigué' (Not even tired) is a rai-zouglou fusion from Algerian rai superstar Khaled and the Ivory Coast's Magic System.[37] It sat atop the French charts for seven weeks in 2009, making it Khaled's first Top Ten hit in France since 'Abdel Kader (Live à Bercy)' with Rashid Taha and Faudel, #6 in 1998.[38]

Khaled, who was born in Oran, Algeria and resided in France from the late 1980s until 2008, is *the* major rai star in France, a position he has occupied ever since his single 'Didi' hit the Top Ten in 1992. His 1996 chart-topping single 'Aïcha' (in French and Arabic) won him a Victoires de la Musique award (France's Grammy equivalent) for (French) Song of the Year; he won again in 2013 for his hit (#4) 'C'est La Vie'. Despite, or maybe in part because of, his embroilment in the occasional scandal, Khaled is a beloved figure in France. He projects a persistently upbeat image, his legendary smile never seeming to vanish from his ever-boyish face.[39] Khaled has been at the forefront of the ever-growing group of artists of Maghribi background who, over the past two decades, have brought the sounds of Arabic music and language into French mainstream culture, a remarkable feat, given that Arabic is the language of the true Other in France, the Algerian/Arab/Muslim, who is much more derided and hated than are any other racial or ethnic group.

The 'hybrid' sound of 'Même pas fatigué' is nothing new for Khaled. Modern rai emerged out of the polyglot and multicultural environment prevalent in the Oran region of northwest Algeria during the colonial period. Khaled recalls growing up in the 1960s and 1970s and listening to Johnny Hallyday (French rock'n'roll), Elvis Presley, Edith Piaf, Adamo (French pop), Joselito (Spanish pop), Farid al-Atrash (Egyptian neo-classical), Algerian chaabi, Moroccan music (Nass El Ghiwane), ouahrani (modern urban Orani), and traditional 'folk' rai (Khaled 1998, 65–67). His hit 'Didi', propelled by funk beats, was produced by the well-regarded Unitedstatesian Don Was, who has worked with the Rolling Stones, Bonnie Raitt, the B-52s, and Bob Dylan. Asked about the salsa–rai fusions on his 1999 album *Kenza*, Khaled replied that he grew up with flamenco, had always performed salsa and rumba, and that such genres were part of his 'roots' (Tenaille 2002, 92–93).

Magic System, one of the Ivory Coast's biggest zouglou bands, had already enjoyed hits in France, including two in the Raï'n'B vein, before recording with Khaled. Their first single to chart in France (#4) was '1er Gaou'[40] (First fool) in 2001. They appeared with rai singer Mohamed Lamine on 113's 2004 dance hit (#9) 'Un Gaou à Oran' (on *Raï'n'B Fever*), noteworthy for its vocals in French, Arabic and an Ivorean dialect. They also sang on the upbeat dance hit 'C'chô, ça brûle' (It's hot, it burns), from *Raï'n'B Fever 2*. Recorded with rai singers Akil and Cheb Bilal and rapper Big Ali, it charted at number four in 2006.

Unlike 'Partir Loin' or 'Don't Panik', which focus on the difficulties of the migration and cultural integration experience, 'Même Pas Fatigué' is a celebratory paean to multiculturalism that depicts France's diverse ethnic population as non-threatening, unproblematic, and entertaining. 'Même pas fatigué' is dominated by an urgent dance beat, and unlike the typical rai track, possesses not a hint of Middle Eastern sound decoration. Instrumentation is simple and basic, with beats supplied by prominent bass and drums, and electronic keyboards that mostly follow the melody. Magic System, the musical group that does most of the vocals, sings an upbeat chorus that is all about fun and partying all night. 'We make the mood/There's no problem/Khaled, Magic System/That's the sound you love/Everywhere it's the same/Not tired is the theme/Not even tired/Tonight we've gotta dance/We'll give it our all'. Magic System repeats this chorus four more times over the course of the song, with Khaled at times singing or ululating along. The other verse Magic System sings includes the lines, 'We can't help/Being hot Raï'n'B fever', positioning the song within that popular generic brand.

The track's video clip shows Khaled and Magic System on a modest neighbourhood soccer pitch (all dirt, no grass), playing a friendly pick-up game with a multi-ethnic crew. The players mug, smile, and dance to the music along with the singers. They include Franck Ribéry, one of France's soccer greats, a regular 'native' working-class 'bloke' who is a convert to Islam and whose wife Wahiba is of Algerian descent. The clip's mood, like the song's, is overwhelmingly happy. 'Y'a pas d'problème' (No problem) they sing, again and again. Khaled contributes a verse in French in the same vein: 'No, no, there's no hate/Hand in hand/No, no, there's no trouble'.

The song and video put a feel-good, joyous face on multi-ethnic France, and depict the *banlieue* environment as anything but threatening. What could be more appealing to a mainstream audience than football mixed with infectious, joyous dance music, a cheery party song that revels in the nation's rich blend of peoples, sounds, and customs? The adult musicians and soccer players are not the dangerous delinquent *banlieue* youth nor are there any 'veiled' women or men with *salafi* beards. The video is a recurrence of the optimistic image projected by France's victorious multi-ethnic soccer squad in the 1998 World Cup, led by Zinedine Zidane (McMurray 1998), as well as the somewhat limited optimism about prospects for a more inclusive sense of national identity in France that prevailed between 1998 and 2002 (George 2007, 94). Soccer, Ahmed (2007/08) has shown, often serves as an ideological technique to generate happy diversity, as evidence that the migrant can successfully integrate and that racism has been overcome. 'Même Pas Fatiguée' was produced in the wake of the 2005 events, when French politicians had begun to talk a great deal about 'diversity', and shortly after law-and-order President Nicolas Sarkozy famously appointed ethnic minorities to his cabinet in 2007.[41] The video does of course reflect the banlieues' multi-ethnic character, and the song's chart-topping meant that Arabic singing again blasted over France's mainstream airwaves. But as wonderful as the song and vid are, they seem overly utopian and self-congratulatory. The words and imagery suggest precisely the sort of 'positive', de-politicised and often state-sponsored 'anti-racism' that community-based *banlieue* movements as well as rappers so frequently protest against (Soumahoro 2008, 59).

Perhaps this helps to make sense of Khaled's happy/melancholic verse in Arabic:

[indistinct] *Sa'dī ejjī l'endī* (I'm happy, come to me)
N'dīrū līl wi n'hār fī bled az-zawālī (We'll spend night and day in the country of the poor)
'Ayish zahwānī ghrīb wi barrānī (Living happy, an exile and a foreigner)
'Ānā megwānī 'ayish būhālī yé yé yé yé (I'm burning, living in a daze like a fool ye ye ye ye)

The lyrics speak of living happily, but the felicity is that of an immigrant who simply 'manages' under conditions of exile, in a France that is no Eldorado, but the land of poverty. The 'happy' situation is also one that hurts, burns, and reduces one to a *būhālī*, a crazy nit-witted, if lovable, simpleton. In the video, Khaled displays his patented smile as he sings over a bouncy beat, but his Arabic lines interject a momentary bittersweetness, a hint of the hard realities faced by migrants and uprooted people.

But do any listeners grasp the ambiguities? Certainly not monolingual French speakers. But Khaled's core audience, speakers of Maghribi dialect, would get the point, and perhaps also some other *banlieue* residents with a bit of Arabic knowledge. Maybe, Khaled's purpose is to remind his Arab fans that despite his star stature, he remains at heart one of them and still understands their issues. Khaled has, of course, routinely been represented by the institutions of public meaning as a symbol of the 'good Arab' one who assimilates and is the antithesis of the fanatic Arab fundamentalist.[42] Khaled himself often asserts that he is not 'political', that he wants just one thing: to party, live, drink, and dance (Khaled 1998, 17) – but he has on occasion complained about French racism and asserted support for Palestinian rights (Daniel 1997; Siclier 2002).

Conclusion

I have presented a small but not unrepresentative sample of the ways in which Maghribi residents of France use popular music in an effort to bring their cultural and socio-political issues into the mainstream of French cultural life. I do not, however, want to overstate their activity's political significance. In the absence of studies of the reception of these cultural artefacts, one can do little more than speculate about their impact on audiences. Any work of art, of course, is available to multiple readings, and dominant discourses frequently guide how an artefact is consumed. Even native speakers frequently misidentify or misread lyrics, as my search for authoritative versions of song lyrics and translations confirms. Even when there is agreement about a song's words, interpretations can vary widely. The problem is compounded when songs employ more than one language, liberally use slang, and are grounded in localised references and insider knowledge. And yet, many in the audience beyond those of Maghribian background may understand the Arabic in such songs. Caubet (2002, 126) argued in 2002 that the presence of Arabic (Maghribi) dialect in the French landscape was 'undeniable', especially in the domains of popular music and comedy. Caubet (2002, 130) reported too that French people of all origins were memorising the words to 'Ya Rayah' (O Exile), Rachid Taha's 1997 hit, a cover of Dahmane El Harrachi's celebrated 1970s' number about migration, to sing in karaoke bars.

We should not overvalue the political significance and potential of such cultural activity in France. There is little political activism in the *banlieues*, where the base audience and practitioners of the music in question are located. The leaders of the major organised political tendencies among French Maghribis – the secular Beur movements that arose in the 1980s and the Islamist movements that emerged in the 1980s – are middle class, clientelist and mostly disconnected from the *banlieues*. Jihadists and salafists have been active in the *banlieues*, but their organising efforts do not focus on the main social issues of concern to *cité* residents. Neither jihadis nor salafis played a significant role in the 'riots' of 2005, and the fact that the unrest was mostly spontaneous and chaotic was a symptom of the absence of grassroots political organising in the *banlieues* (International Crisis Group 2006). The rappers of *cité* origins are mostly not political activists either, simply artists who report on local realities and grievances. This relative vacuum means that musicians' political role is exaggerated. Effective, transformative political action, however, will not come through the leadership of artists, however intelligent, well-intentioned, or activist.[43]

The chief achievement of the work discussed here is nevertheless not insignificant: the simple airwave presence of the language and culture of the social element many in France regard as the enemy, as a demographic threat, a social force that will impose *shari'a*. Khaled's 'Même pas fatigué' has undoubtedly given some 'native' French people a more nuanced and positive view of the *banlieues*. Similarly, Rim'K and Reda Taliani's 'Partir Loin' has generated additional understanding of the issues of the migrant and the culturally displaced, and helped to legitimise the transnational positioning of French Arabs, who are 'd'ici et de là-bas continuellement' (continuously from here and there) (Daoudi and Miliani 2002, 125). And some French rap fans may regard Islam and the *banlieusards* more favourably due to Médine.

There are other concrete positive effects as well. Médine argues in several songs that today's anti-Arab racism, Islamophobia and urban crises have their roots in France's colonial period, and that better understanding is only possible with public acknowledgement of the full extent of colonial crimes, committed by republican governments. It is therefore quite remarkable that in 2012 the text of Médine's song, '17 Octobre', was taught in the French public high school history curriculum.[44] The song, from his 2006 album *Table d'écoute*, addresses the October 1961 Paris police massacre of as many as 200 French Algerians who were peaceably demonstrating against curfews and in support of the FLN (Front de Libération Nationale) (Derderian 2004, 164–165; House and MacMaster 2006). This bloody event, in which some deaths resulted when police tossed men they had beaten unconscious into the Seine, is one that French officialdom has tried for decades to keep forgotten. No one has ever been prosecuted for participation in the killings, due to the general amnesty declared at the end of the Algerian war. It quite is an achievement, therefore, for '17 Octobre' to be taught in state schools.

Moreover, the presence on the airwaves and everyday speech of Arabic, and particularly Maghribi dialect, may in fact have helped to revive its use in France. Caubet claims that crossover successes of artists like Khaled and Reda Taliani have led to an upsurge of pride and valorisation in Arabic language among the scion of Maghribis, who might previously have regarded it of lesser value than the higher prestige French (Caubet n.d., 7, 9; Zelenková 2013, 26). Moreover, the use of Arabisms has become a kind of identity marker for French youth in general, especially *banlieusards* (Zelenková 2013, 27). In a sense, the successes of these artists are part of a wider challenge to French language hegemony.

These then are not inconsequential achievements. Of course, it is urgent that much more be done to improve conditions for French Maghribis and Muslims, particularly the young and unemployed. But in a different context, such cultural work could form the basis for more profound and thoroughgoing political action.

Acknowledgements

Special thanks to Hisham Aidi and John Schaefer for help with translations.

Notes

1. Benny B's 1990 'Vous êtes fous' was the first French rap hit (#3 in the charts). Khaled's 1992 'Didi' (#9) was the first rai hit. Beurs are also involved in several other musical genres that have crossed over (Daoudi and Miliani 2002).
2. On media constructions of the banlieues as a 'synonym of alterity, deviance, and disadvantage', see Hargreaves (1996).
3. On gangsta rap's rise in the USA (Reeves 2008, 93–115; Chang 2005, 299–329).
4. The situation is analogous to the UK's 'ethnic love and hate fest' of the late 1990s Hesse and Sayyid (2005, 27), when an upsurge in extreme-rightist attacks and racist state policies aimed at British Asians, especially Muslims, occurred at the same time as a 'mainstream passion for all things culturally diverse', especially produced by the suddenly 'cool' (South) Asians.
5. Notable rai–rap releases include Rim'K and Chaba Zahouania, 'Rachid Sytem' (2004, #35 on the charts); Rim'K and Chaba Zahouania, 'Clandestino' (2008, #25); and Rim'K and Chaba Maria, 'Le Jour Maghrib United' (2009).
6. K'Mel: 'You're hired as long as we 've not seen your face' – a reference to racist hiring practices. Cheb Mami: "Alā wijhī inkartūnī, ū gultu étranger" (You did not accept me because of my appearance, and you called me a foreigner). It appears on Cheb Mami's 1999 album *Melli Melli*. Béru (2011, 71) observes that between 1990 and 2000, duos between rappers and singers from North and sub-Saharan Africa partially supplemented those involving or evoking US rappers.
7. Additional volumes are *Raï N'B Fever 2* (2006), *Raï N'B Fever 3* (2008), *Raï'n'B Fever 3 Même pas fatigué* (2009), and *Raï N'B Fever 4* (2011). Another influential raï'n'b collection was *Des 2 côtés* (2004), produced by DJ Kim, a rai DJ, and hip-hop producer DJ Goldfingers. There are many other such collections, many produced in Algeria, sometimes under the name 'rai r'n'b'.
8. Four of 113's five albums have been certified either gold or platinum.
9. Rim'K (born Abdelkrim Brahmi-Benalla) is *verlan* (hip French backslang) for Karim.
10. Taliani was born Tamni Réda in 1980 in Algiers' El Biar district and grew up in Kolea, a town 20 miles southwest of Algiers, where he earned the nickname 'Taliani' (Italian) because of his style of dress. His other notable rai–rap collaborations include 'Cholé Cholé' (2006), with Rappeurs d'Instinct (on *Raï N' B Fever 2*), and 'Inch'Allah', with Grand Corps Malade (2011, #59).
11. Autotune is an audio processor technology used to alter pitch and distort the voice. Ever since Algerian rai artist Chaba Djenet's 2000 hit single, 'Kwit Galbi Wahdi' (You Broke My Heart by Leaving Me), auto-tuning technology has been used heavily on rai vocal recordings in Algeria and France (Clayton 2009) Maghrib.
12. Such codeswitching and borrowing dates to the colonial period. On contemporary codeswitching and borrowing between Arabic and French in Algeria and France (Boumedini and Hadria 2013; Caubet 2002, 2006; Davies and Bentahila 2002, 2006; Miliani 2004; Taleb-Ibrahimi 2004; Zelenková 2013).
13. A *verlan* rendering of *racaille*, a term of official opprobrium that tough banlieue youth have embraced as a positive designation. Silverstein (2012b) describes French gangsta rap as characterised by a harsh vocal flow, complex layering of samples, and a lyrical concentration on issues of racism and violence. As he shows, on their songs 113 have typically self-represented as 'marginal' figures 'outside the law', as 'fugitives...presumed to be dangerous',

and as 'street niggaz (*négros*), ruff in spirit and 100% insubordinate (*insoumis*)'. Two members of Sarkozy's party, the Union for Popular Movement, publicly condemned Rim'K in 2010 for being 'racist against whites and the French in general', basing their claim on lyrics ('Fuck your nation...We've hated the blue uniform since we were young') from 'Face à la police', on 113's 1999 album, *Les Princes de la ville* (Khatibi 2012). For an overview of 113's career (Mortaigne 2010).

14. 'Rap is social music by definition, it's the cry of the street', Rim'K has stated (S.-J. T 2012).

15. Aomar Boum (personal communication) has found nineteenth-century travel accounts describing the Algerian term for hashish as benji. Possibly 'benji' is related to 'bango', Egyptian slang for hash, and may also refer to 'banj', or 'anesthetic', in the Levant. I can find no reference to '350'. Laurie King, Bill Lawrence, Alyssa Miller, Laleh Khalili, Bill Kelsey, and Jean-Baptiste Gallopin help me determine benji's meanings.

16. His family is from the town of Barbacha, in Bejaïa Province.

17. As a young man Rim'K used to vacation in Algeria each summer with his family (Binet 2012).

18. Benachour is referring to 'Partir Loin', often called 'Ya l'babour' or 'Al-Babour'.

19. Unemployment rates for Algerians aged 16–25 were estimated to be as high as 55% in 2005 (Beaugé 2005).

20. The late Cheb Hasni recorded some dozen songs about the problems of obtaining a visa, including the hit 'El Visa', lamenting how these difficulties prevented the song's subject from joining his beloved (Miliani 2005, 120).

21. From Médine's 2008 mixtape *Don't Panik* and his 2008 album *Arabian Panther*.

22. Médine adopts the term from US rap, where it refers to artists like Public Enemy, Dead Prez, KRS-One, or Lupe Fiasco. Médine has, nonetheless, collaborated with several French hardcore artists (Silverstein 2012b, 27), including Rim'K*Maghrib*.

23. On Médine, see Aidi (2011, 2012) and Silverstein (2012b). His performance name refers to Medina, the second holiest city in Islam.

24. The Open Society Institute and the French National Center for Scientific Research's 2009 study found that in France, black people were six times, and Arabs almost eight times, as likely as white people to be stopped by police for i.d. checks (Open Society Institute 2009). See also Human Rights Watch (2012). On youth–police *banlieue* relations (Soumahoro 2008).

25. Overall unemployment for French university graduates is 5%, for graduates of North African origin, over 26% (BBC 2005).

26. As of 2009, only one National Assembly member out of 577 was of Maghribi origin (Hargreaves 2009, 313).

27. Of a population of 60 million (2005) about 4–4.5 million are Muslims, about 3 million of whom of North African origin. An estimated three million French Muslims, 5% of the population, are citizens.

28. *Bouléhia* (*būliḥya*) is Arabic for 'bearded guy'.

29. The use of English expressions is quite common in French rap (Zelenková 2013).

30. De Wenden (1991, 99, 108) discusses the emergence during the 1980s of the myth that Islam was a virtually insuperable obstacle to social integration in France. Bayat (2007, 508) reports that a survey of French Muslims found that 87% considered Islam compatible with the French Republic, suggesting that they are much more secularist than mainstream pundits imagine.

31. Fadela Amara, long-time Socialist Party member and founder of Ni Putes Ni Soumises (Neither Whores Nor Submissive), a feminist organisation that fights violence against women in the *banlieues*, famously contrasted the image of the Beurette, the young French Arab woman who dons mini-skirts and desires liberation, with that of the oppressed woman in a veil (Costa-Kostritsky 2012). Amara has stated that the hijab conveyed a 'negative image of women' and constituted 'a real danger for young women in poor districts' (De la Baume 2013).

32. Particularly after 1995 when, in response to France's support for Algeria's military regime in the civil war, the Islamist militant group GIA used local recruits, most famously Khaled Kelkal, to launch several terrorist attacks in France.

33. I've not determined whether Mesrine took 'revenge' on journalists.

34. Police killing of local youths was a trigger in at least 29 (and possibly 34) of the 48 major banlieue 'riots' between 1990 and 2000 (Dikeç 2004, 203).

35. His album *Arabian Panther* (2008), an independent label release, sold a respectable 25,000 plus copies ('Médine' [rappeur]). His 2013 album *Protest Song* hit #9 on its first week of sales (http://www.chartsinfrance.net/Medine/ProtestSong-a117067024.html).

36. In his 2012 Youtube video, 'I'm Migrant Don't Panik', Médine elaborates on his artistic and political aims and projects (http://www.youtube.com/watch?v=rnKtEkNZWcI).

37. On Khaled's 2009 album *Liberté* as well as *Raï'n'B Fever 3: Même pas fatigue* (2009), but left off the US release of *Liberté*.

38. In between, he had three Top Twenty singles: 'El harba wine' (#20, 2000), 'Ya-Rayi' (#11, 2004), and 'Zine Zina' (#18, 2004).
39. Hence, the title of his 1998 autobiography, *Khaled: Derrière le sourire* (Behind the Smile). Khaled turned 54 in February 2014.
40. 'Gaou' is rube or fool in Ivoirean slang.
41. Rachida Dati (Minister of Justice), Rama Yade (Secretary of State for Human Rights under the Minister of Foreign and European Affairs), and Fadela Amara (Secretary of State for Urban Policies).
42. In his preface to Khaled's autobiography, Gilles Lhote presents the singer as a symbol of the struggle against fundamentalism and its horrors (Khaled 1998, 9).
43. Médine is active in the anti-racist Mouvement des Indigènes de la République. Reda Taliani performed at a September 2010 concert called Rock sans papiers, aimed at criticising the government's shameful treatment of the undocumented (Lafitte 2010).
44. According to his documentary 'I'm Migrant Don't Panik'.

References

Abderrazzak, Hakim. 2009. "'Burning the Sea': Clandestine Migration Across the Strait of Gibraltar in Francophone Moroccan 'Illiterature'." *Contemporary French & Francophone Studies* 13 (4): 461–469.

Abderrazzak, Hakim. 2011. "'To Sea' or 'Not To Sea': North African Clandestine Crossings in the Mediterranean." Paper presented at the symposium, "Porous Nations? Migrants, Transnationals and Illegals in the Cinemas of the Maghrib, Quebec and France". Georgetown University, November 2.

Ahmed, Sara. 2007/08. "Multiculturalism and the Promise of Happiness." *New Formations* 63: 121–137.

Aidi, Hisham. 2011. "The Grand (Hip-Hop) Chessboard: Race, Rap and Raison d'Etat." *Middle East Report* 260: 25–39.

Aidi, Hisham. 2012. "Don't Panik! Islam and Europe's 'Hip Hop Wars'." *Al Jazeera English*, June 5. http://www.aljazeera.com/indepth/opinion/2012/06/20126310151835171.html

Bayat, Asef. 2007. "When Muslims and Modernity Meet." *Contemporary Sociology: A Journal of Reviews* 36 (6): 507–511.

BBC. 2005. "French Muslims Face Job Discrimination." BBC News. November 2. news.bbc.co.uk/1/hi/world/europe/4399748.stm

Beaugé, Florence. 2005. "En rentrant au pays, des expatriés se découvrent une âme de 'pionnier'." *Le Monde*, June 25.

Benachour, Djamel. 2007. "Oran-Festival du rai." *El Watan*, August 7.

Béru, Laurent. 2011. "Mémoire et musique rap: L'indissociabilité de l'esclavage et de la colonisation." *Mouvements* Hors-Série No. 1: 67–76.

Binet, Stéphanie. 2012. "Rim'K, Médine et Imhotep: paroles de rappeurs français sur le poids de ce passé enfoui." *Le Monde*, September.

Boniface, Pascale, and Médine. 2012. *Don't Panik*. Paris: Desclée De Brouwer.

Boumedini, Belkacem, and Nebia Dadoua Hadria. 2013. *La créativité langagière dans la chanson algérienne, rai et rap*. Saarbrücken: Presses Académiques Francophones.

Caubet, Dominique. 2002. "Métissages linguistiques ici (en France) et là-bas (au Maghrib)." *Ville – École – Intégration Enjeux* 130: 117–132.

Caubet, Dominique. 2006. "Banalisation Salutaire d'une 'Langue de France': L'Arabe Maghrébin-Darja Sur La Scène Culturelle Française." In *Langue française et diversité linguistique*, edited by Conseil supérieur de la langue française and Service de la langue française de la Communauté française de Belgique, 161–168. Brussels: De Boeck Supérieur.

Caubet, Dominique. n.d. "About the Transmission of Maghribi Arabic in France." https://www.utexas.edu/cola/insts/france-ut/_files/pdf/resources/caubet.pdf

Chang, Jeff. 2005. *Can't Stop Won't Stop: A History of the Hip-hop Generation*. New York: St. Martin's Press.

Clayton, Jace. 2009. "Pitch Perfect." *Frieze*, 123, May. http://www.frieze.com/issue/article/pitch_perfect/

Costa-Kostritsky, Valeria. 2012. "France and the Veil – the Dark Side of the Law." *openDemocracy*, November 28. http://www.opendemocracy.net/5050/valeria-costa-kostritsky/france-and-veil-%E2%80%93-dark-side-of-law

Daniel, Jean. 1997. "Le prince de Strasbourg." *Nouvel Observateur*, 1690, March 27.

Daoud, Kamel. 2011. "Kamel Daoud's Daily Dose of Subversion." Translation and introduction, Suzanne Ruta. *Berfrois*, April 8. http://www.berfrois.com/2011/04/kamel-daouds-daily-dose-subversion/

Daoudi, Bouziane, and Hadj Miliani. 2002. *Beurs' mélodies: Cent ans de chansons immigrées maghrébine en France*. Paris: Séguier.

Davet, Stéphane. 2004. "Venu des casbahs et des ghettos, le raï'n'b veut être la jouvence de la scène française." *Le Monde*, December 20.

Davies, Eirlys E., and Abdelali Bentahila. 2002. "Language Mixing in Rai Music: Localisation or Globalisation?" *Language and Communication* 22 (2): 187–207.

Davies, Eirlys E., and Abdelali Bentahila. 2006. "Code Switching and the Globalisation of Popular Music: The Case of North African Rai and Rap." *Multilingua* 25 (4): 367–392.

De Koning, Martijn. 2006. "Islamization of the French Riots." *ISIM Review* 17: 30–31.

De la Baume, Maïa. 2013. "More in France Are Turning to Islam, Challenging a Nation's Idea of Itself." *New York Times*, February 3.

De Wenden, Catherine Withol. 1991. "North African Immigration and the French Political Imaginary." In *Race, Discourse and Power in France*, edited by Maxim Silverman, 98–109. Aldershot: Averbury.

Derderian, Richard L. 2004. *North Africans in Contemporary France: Becoming Visible*. New York: Palgrave MacMillan.

Derville, Grégory. 1997. "La stigmatisation des 'jeunes de banlieue.'" *Communication et langages* 113: 104–117.

Dikeç, Mustafa. 2004. "Voices into Noises: Ideological Determination of Unarticulated Justice Movements." *Space and Polity* 8 (2): 191–208.

Fara, C. 2009. "Medine et Sefyu. Le hip-hop en liberté … égalité, fraternite." *L'Humanité*, August 29. http://www.humanite.fr/node/20350

Gastaut, Yvan. 2006. "Chansons et Chanteurs Maghrébins en France (1920–1986)." *Migrations Société* 18: 105–115.

George, Brian. 2007. "Rapping at the Margins: Musical Constructions of Identities in Contemporary France." In *Music, National Identity and the Politics of Location: Between the Global and the Local*, edited by Ian Biddle and Vanessa Knights, 93–113. Farnham, Surrey: Ashgate.

Gross, Joan, David McMurray, and Ted Swedenburg. 1996. "Arab Noise and Ramadan Nights: Rai, Rap, and Franco-Maghribi Identities." In *Displacement, Diaspora, and Geographies of Identity*, edited by Smadar Lavie and Ted Swedenburg, 119–155. Durham: Duke University Press.

Hargreaves, Alec G. 1996. "A Deviant Construction: The French Media and the 'Banlieues'." *New Community* 22 (4): 607–618.

Hargreaves, Alec G. 2009. "La culture française à l'heure du mélange." In *Générations: Un siècle d'histoire culturelle des Maghrébins en France*, edited by Driss El Yazami, Yvan Gastaut, and Naïma Yahi, 308–313. Paris: Gallimard.

Hesse, Barnor, and S. Sayyid. 2005. "Narrating the Postcolonial Political and the Immigrant Imaginary." In *A Postcolonial People: South Asians in Britain*, edited by N. Ali, V. S. Kalra, and S. Sayyid, 13–31. London: Hurst & Company.

House, Jim, and Neil MacMaster. 2006. *Paris 1961: Algerians, State Terror, and Memory*. Oxford: Oxford University Press.

Human Rights Watch. 2012. "'The Root of Humiliation': Abusive Identity Checks in France." http://www.hrw.org/sites/default/files/reports/france0112ForUpload.pdf

International Crisis Group. 2006. "La France Face à Ses Musulmans: Émeutes, Jihadisme et Dépoliticisation." Rapport Europe N°172. http://www.crisisgroup.org/~/media/Files/europe/172_la_france_face_a_ses_musulmans_emeutes__jihadisme_amended

Jouili, Jeanette. 2013. "Rapping the Republic: Utopia, Critique, and Muslim Role Models in Secular France." *French Politics, Culture & Society* 31 (2): 58–80.

Khaled. 1998. *Khaled: Derrière le sourire*. Paris: Michel Lafon.

Khatibi, Saïd. 2012. "Rim'K: The Algerian Beats of Nostalgia." *Al-Akhbar English*, March 15. http://english.al-akhbar.com/node/5256/

Lafitte, Romain. 2010. "Du son, des mots, des images pour les sans-papiers." *L'Humanité*, September 20. http://www.humanite.fr/node/453815

Madjid, Talbi. 2009. "Dossier: Les Harragas en Algérie." *Algérie Actualité*, February 23. http://www.algerie-actualites.com/article.php3?id_article=8548

Manach, Jean Marc. 2011. " [APP] Fortress Europe: a deadly exodus." *OWNI.eu*, March 4. http://owni.eu/2011/03/04/app-fortress-europe-a-deadly-exodus/

McMurray, David. 1998. "Sports as an Integrative Force? North African Players and the Équipe de France." *MERIP Newsletter* (Fall): 2–3.

Merzouk, Zineb. 2004. "La nouvelle mode du raï'n'b." *El Watan*, August 29.

Miliani, Hadj. 2002. "De la nostalgie du local aux mythologies de l'exil: chanteurs et chansons dans l'émigration algérienne en France (des années 1920 au début des années 80)." *Insaniyat* 12: 209–228.

Miliani, Hadj. 2004. "Variations linguistiques et formulations thématiques dans la chanson algérienne au cours du XXe siècle: Un parcours." In *Trames de langues: Usages et métissages linguistiques dans l'histoire du Maghrib*, Jocelyne Dakhlia, dir., 423–438. Paris: Maisonneuve et Larose.

Miliani, Hadj. 2005. *Sociétaires de l'emotion: études sur les musiques et les chants d'Algérie d'hier et d'aujourd'hui.* Oran: Éditions Dar El Gharb.

Mortaigne, Véronique. 2010. "Le 113 place le rap dans l'orbite de la dance." *Le Monde*, December.

Mundy, Jacob. 2009. "Bouteflika's Triumph and Algeria's Tragedy." *Middle East Report Online*, April 10. http://www.merip.org/mero/mero041009

Open Society Institute. 2009. "Profiling Minorities: A Study of Stop-and-Search Practices in Paris." http://www.opensocietyfoundations.org/sites/default/files/search_20090630.Web.pdf

Planet Hip Hop. 2005. "Médine" (interview), July. www.planet-hiphop.ch/v2/index.php?select=interviews&id=131

Prévos, André. 1998. "Hip-Hop, Rap, and Repression in France and in the United States." *Popular Music and Society* 22 (2): 67–84.

Prévos, André. 2001. "Postcolonial Popular Music in France: Rap Music and Hip-Hop Culture in the 1980s and 1990s." In *Global Noise, Rap and Hip-Hop Outside the USA*, edited by Tony Mitchell, 39–56. Middletown: Wesleyan University Press.

Reeves, Marcus. 2008. *Somebody Scream! Rap Music's Rise to Prominence in the Aftershock of Black Power.* New York: Faber and Faber.

Rekacewicz, Philippe. 2013. "Mapping Europe's War on Immigration." *Le Monde Diplomatique* (English Edition), October. http://mondediplo.com/blogs/mapping-europe-s-war-on-immigration.

Schade-Poulsen, Marc. 1999. *Men and Popular Music in Algeria: The Social Significance of Raï.* Austin: University of Texas Press.

Sekaninová, Tereza. 2012. "Stéréotypes lies au verlan: variation diatopique dans le rap français." MA thesis, Masaryk University.

Sherwood, Seth. 2005. "In the Heart of Paris, an African Beat." *New York Times*, December 18, Travel Section.

Siclier, Sylvain. 2002. "Khaled célèbre le passé et le futur du rai." *Le Monde*, June 6.

Silverstein, Paul A. 2012a. "Le Patrimoine du ghetto: Rap et racialisation des violences urbaines en France." In *L'Atlantique Multiracial*, edited by James Cohen, Andrew J. Diamond, and Philippe Vervaecke, 95–118. Paris: Karthala.

Silverstein, Paul A. 2012b. "Sounds of Love and Hate: Sufi Rap, Ghetto Patrimony, and the Concrete Politics of the French Urban Periphery." Unpublished ms.

Soumahoro, Maboula. 2008. "On the Test of the French Republic as Taken (and Failed)." *Transition: An International Review* 98: 42–66.

S.-J. T. 2012. "Rim'K: 'C'est une fierté de venir voir les jeunes à Alès'." *Midi Libre*, July 6.

Taleb-Ibrahimi, Khaoula. 2004. In Jocelyne Dakhlia, dir., *Trames de langues: Usages et métissages linguistiques dans l'histoire du Maghrib*, 439–454. Paris: Maisonneuve et Larose.

Tenaille, Frank. 2002. *Le Rai: De La Bâtardise à La Reconnaissance Internationale.* Paris: Cité de la musique.

Zelenková, Anna. 2013. "Arabismes dan les chansons de rap français: traitement lexicographie, adaption phonique et role de l'origine des rappeurs." MA thesis, Masaryk University.

Z.M. 2005. "Raï'N'B: Concert explosif à la Coupole." *El Watan*, February 24.

Index

www.ingramcontent.com/pod-product-compliance
Ingram Content Group UK Ltd.
Pitfield, Milton Keynes, MK11 3LW, UK
UKHW020348010325
455677UK00021B/343